Regulating Private Military Companies

This work examines the ability of existing and evolving PMC regulation to adequately control private force, and it challenges the capacity of international law to deliver accountability in the event of private military company (PMC) misconduct. From medieval to early modern history, private soldiers dominated the military realm and were fundamental to the waging of wars until the rise of a national citizen army. Today, PMCs are again a significant force, performing various security, logistics, and strategy functions across the world. Unlike mercenaries or any other form of irregular force, PMCs acquired a corporate legal personality, a legitimising status that alters the governance model of today. Drawing on historical examples of different forms of governance, the relationship between neoliberal states and PMCs is conceptualised here as a form of a 'shared governance'. It reflects states' reliance on PMCs relinquishing a degree of their power and transferring certain functions to the private sector. As non-state actors grow in authority, wielding power, and making claims to legitimacy through self-regulation, other sources of law also become imaginable and relevant to enact regulation and invoke responsibility.

Katerina Galai is a defence and security analyst at RAND Europe, a not-for-profit research institute, based in Cambridge, UK.

Regulating Private Military Companies

Conflicts of Law, History and Governance

Katerina Galai

Routledge
Taylor & Francis Group
LONDON AND NEW YORK

First published 2019 by Routledge

2 Park Square, Milton Park, Abingdon, Oxfordshire OX14 4RN
52 Vanderbilt Avenue, New York, NY 10017

Routledge is an imprint of the Taylor & Francis Group, an informa business

First issued in paperback 2020

British Library Cataloguing-in-Publication Data
A catalogue record for this book is available from the British Library

Library of Congress Cataloging-in-Publication Data
Names: Galai, Katerina, author.
Title: Regulating private military companies: conflicts of law, history, and governance / Katerina Galai.
Description: Abingdon, Oxon [UK]; New York, NY: Routledge, 2019.
Identifiers: LCCN 2018058884 (print) | LCCN 2018059735 (ebook) | ISBN 9780429465888 (ebk) | ISBN 9781138610057 (hbk)
Subjects: LCSH: Private military companies (International law) | Mercenary troops (International law) | Private security services.
Classification: LCC KZ6418.5 (ebook) | LCC KZ6418.5 .G35 2019 (print) | DDC 343/.015354—dc23
LC record available at https://lccn.loc.gov/2018058884

ISBN: 978-1-138-61005-7 (hbk)
ISBN: 978-0-367-67103-7 (pbk)

Typeset in Galliard
by codeMantra

Contents

Acknowledgements

Unlike most projects on private security, my work did not begin with Blackwater and the Nisour Square shootings. Instead, the enquiry and the method developed in the process were urged by the short-termism and short-sightedness of international law, accentuated by the ageless phenomenon, that is, private security.

The journey of this book began with PhD research at the University of Sussex as I unsuccessfully tried convincing supervisors of the School of Global Studies of the added value an interdisciplinary PhD could bring, combining insights of law and historical sociology.

The project was conducted and completed at the University of Sussex Law School under the supervision of a brilliant critical legal theorist Dr Tarik Kochi, who enabled, challenged, and believed in the interdisciplinarity and the topic that drew commentary from a number of faculty colleagues from corporate and international criminal lawyers to critical thinkers and sociologists.

Inspiration, ideas, and critique were not limited to Sussex Law School. Meeting James G Stewart and hearing him present at the Institute for Global Law and Policy at Harvard Law School drew my attention to the importance of corporate accountability in the overall question of PMC regulation. Further, I received much hands-on support during my two weeks at the Transnational Summer Law School at King's College London with the chapter on decolonisation and the Nicaragua case discussed in detail as part of a working group.

I would like to gratefully acknowledge the Modern Law Review Scholarship which afforded both the funding and the intellectual encouragement and recognition at critical junctures.

I would also like to thank my examiners, Professors Nigel White and Christian Henderson, for their insightful comments and suggestions for developing the thesis into this monograph.

Finally, and most importantly, I would like to express my gratitude to my husband, Adrian, who encouraged me to start and certainly made it possible to finish, providing support, instilling confidence and maintaining composure every step of the way.

Introduction

From medieval to early modern history, private soldiers have dominated the security landscape. Their existence was fundamental to the waging of the wars between feudal lords, dynastic monarchies, and the city-republics of Italian Renaissance. Identified by Machiavelli as a threat to republican ideals and good governance,[1] mercenaries were also more expensive than the emerging citizen conscripts, putting a financial strain on the large-scale belligerent demands of sixteenth- and seventeenth-century monarchies. Modern mercenaries, or private military companies (PMCs), largely inherited their unenviable reputation from their counterparts in the latter half of the twentieth century, when mercenaries were criminalised by the Geneva Conventions in the context of proxy wars and involvement in wars of national liberation.[2]

Today, private security providers dispose of vast resources, performing various security functions across the world. Most such companies mainly offer security-related services, such as provision of personnel, assistance of law enforcement, and civilian-level security. Some of the big players, such as British G4S (620,000 employees[3]), American DynCorp (13,540 employees[4] with 96 per cent of revenue generated by the US government defence contracts[5]), and Canadian GardaWorld (45,000 employees[6]), operate globally, supporting national governments in foreign operations,[7] international organisations for peacekeeping purposes[8] or contracted by other companies to protect extraction facilities abroad.[9] As a result of growing PMC activity and several high-profile scandals involving PMCs,[10] the issue of PMC regulation has sparked considerable debate amongst legal and political scholars, policymakers, and the international community. Because of this focus, a wide range of possible responses have emerged, varying between industry attempts at self-management through voluntary norms and non-binding standards,[11] to numerous approaches that critique private force, offering solutions grounded in ethics[12] and human rights.[13]

This work examines the ability of existing and evolving PMC regulation to adequately control private force and challenges the capacity of international law to deliver accountability in the event of PMC misconduct. While the contemporary legal analysis can expose the inefficiencies and legal loopholes created by the overlapping regulation (ranging from industry standards, to human rights guidelines and voluntary norms, to the binding framework provided by the corporate, contract, and tort law), it still only offers incomplete answers.

To help inform the legal question of PMC regulation, I draw insights from historical sociology[14] and military history[15] through a historical examination of private violence and its use and regulation in varying governance models from the fourteenth century to the present day. By challenging the customary notions of what constitutes public and private force, I seek to attain a wider scope for analysis, adopting a more critical and informed approach when analysing contemporary challenges in international law posed by the use of private force.

Establishing the need for a more historically aware means to regulating private military actors, this work, therefore, also critiques a state-centric approach to regulation that dominates the international legal landscape. Underpinning the critical approach are the timeless and politically agnostic concepts of power and legitimacy that are used throughout the monograph to identify different governance models beyond the Westphalian concept of nation-state. While the sources of power and legitimacy are identifiable in other governmental structures, states cease to be the only that are recognised by the global governance system.

State-centric theorisation, on the contrary, flattens out this historical variability in forms of governance,[16] thus limiting the applicability of international law as a contemporary discipline. Furthermore, as non-states actors grow in authority (despite their limited theoretical significance under international law),[17] other sources of law also become imaginable and relevant to enact regulation and invoke responsibility.

The changing form of governance informs the legal question of PMC regulation in two ways: first, by articulating the existing relationship between the states and PMCs in a form of a 'shared governance' model, whereby neoliberal states rely on PMCs relinquishing a degree of their power and transferring certain functions to the private sector. Meanwhile, PMCs and corporations more generally are making claims to a form of legitimacy through industry self-regulation. The second way in which the critical approach of historical sociology helps to inform the question of PMC regulation is by pointing out the normative gaps of existing and emerging regulatory frameworks and their incompatibility with the model of shared governance.

The task of evaluating the effectiveness of PMC regulation is, on the one hand, hamstrung by the parameters of existing legal and regulatory frameworks and, on the other hand, cultivated by the diversification of regulatees; actors that ought to bear responsibility for PMC conduct. PMC contractors as individuals, states as clients and corporations as the new form of PMCs themselves, are all thus considered when thinking about regulating private force and allocating the responsibility in the event of gross offences committed by PMCs.

Conceptual framework

Critical approaches found in Mann,[18] Geuss,[19] Weber,[20] Tilly,[21] and Dorsett and McVeigh[22] highlight the evolving nature of states, authority, law, and economic power, and the way these shifts influence the relationships between the concepts from a socio-historical perspective. My socio-historical approach builds upon this critical debate and seeks to establish normative patterns by examining the use and regulation of private military force in different types of governance.

Power and legitimacy

Power and legitimacy are the two conditions through which a type of governance can be identified. Power broadly represents the successful monopoly of the legitimate use of violence while legitimacy is envisioned through the mandatory adherence to the rules by all members of a designated group of people.[23] While both notions have been conceptualised with a degree of variance in categorisation, the essence of power and legitimacy remains recognisable across the work of historical sociologists and critical thinkers.

Power is versatile and omnipresent throughout history as it manifests itself at all times through one form or another. For example, Geuss's notion of '*de facto* political authority' can be likened to power as it is concerned with factual control of certain people over a certain area and is likely to contain "a strong element of compulsion of the threat of use of physical force".[24] Mann differentiates between despotic and infrastructural power, whereby despotic power refers to the distributive power of the ruling class over civil society, and infrastructural power describes the state's institutional capacity to penetrate its territories and implement decisions,[25] for instance, early medieval empires who had enormous military capacity but only limited administrative authority.[26] Although more prominent and explicit in Tilly and Mann, a relationship between political and military power is also set out by Weber: "all political structures use force, but they differ in the manner in which and the extent to which they use or threaten to use it against other political organisations".[27]

Legitimacy is best understood in terms of justification of authority. Coined by Geuss as '*de jure* authority', legitimacy derives from law and assumes "there is a law that prescribes that people should obey them".[28] Whether deriving from the Church (in feudalism and the Holy Roman Empire), dynasty (in absolute monarchies), reason (Machiavellian republicanism), the state and the people (territorial and popular sovereignty of a nation-state), or law, these accounts demonstrate a variety of historical and normative justifications of resort to power.[29]

Identifying forms of governance

The confluence of power and legitimacy in different institutional practices forms the notion of governance, as used throughout this monograph. Along the same methodological lines, in their analysis of the plurality of jurisdictional forms of authority, Dorsett and McVeigh consider earlier forms of state and authority that predated the modern nation-state.[30] I echo Geuss as he envisages a state as "merely an agency operating and exercising powers in a certain way".[31] 'State' is therefore used as a shorthand for a form of authoritative governance that fluctuates and adopts different models throughout history. Examining historical examples of different forms of governance, namely feudalism,[32] Italian city-republics,[33] absolutism,[34] imperialism,[35] nation-states,[36] and material on neoliberalism,[37] helps to outline structural commonalities in state practice with regard to military power, identifying transformation and lineages of regulation of private forces into modernity.

Like the concept of a 'state', 'sovereignty' acquired its modern meaning only following the Peace of Westphalia in 1648.[38] Since then, sovereignty had served as a definition of the modern international system, as it accordingly marked the "division of the world into sovereign states".[39] The same applies to the contemporary international legal order which is both characterised and constrained by the prominence of sovereign territorial states.[40] The disciplines of international law and international relations alike are dominated by state-centric and ahistorical theories lacking normative dynamism and the ability to tackle different actors within the evolving governance model.[41] Therefore, separating the notion of sovereignty from the modern state[42] opens up possibilities to explore various forms of governance instead of focusing solely on one, epitomised by territoriality and autonomy.[43]

Chapter outline

Chapter 1 outlines the issues associated with the classification of private military actors, situating them in the broader historical context of private security and different forms of governance. Outlining the distinctions between mercenaries, civilians, private contractors, and PMCs as corporations, this chapter interprets the nuance of private force in the context of accepted definitions. Furthermore, it conceptualises PMCs as a modern manifestation of a private military phenomenon that pre-dates nation-states and standing armies. This chapter also introduces the questions of regulation and responsibility with regard to private force. Given the international scope of PMC activity, the corporate status of PMCs, and the close proximity to hostilities of armed civilian personnel, accountability for PMC conduct could give rise to individual, state, and corporate responsibility. Explaining the different approaches to regulation, it considers who should be regulated and to what end.

Chapter 2 develops an account of the changing nature of war and military power in modernity, providing the necessary context to critique contemporary attempts by international law (IL) to regulate mercenaries and PMCs. By applying the concepts of power and legitimacy, this chapter traces the changing relationship between forms of governance and the military power that they use in order to identify elements of private military powers and the ways in which these were regulated. It analyses the shift from vassals serving multiple feudal lords and private armies to a move towards a professional standing army in the absolute monarchies of continental Europe, to mercenaries and the unconsolidated militaries of Italian city-states, as well as contrasting models of *levée en masse* of the early nation-state of Revolutionary France, and to the outsourced colonial army of the English East India Company. The chapter offers normative conclusions that each attempt to explain, within their own historical circumstances, the choice of deploying a certain type of military force within a certain type of governance model. While considering some of the normative approaches grounded in these relationships, it introduces different forms of military force, revealing varying interpretations of its classification into public and private through changing conflict paradigms.

Chapter 3 continues the historical analysis into the twentieth century by drawing on the changing nature of war and tracing international legal response to mercenaries in the context of decolonisation and proxy warfare. The re-emergence of private force is juxtaposed with the total centralisation of military resources at the beginning of the twentieth century, particularly during the period of the two World Wars. Despite the codification of provisions relating to mercenaries under the Geneva Conventions and active anti-mercenary movements, relevant treaties and norms have failed to achieve universality in their relevance and applicability. The analysis of *Nicaragua case* with regard to the use of the Contras also demonstrates the highly political nature of twentieth-century international law.

Chapter 4 examines the rise of PMCs at the end of the twentieth century as a by-product of the demand created by the 'new wars' and the supply of disposed military personnel following the end of the Cold War. During this time, the conflict paradigm shifted from large-scale interstate tensions to far more ambiguous internal ethnic struggles, powered by the growing private security market and the absence of the US-Soviet balance of power. The rise of PMCs was further shaped by the failure to criminalise the act of mercenarism, coupled with the spread of neoliberal ideas from the 1980s onwards. With its characteristics of small government, privatisation, and outsourcing trends, neoliberal policy also affects the security landscape. Along with the normalisation of private security in terms of government policy, failure to criminalise the act of mercenarism allowed for the incorporation of PMCs as legitimate businesses, while extensive privatisation and outsourcing created room for PMCs, and changed the perception of normality and legality of private actors in the defence and security landscape.

Chapter 5 explores legal constructs available to administer PMC conduct and hold individual contractors and states accountable when gross misconducts occur. Setting the scene for an analysis of corporate responsibility of PMCs, this chapter focuses on the contemporary legal regulation of PMCs and the role of international legal institutions in shaping normative conditions in favour of and against their use. It explores contemporary problems posed by the overlapping regulation of PMCs and the limitations that derive from the existence of different bodies of law in their efforts to invoke individual and state responsibility. This chapter subsumes the lessons learned from the historical analysis in terms of the relationship between the government and the military, as these patterns help identify weaknesses in existing regulatory approaches.

Chapter 6 explores existing and emerging international regulatory tools and mechanisms that address PMCs as corporations. It further evaluates the effectiveness of industry self-regulation, contemplating the narrative it creates for the legitimacy of international corporations in the private military sector. The purpose of this chapter is to navigate through the complex channels of existing regulation and to identify key legal gaps that lead to corporate impunity of PMCs. This chapter also portrays PMCs as a form of power that exists in parallel to that of a state while PMC efforts in self-governance can be understood as claims to legitimacy that solidify their position further in the contemporary and future security landscape. Created by the horizontal nature of a contract between states and PMCs and amplified by the growing authority of PMCs, parallel power relationship between states and PMCs creates a model of a 'shared governance' in which PMCs are currently not recognised as actors under international law. However, the corporate status of PMCs introduces additional sources of law to invoke responsibility.

Chapter 7 thus assesses both domestic and transnational legal frameworks that claim jurisdiction over corporations and, more importantly, it identifies their weaknesses, omissions, and gaps which could lead to corporate impunity. Unlike states and international organisations who are the recognised subjects of IL,[44] corporations fall outside this remit. Nor are they effectively governed by international criminal and humanitarian laws concerning genocide, war crimes, and crimes against humanity, applying to natural persons.[45] This chapter considers how companies fit into a criminal justice system as it identifies precedent of corporate criminal responsibility in different national jurisdictions. Furthermore, by analysing examples of domestic criminal procedure for prosecuting corporations charged with international crimes it allows for international criminal law to be explored as a possible source of regulation.

Finally, **Chapter 8** reaps the benefits of previously evaluating the legal question of PMC regulation through a critical lens of historical sociology. Based on the claim of a 'shared governance' model established in Chapter 6, and the availability of private law sources, PMCs and corporations more generally have developed an extent of authority that requires a proportionate degree and extent of responsibility. This chapter explores why we need corporate criminal liability for PMCs internationally and offers potential future legal responses for its implementation. It considers different avenues within international criminal law for a more effective and tailored regulation of the private military space, mindful of the doctrinal limitations and taking into consideration the evolving shared governance model.

Notes

1 Machiavelli (1994a, b, p. 140).
2 The Protocol Additional to the Geneva Conventions of 12 August 1949, relating to the Protection of Victims of International Armed Conflicts, Protocol I, Article 47 (2), June 1977.
3 See: www.g4s.com/en/Who%20we%20are/Our%20people/Our%20employees/.
4 See: www.linkedin.com/company/dyncorp-international.
5 See: www.securitydegreehub.com/most-powerful-private-security-companies-in-the-world/.
6 See: www.garda.com.
7 Scahill (2007); Shearer (1998); Howe (1998, pp. 307–331).
8 Ostensen (2011); Colonel Russell (1997).
9 Paying for Protection (2005); Arduino (2015).
10 Such as Blackwater in Iraq or DynCorp in Bosnia.
11 Such as: International Code of Conduct for Private Security Providers; The Montreux Document; American Society for Industrial Security (ASIS) International; International Organisation for Standardisation (ISO/PAS 28007-1:2015); OECD Guidelines for Multinational Enterprises, etc.
12 Percy (2007); Pattison (2010, pp. 425–447); Tesón (2011, pp. 192–212); Alexandra, Baker and Caparini (2008).
13 Such as the efforts of the UN Working Group on Mercenaries and the UN Intergovernmental Group on Business and Human Rights.
14 Cutler and Dietz (2017); Rosenau and Czempiel (1992); Cutler (2003); Hobden and Hobson (2002); Cutler (2002); Dorsett and McVeigh (2012).
15 Parker (1988); McNeil (1982); Tilly (1990); Held, McGrew et al. (1999); Kaldor (2002).

16 Krasner (1993, pp. 235–264; 1997, pp. 651–680).
17 Cutler (2002, p. 191).
18 Mann (1993; 2012; 2013).
19 Geuss (1981; 2001; 2008).
20 Weber (2004); Gerth and Wright Mills (1993).
21 Tilly (1990; 1975).
22 Dorsett and McVeigh (2012).
23 Geuss (2001, Chapter 3).
24 Geuss (2001, p. 40).
25 Mann (1993, p. 59).
26 Held, McGrew, et al. (1999, p. 33).
27 Gerth and Wright Mills (1993, p. 159).
28 Geuss (2001, p. 40).
29 Dorsett and McVeigh (2012, p. 11).
30 Dorsett and McVeigh (2012, p. 32).
31 Geuss (2001, p. 43).
32 On feudalism, see: Stephenson (1941, pp. 788–812); Coulborn and Strayer (1956); Ganshof (1964); Brown (1974, pp. 1063–1088); Strayer (1970); Fischer (1992, pp. 427–466).
33 On Italian city-republics, see: Bock, Skinner and Viroli (1990); Machiavelli (1994a, b); Kent (1975, pp. 575–638); Rubinstein (1960).
34 Anderson (1974); Kiernan (1957, pp. 66–86); Wallerstein (1974).
35 Anghie (1999, pp. 1–80); Scott (1995, pp. 191–220); Ruskola (2002, pp. 179–234); Killingray (1979, pp. 421–436); Cohn (1996).
36 Mann (1993); Tilly (1990); Hobsbawm (1990).
37 Hayek (2001); Friedman 2002; Chomsky (1999); Wapshott (2012); Prasad (2006); Harvey (2005); Odysseos (2010, pp. 747–772); on military privatisation see: Abrahamsen and Williams (2011); Singer (2004).
38 Singer (2004, p. 35); see other critical and historical literature on sovereignty: Croxton (1999, pp. 569–582); MacCormick (1999); Osiander (2001, pp. 251–287).
39 Barkin and Cronin (1994, p. 107).
40 Dorsett and McVeigh (2012, p. 5).
41 Cutler (2002, p. 181); Franck (1990).
42 Westphalian model limits the scope of inquiry to nation-states only, however, I am taking a more comprehensive approach to locate sovereignty to a greater or lesser extent in every form of governance from the fifteenth century onwards. See: Beaulac (2004); Croxton (1999, pp. 569–582); Osiander (2001, pp. 251–287).
43 Krasner (1995–1996, pp. 119); Philpott (2001, p. 311).
44 Akande (2014, p. 251).
45 Fafo Report (2005, p. 19).

References

Abrahamsen, R. and Williams, M. C.: *Security beyond the State: Private Security in International Politics*, CUP, Cambridge, 2011.

Akande, D.: "International Organisations" in Evans, M. D. (ed.): *International Law*, 4th edition, OUP, Oxford, 2014.

Alexandra, A., Baker D.-P. and Caparini, M. (eds): *Private Military and Security Companies: Ethics, Policies, and Civil-Military Relations*, Routledge Military Studies, New York, 2008.

American Society for Industrial Security (ASIS) International, available at: www.asisonline.org

Anderson, P.: *Lineages of the Absolutist State*, NLB, London, 1974.

Anghie, A.: "Finding the Peripheries: Sovereignty and Colonialism in Nineteenth-Century International Law", 1999, Vol. 40 (1), *Harvard International Law Journal*, pp. 1–80.

Arduino, A.: Security Privatisation with Chinese Characteristics: The Role of Chinese Private Security Corporations in Protecting Chinese Outbound Investments and Citizens, Policy Report, S. Rajaratnam School of International Studies, June 2015.

Barkin, J. S. and Cronin, B.: "The State and the Nation: Changing Norms and the Rules of Sovereignty in International Relations", 1994, Vol. 48 (1), *International Organization*, pp. 107–130.

Beaulac, S.: *The Power of Language in the Making of International Law: The Word Sovereignty in Bodin and Vattel and the Myth of Westphalia*, Martinus Nijhoff, Leiden, 2004.

Bock, G., Skinner, Q. and Viroli, M. (eds): *Machiavelli and Republicanism*, CUP, Cambridge, 1990.

Brown, E. A. R.: "The Tyranny of a Construct: Feudalism and Historians of Medieval Europe", 1974, Vol. 79 (4), *The American Historical Review*, pp. 1063–1088.

Chomsky, N.: *Profit over People: Neoliberalism and Global Order*, Seven Stories Press, New York, 1999.

Cohn, B. S.: *Colonialism and Its Forms of Knowledge: The British in India*, Princeton University Press, Princeton, 1996.

Colonel Russell, D. W.: *Understanding the Application of Army's Logistics Civil Augmentation Program (LOGCAP)*, U.S. Army War College, Carlisle Barracks, Pennsylvania, 1997.

Coulborn, R. and Strayer, J. R: *Feudalism in History*, Princeton University Press, Princeton, 1956.

Croxton, D.: "The Peace of Westphalia of 1648 and the Origins of Sovereignty", 1999, Vol. 21, *International History Review*, pp. 569–582.

Cutler, A. C.: "Critical Historical Materialism and International Law: Imagining International Law as Praxis" in Hobden, S. and Hobson, J. M. (eds): *Historical Sociology of International Relations*, CUP, Cambridge, 2002.

Cutler, A. C.: *Private Power and Global Authority: Transnational Merchant Law in the Global Political Economy*, CUP, Cambridge, 2003.

Cutler, A. C. and Dietz, T. (eds): *The Politics of Private Transnational Governance by Contract*, Routledge, London, 2017.

Dorsett, S. and McVeigh, S.: *Jurisdiction*, Routledge, Abingdon, 2012.

Fafo Report: Business and International Crimes: Assessing the Liability of Business Entities for Grave Violations of International Law (2005), available at: www.fafo.no/index.php?option=com_zoo&task=item&item_id=3742&Itemid=927&lang=en.

Fischer, M.: "Feudal Europe, 800–1300: Communal Discourse and Conflictual Practices", 1992, Vol. 46 (2), *International Organization*, pp. 427–466.

Franck, T.: *The Power of Legitimacy among Nations*, OUP, Oxford, 1990.

Friedman, M.: *Capitalism and Freedom*, The University of Chicago Press, London, 2002.

Ganshof, F. L.: *Feudalism*, Harper & Row, New York, 1964.

Gerth, H. H. and Wright Mills, C. (eds): *From Max Weber: Essays in Sociology*, Routledge, London, 1993.

Geuss, R.: *A Critical Theory. Habermas and the Frankfurt School*, CUP, Cambridge, 1981.

Geuss, R.: *History and Illusion in Politics*, CUP, Cambridge, 2001.

Geuss, R.: *Philosophy and Real Politics*, Princeton University Press, Woodstock, 2008.

Harvey, D.: *A Brief History of Neoliberalism*, OUP, Oxford, 2005.

Hayek, F. A.: *The Road to Serfdom*, Routledge, Abingdon, 2001.

Held, D., McGrew, A. et al. (ed.): *Global Transformations: Politics, Economics and Culture*, Polity, Cambridge, 1999.

Hobden, S. and Hobson, J. M. (eds): *Historical Sociology of International Relations*, CUP, Cambridge, 2002.

Hobsbawm, E. J.: *Nations and Nationalism since 1780*, CUP, Cambridge, 1990.

Howe, H. M.: "Private Security Forces and African Stability: The Case of Executive Outcomes", 1998, Vol. 36 (2), *The Journal of Modern African Studies*, pp. 307–331.

www.garda.com.

www.linkedin.com/company/dyncorp-international.

www.securitydegreehub.com/most-powerful-private-security-companies-in-the-world/.

International Code of Conduct for Private Security Providers, available at: www.icoca.ch/en/the_icoc.

International Organisation for Standardisation (ISO/PAS 28007-1:2015), available at: www.iso.org/standard/63166.html.

Kaldor, M.: *New and Old Wars: Organized Violence in a Global Era*, Polity Press, Cambridge, 2002.

Kent, D.: "The Florentine Reggimento in the Fifteenth Century", 1975, Vol. 28 (4), *Renaissance Quarterly*, pp. 575–638.

Kiernan, V. G.: "Foreign Mercenaries and Absolute Monarchy", 1957, Vol. 11, *Past and Present*, pp. 66–86.

Killingray, D.: "The Idea of a British Imperial African Army", 1979, Vol. 20 (3), *The Journal of African History*, pp. 421–436.

Krasner, S. D.: "Compromising Westphalia", 1995–1996, Vol. 20 (3), *International Security*, pp. 115–151.

Krasner, S. D.: "Pervasive Not Perverse", 1997, Vol. 30 (3), *Cornell International Law Journal*, pp. 651–680.

Krasner, S. D.: "Westphalia and All That" in Goldstein, J. and Keohane, R. O. (eds): *Ideas and Foreign Policy*, Cornell University Press, Ithaca, 1993.

MacCormick, N.: *Questioning Sovereignty: Law, State, and Nation in the European Commonwealth*, OUP, Oxford, 1999.

Machiavelli, N. (ed. Wootton, D.): *Selected Political Writings*, Hackett Publishing Company Inc., Cambridge, 1994a.

Machiavelli, N.: "The Discourses" in Wootton, D. (ed.): *Selected Political Writings*, Hackett Publishing Company Inc., Cambridge, 1994b.

Mann, M.: *The Sources of Social Power, Vol. II The Rise of Classes and Nation-States, 1760–1914*, CUP, Cambridge, 1993.

Mann, M.: *The Sources of Social Power, Vol. III Global Empires and Revolutions, 1890–1945*, CUP, Cambridge, 2012.

Mann, M.: *The Sources of Social Power, Vol. IV Globalizations, 1945–2011*, CUP, Cambridge, 2013.

McNeil, W. H.: *Pursuit of Power: Technology, Armed Force and Society Since A.D. 1000*, University of Chicago Press, Chicago, 1982.

OECD Guidelines for Multinational Enterprises.

Odysseos, L.: "Human Rights, Liberal Ontogenesis and Freedom: Producing a Subject for Neoliberalism?", 2010, Vol. 38 (3), *Millennium—Journal of International Studies*, pp. 747–772.

Osiander, A.: "Sovereignty, International Relations, and the Westphalian Myth", 2001, Vol. 55, *International Organization*, pp. 251–287.

Ostensen, A. G.: "UN Use of Private Military and Security Companies: Practices and Policies", The Geneva Centre for the Democratic Control of Armed Forces, SSR Paper 3,

2011, available at: www.dcaf.ch/Publications/UN-Use-of-Private-Military-and-Security-Companies-Practices-and-Policies.

Parker, G.: *The Military Revolution: Military Innovation and the Rise of the West 1500–1800*, CUP, Cambridge, 1988.

Pattison, J.: "Deeper Objections to the Privatisation of Military Force", 2010, Vol. 18 (4), *The Journal of Political Philosophy*, pp. 425–447.

Paying for Protection: The Freeport Mine and the Indonesian Security Forces, A Report by Global Witness, July 2005.

Percy, S.: *Mercenaries: The History of a Norm in International Relations*, Oxford University Press, Oxford, 2007.

Philpott, D.: "Usurping Sovereignty of Sovereignty?", 2001, Vol. 53 (1), *World Politics*, pp. 297–324.

Prasad, M.: *The Politics of Free Markets: The Rise of Neoliberal Economic Policies in Britain, France, Germany, & the United States*, The University of Chicago Press, London, 2006.

Rosenau, J. and Czempiel, E. O. (eds): *Governance without Government. Order and Change in World Politics*, CUP, Cambridge, 1992.

Rubinstein, N.: "Politics and Constitution in Florence at the End of the Fifteenth Century" in Jacob, E. F. (ed.): *Italian Renaissance Studies*, Barnes and Noble, New York, 1960.

Ruskola, T.: "Legal Orientalism", 2002, Vol. 101 (1), *Michigan Law Review*, pp. 179–234.

Scahill, J.: *Blackwater: The Rise of the World's Most Powerful Mercenary Army*, Serpent's Tail, London, 2007.

Scott, D.: "Colonial Governmentality", 1995, Vol. 43 (3), *Social Text*, pp. 191–220.

Shearer, D.: "Private Armies and Military Intervention", 1998, Vol. 38, *The Adelphi Paper* 316.

Singer, P. W: *Corporate Warriors: The Rise of the Privatized Military Industry*, Cornell University Press, New York, 2004.

Stephenson, C.: "The Origin and Significance of Feudalism", 1941, Vol. 46 (4), *The American Historical Review*, pp. 788–812.

Strayer, J. R.: *On the Medieval Origins of the Modern State*, Princeton University Press, Princeton, 1970.

Tesón, F.: "Humanitarian Intervention: Loose Ends", 2011, Vol. 10 (3), *Journal of Military Ethics*, pp. 192–212.

The Montreux Document on Private Military and Security Companies, 17 September 2008, available at www.eda.admin.ch/eda/en/home/topics/intla/humlaw/pse/psechi.html.

The Protocol Additional to the Geneva Conventions of 12 August 1949, relating to the Protection of Victims of International Armed Conflicts, Protocol I, Article 47 (2), June 1977.

Tilly, C.: *Coercion, Capital, and European States, AD 990–1990*, Basil Blackwell, Oxford, 1990.

Tilly, C.: *The Formation of National States in Western Europe*, Princeton University Press, Princeton, 1975.

Wallerstein, I.: *The Modern World-System I. Capitalist Agriculture and the Origins of the European World-Economy in the Sixteenth Century*, Academic Press, London, 1974.

Wapshott, N.: *Keynes. Hayek: The Clash that Defined Modern Economics*, W. W. Norton & Company, London, 2012.

Weber, M.: *The Vocation Lectures*, Hackett Publishing Company, Cambridge, 2004.

www.g4s.com/en/Who%20we%20are/Our%20people/Our%20employees/.

1 Private military companies, a contemporary problem?

While the growth of the private military industry can be observed in the media and through general privatisation trends,[1] it can be problematic to obtain comprehensive data about private military company (PMC) activity. Unlike national armies and official governmental agencies, PMCs are more obscured because they are not subject to the Freedom Information Act or similar legislative tools that impose transparency. Government enquiry into the private military industry is also limited with little reporting or regulation of the industry.[2] Similarly, the contracts between national governments and PMCs carry commercial and security sensitivities and are generally not available for public, scholarly, or advocacy scrutiny.[3] This level of secrecy and ambiguity surrounding private military companies is certainly adds to the puzzle of PMC classification and partially explains why these actors are difficult to regulate. Another challenge arises from the codification itself, with existing legal definitions formulated within a particular political context which has since shifted.

Private force has always found room to exist within different forms of governance. Understanding the limitations of existing codification sets the stage for the broader conceptualisation of private military power and its regulation. In addition, this chapter provides a high-level introduction to PMC regulation, discussing its purpose and considering different facets of accountability regulation offers in the context of PMC conduct.

Mercenaries, contractors, civilians

In the absence of a universally accepted definition of mercenaries, the term has been stretched from hired individuals, to private security firms contracted by the state, to cross-border troops providing military services.[4] Historically, as discussed in *Chapter 2*, mercenaries were ascribed a more colloquial meaning, exemplifying the nature of medieval privateering and the professional aspect of the absolutist standing armies. In the twentieth century, the national liberation movements of the Cold War era urged for criminalisation of mercenaries through the ratification of the 1972 Convention for the Elimination of Mercenaries in Africa by the Organisation of African Unity (OAU). Combining the elements of nationality and motive, the first regional definition of mercenaries was comprehensively drafted in order to address the challenges that mercenaries posed for the national liberation movements and the sovereign integrity of the newly established African states.[5] While binding on the signatory states, the OAU definition of mercenaries was subsequently altered in 1980 by the addition of Appendix III, aligning it with the most widely accepted international definition of a mercenary, codified in the 1977 Additional Protocol (AP) I to the Geneva Conventions.[6] AP I articulates the parameters of motivation in order to define mercenaries under IL. Article 47 (2) of Protocol I states that a mercenary is any person who:

a is especially recruited locally or abroad in order to fight in an armed conflict;
b does, in fact, take a direct part in the hostilities;
c is motivated to take part in the hostilities essentially by the desire for private gain and, in fact, is promised, by or on behalf of a Party to the conflict, material compensation substantially in excess of that promised or paid to combatants of similar ranks and functions in the armed forces of that Party;
d is neither a national of a Party to the conflict nor a resident of territory controlled by a Party to the conflict;
e is not a member of the armed forces of a Party to the conflict; and
f has not been sent by a State which is not a Party to the conflict on official duty as a member of its armed forces.

Later, the 1989 United Nations (UN) Mercenary Convention[7] broadened the definition to include non-nationals recruited to overthrow a "government or otherwise undermining the constitutional order of a State; or undermine the territorial integrity of a State". While this definition of mercenaries was largely based on AP I, it was expanded by being applied to "armed conflict"[8] and to "any other situation".[9] The 2015 UN General Assembly annual report from the Working Group (WG) on the use of mercenaries compares and contrasts the concepts of mercenaries and foreign fighters. The report considers "motivation and recruitment practices, the linkages between foreign fighters and mercenaries and the human rights implications".[10] The WG concluded that while both may be recruited abroad or locally, "foreign fighter mobilisations may encompass nationals of a party to the conflict, such as from the diaspora, while mercenaries are necessarily non-nationals".[11]

Although AP I did not produce a timeless and universally accepted definition, it formalised the legal status of a mercenary as a non-combatant under international law (IL), marking an important change in the normative classification of private military actors. The status of PMC contractors does not have a separate definition under IL. According to the Montreux Document, the personnel of private military and security companies (PMSCs)

> are protected as civilians under international humanitarian law, unless they are incorporated into the regular armed forces of a State or are members of organised armed forces, groups or units under a command responsible to the State; or otherwise lose their protection as determined by international humanitarian law.[12]

In 2013, the Geneva Academy of International Humanitarian Law and Human Rights published a revised document on the topic of regulation of private security, "The international Code of Conduct for Private Security Providers" (ICoC). The ICoC does not define contractors or civilians; their definition refers to private security companies and other private security service providers (PSCs) personnel as:

> persons working for a PSC, whether as employees or under a contract, including its staff, managers and directors. [...] Persons are considered to be personnel if they are connected to a PSC through an employment contract (fixed term, permanent or open-ended) or a contract of assignment (whether renewable or not), or if they are independent contractors, or temporary workers and/or interns (whether paid or unpaid), regardless of the specific designation used by the Company concerned.[13]

It is particularly important to highlight that PMC contractors are non-combatants and, therefore, civilians, if they are not incorporated into the military forces of the state. However, the idea of civilians who provide military and security services on behalf of a private company, which in turn is contracted by a state, but not formally incorporated in its military structure, is a rather problematic one. Whether referred to as civilians, non-combatants, or PMC contractors, this particular segment of non-military personnel who, by the nature of their work, have access to arms and tend to operate in conflict or post-conflict areas, challenges contemporary international legal norms and is not appropriately regulated.

Definition of private military companies

Although most advocates of the private military industry, and even some critics,[14] insist on the separation between private military companies and mercenaries, the nature of their activities has substantial similarities, and their motives and methods often overlap. Putting aside the political context of the AP I definition of mercenaries, rooted in the rhetoric of decolonisation and national liberation movements, the aim of international community is to criminalise inappropriate participation in hostilities by groups and individuals who have no national or ideological relation to either party to the conflict.

The WG defines a PMSC as "a corporate entity which provides on a compensatory basis military and/or security services by physical persons and/or legal entities".[15] By acknowledging that PMC activities fall outside of the UN Mercenary

Convention's definition, they become excluded from its regulatory scope.[16] Meanwhile, the AP I mercenary definition disregards most PMC personnel, many of whom are nationals of one of the parties to the conflict and are not contracted to fight in military operations.[17] The WG has been following the development of the Policy and the Operations Manuals on the use of armed services from private security companies and engaging with the UN Department of Safety and Security in order to produce a comprehensive, human rights-compliant policy framework for the procurement and use of armed private security companies by UN organs and bodies.[18] This initiative clearly indicates the WG's intention to legitimise the deployment of armed private contractors by the UN.

Another definition of PMCs was proposed by the International Committee of the Red Cross (ICRC). At the fourth meeting on the 'Swiss Initiative' in September 2008, the Montreux Document was finalised and adopted by consensus of participating governments.[19] This intergovernmental initiative intended to promote respect for international humanitarian law (IHL) and human rights law whenever PMCs are present in armed conflicts.[20] It states that

> PMSCs are private business entities that provide military and/or security services, irrespective of how they describe themselves. Military and security services include, in particular, armed guarding and protection of persons and objects, such as convoys, buildings and other places; maintenance and operation of weapons systems; prisoner detention; and advice to or training of local forces and security personnel.[21]

The industry as well as academic literature provides a variety of terms: private security company (PSC), private military company (PMC), private military and security companies (PMSCs), private security companies and other private security service providers (PSCs). Interestingly, the Montreux Document and the ICoC do not differentiate between PMSCs based on the nature of the contribution they make (or do not make) to the conduct of hostilities.[22] While this monograph uses the term PMC to distinguish companies engaged in the provision of armed contractors, it is also concerned with how accountability for misconduct is invoked regardless of the specific naming of the company. Therefore, to an extent, the term PMC, as used in this analysis, is interchangeable with PMSC and PSC and should be recognised as a limitation. Although I critique the regulatory application and highlight limitations of the Montreux Document in the following chapters, its definition of PMCs closely supports the proposed scope of my analysis. In other words, all functions listed above, except for advisory services, apply to armed private contractors. While the ICoC builds upon the foundation of the Montreux Document, attempting to address some of its regulatory gaps, the proposed definition only covers private security companies and private security service providers (PSCs). Similar to its predecessor, the ICoC describes a PSC as "any Company (as defined in this Code) whose business activities include the provision of Security Services either on its own behalf or on behalf of another, irrespective of how such a Company describes itself".[23]

Although omitting 'military' companies or services from their terminology, the ICoC recognises the military aspect of PSC activity in its Preamble, stating that "PSCs play an important role in protecting state and non-state clients engaged in relief, recovery, and reconstruction efforts, commercial business operations, diplomacy and military activity".[24] Such codification mechanisms adopted by the recognised international regulatory authorities inadvertently distance PMCs from their contentious mercenary association, thereby further normalising and legitimising PMC activity.

Challenges of the definitions

One of the challenges of defining the legitimacy of mercenaries, or their corporate successors, private military companies, is not a legal, but mainly a political one. Whether examined from a historical angle, or that of nationality or motive, there is always a degree of irregularity present in the field of private military force. Echoing O'Brien, the definition of a 'mercenary' contained in AP I is generally unworkable as a legal instrument as first, it describes the actor and not the act of mercenarism, and second, all six parameters of the definition must apply to the actor in order to meet the criteria.[25]

One broad criterion for defining a mercenary is grounded in nationality or citizenship, i.e. foreign recruits in a national army. However, countries like the US, the UK, and France have legal mechanisms that enable foreign citizens to serve in their armed forces.[26]

Defining a mercenary based on a motivation of financial gain is too narrow because it excludes contractors who participate in a conflict for ideological reasons.[27] It also omits a large number of ex-military personnel who continue their profession outside of the state army. Motives are hard to establish, as they may vary depending on the individual. Moreover, they are subjective and open to interpretation. Basing the entire set of regulations purely on motivation makes the law easy to manipulate, depending on political agendas. As noted in the Diplock Report, released in 1976 following the involvement of British mercenaries in Angola, the "soldier of conscience may be found fighting side by side with the soldier of fortune".[28] A definition based on motivation questions the neutrality and impartiality of law and once again brings political rhetoric into play. However, if the element of motivation by profit is removed from the definition, its content degrades substantially. If mercenaries are not distinguished from other combatants by commercial gain, then the term would cover all non-nationals and non-residents who enlist to oppose or support any political movement in an armed conflict.[29]

The test of motivation offers another controversial facet found in a more contemporary example of the Indonesian army. Freeport-McMoRan Copper & Gold, Inc. is a prominent US mining company that controls one of the world's largest gold and copper mines in Indonesia. The company collaborated with the Indonesian army who guarded the Grasberg mine. In 2003, two US pension funds that were shareholders in the company raised a concern about "human rights abuses against the indigenous population [of Papua] by the Indonesian military in connection with security operations conducted on behalf of Freeport-McMoRan".[30] As a result of this inquiry, Freeport-McMoRan were found to have made substantial payments to the Indonesian army, often to a single general, to ensure military protection of the extraction business. According to the research conducted by Global Witness, Indonesian reformists considered these payments controversial, and saw them as evidence of the dependency of the Indonesian national army on a private company.[31] This is a question of motivation and loyalty, and an example of a national army pursuing private, mercenary goals instead of serving the state and the nation. The military suggested that the activities conducted by Freeport-McMoRan were a lucrative business ameliorating the military facilities, equipment, and transport.[32] If the security services provided by the military ultimately benefited the Indonesian economy and the state, they could potentially be regarded as catering to public state interests. This argument would stand, had Freeport-McMoRan not been found to be paying the military directly, rather than the Indonesian government. Between May 2001 and March 2003, Global Witness found that "a series of payments totalling US$247,705 appear to have been made by Freeport Indonesia to an Indonesian general named Mahidin Simbolon".[33] In this scenario, an army was a governmental institution that pursued private goals outside of the public framework with security services to the mining company were provided in exchange for monetary gain, therefore evoking a mercenary motive.

To better understand the definition, a historical and at the same time universal example of piracy can be explored in contrast to mercenarism. As a rule, mercenaries and PMCs act upon instruction within the terms of a contract or in exchange for a payment, while pirates pursue their own interests. Although piracy fundamentally differs from mercenarism in this respect, there have been historical examples where pirates were used by a state to perpetrate an attack on their opponent. By the 1720s, thousands of pirates had sought to build autonomous, relatively equal, and democratic orders of their own, countering Atlantic capital. Captains were often elected and accountable to their crews, attitudes were liberal, and decisions were democratic.[34] Despite these positive characteristics, for hundreds of years, IL has treated the pirate as a *hostis humani generis* – an enemy of all mankind.[35] The rationale behind the universality of the pirate as an enemy was the indiscriminate threat that piracy posed to trade, other sailors, and even the established world order. However, before sailors-turned-pirates could claim their own ship, they commonly "served the needs of the maritime state and the merchant community in England".[36] Some seamen were recruited to serve on Jamaican privateers during the War of Spanish Succession.[37] A mercenary motive or a legitimating state action could draw distinctions between a pirate and a privateer. In 1817, William Hutchings was accused of piracy for sailing an American ship under a "Buenos Aires commission and colours as a part of their independence struggle against Spain".[38] In *United States v. Hutchings*,[39] the court established that *animo furandi*, a necessary component of piracy, could be disproved if the accused was acting under a commission or acting on government service without a commission.[40] In addition, Woodes Rogers was known for both recruiting pirates in his capacity as a captain of a large-scale privateering trip, and denouncing them in the West Indies as royal governor of the Bahama Islands.[41]

While nationality and motive have been prominently used to distinguish and define mercenaries, both tests can also be problematic in terms of context and universality. Unlike pirates, terrorists, freedom fighters, and militias, mercenaries and PMCs are typically hired to provide their services on behalf of another party, rather than waging a conflict to pursue their own political or ideological goals. Also, under current provisions of IL, only states can commit the acts of aggression, using mercenaries as their implements; mercenaries themselves cannot be the perpetrators.[42] So, rather than focusing on the monetary gain, I propose to envisage a transactional relationship between supply and demand of private security that existed long before modern sovereign states, national armies, and arguments concerning the ethics and morality of private military resources.[43]

For the purposes of socio-historical analysis, in this monograph I consider a broader spectrum of irregular military actors, foregoing the rigidity of the proposed definitions in order to evaluate all forms of private violence used by a state. By extending the scope of my enquiry to various privately organised military forces deployed by a state or a sovereign, regardless of the contemporary classification, different facets of private security can be traced in the changing conflict paradigm. Narrowing down the definition may hinder the broader purpose of understanding the constitutive elements of contemporary issues posed by private military actors. Therefore, in *Chapter 2*, the terms 'mercenary' and 'private military' are used interchangeably. It does not, however, negate the nuanced differences that the two notions have *in the abstract.*

The value of narrow definitions lies in their ability to provide the grounds for critical thought in response to contemporary issues.[44] However, a more historically informed classification of mercenaries enables us to consider patterns of state-military relationships, where a more rigid contemporary legal definition would draw a line. For example, Hampson argues that foreign units that were routinely hired and incorporated into states' own forces before the nineteenth century cannot be considered mercenaries.[45] While Hampson's assessment is accurate if measured against the criteria set out by the AP I definition of 1977, it is crucial to bear in mind the political circumstances of decolonisation under which this definition was drafted. The context of national liberation struggles can hardly apply to the widespread professionally hired private soldiers of the fifteenth and sixteenth centuries. However, the fact alone that mercenaries were not criminalised, but were actually a norm for centuries, insists on the significance of the 'private' element in feudal, absolutist, and imperial military cultures. When a conflict unfolded in sixteenth-century Europe, the king would summon his barons who appeared with *their* troops,[46] leaving him dependent on the patronage and loyalty of feudal lords rather than his own ability to centralise military power. Similarly, nineteenth-century empires were not relying on their own 'home-grown' armies to fight territorial wars. Instead, they would leverage colonial armies, whom they subjected and utilised in a manner that considerably differed from the treatment of national conscripts.

The context in which the definitions of mercenaries were drafted implies that the law is not neutral; instead, it is shaped by various expressions of power and articulated through the concept of legitimacy. This becomes of particular significance when considering current and future legal responses to PMC regulation. Different aspects of violence, traditionally segregated into public and private, are not purely arbitrary. They bear political and normative meaning and are related to a state's choice of security resources, their allocation and distribution, as well as the formation of norms supporting this choice.

PMC classification

According to Robert Mandel, PMCs represent a modified form of organised corporate mercenarism, shielding their home states from international responsibility by concealing their participation or influence in conflicts.[47] While there are plenty of critics blurring the lines between PMCs and mercenaries,[48] it is important to distinguish the basic components of PMCs from a legal rather than ethical or political standpoint. From a corporate legal perspective, PMCs arose from the juxtaposition of civilian corporations and the lack of any clear criminalisation of mercenaries by the instruments of IL.[49] Like mercenary groups, PMCs are still formed and run exclusively by civilians, albeit the majority are former military personnel. However, PMCs acquired a corporate legal personality which distinguishes them from their legally dubious predecessors. The construct of incorporation turned a private business of mercenarism into a company.

While the legitimacy of PMC activity is widely debated under IL, it is important to establish the starting point of their status. Incorporated as companies with employees, subsidiaries, investors, and profit reports, PMCs enjoy the same protection by corporate law as any other company. In other words, all PMCs are *a priori* legitimate, since according to the legal definition of corporate and contract law, no company can be formed with the purpose of engaging in illegal activities.[50] As argued by Hin-Yan Liu and also discussed in *Chapter 3*, IL failed to criminalise the act of mercenarism, therefore leaving a loophole for PMCs to exploit. Although I discuss the regulation of PMCs under corporate and contract law in more detail in *Chapter 5*, the above clarification was necessary to identify the starting point for PMC classification.

There is no one right way to classify a PMC. Peter Singer divides PMCs into three "business sectors": (i) military provider firms supplying "direct, tactical military assistance" that can include serving in front-line combat; (ii) military consulting firms that provide strategic advice and training; and (iii) military support forms that provide logistics, maintenance, and intelligence services to armed forces.[51] Wulf divides the companies into five categories, identifying (i) private security companies, (ii) defence producers, (iii) private military companies, (iv) non-statutory forces, and (v) mercenaries. He further differentiates PMCs by the nature of their activity, i.e. provision of consulting, logistics and support, technical services, training, peacekeeping and humanitarian assistance, and combat forces.[52]

McFate separates PMCs into 'mercenary and military enterprisers'.[53] South Africa's Executive Outcomes[54] and London-based Sandline International[55] fall under McFate's classification of mercenary enterprisers, defining them as a private army conducting autonomous military campaigns. According to McFate, raising rather than commanding military forces is a distinct feature of military enterprisers, such as Blackwater, DynCorp International, or Triple Canopy.[56] Meanwhile, the industry itself classifies PMSCs as "private business entities that provide military and/or security services, irrespective of how they describe themselves".[57]

While as of March 2011, there were 90,339 contractors in Afghanistan, compared to approximately 99,800 uniformed military recruits,[58] the armed contractors represented a minority of approximately 16 per cent of all US Department of Defence (DOD) contractor personnel.[59] This is important when conceptualising the scope of PMC activities, as the majority of contractors fulfil purely civilian functions, such as logistics and transportation of supplies, maintenance, etc. PMC taxonomy is made problematic by the ambiguous use of the term 'security' or 'military' in the context of private civilian-formed companies. The term 'military' is the contentious part of the term 'private military company', as it creates an automatic assumption that the company is belligerent and armed. While PMCs are used by governments to provide support in their military operations abroad, the term 'military' can be somewhat misleading, implying that this is the direct function of the company. It also becomes an oxymoron, as the term 'military' which, according to current rules and regulations of IHL, is inherently governmental, is juxtaposed against the term 'private company', contradicting public state ownership of legitimate means of violence. Therefore, for the purposes of this monograph, when referring to a PMC, I emphasise the corporate status of a PMC as a legal entity that employs contractors who could directly participate in hostilities.

Despite the critique condemning the privatisation and outsourcing of any governmental functions,[60] much of PMC activity, such as logistics support, construction, communication, and maintenance, does not pose codification or accountability issues under IL. While ethical arguments are valid in denouncing the mercenary motive, and the impact on democratic accountability,[61] these are often disproportionate to the reality of the armed contractor issue. On an institutional level, the norm against the use of private force on ethical grounds was demonstrated in 1994, when Executive Outcomes approached Kofi Annan at the outbreak of Rwandan atrocities. Although the UN decision was firmly against using a PMC to address the crisis, the inability to mobilise public forces in a timely manner, and the reluctance to defer to a PMC resulted in over 800,000 casualties, which combined exceeds the number of victims in Iraq and Afghanistan.[62] However, since then, the UN has been using PMCs both directly and through US procurement for their peacekeeping and humanitarian operations.[63]

Regulation and accountability: who should be regulated and to what end?

Since the end of the Cold War, an overwhelming number of PMCs have been running as part of foreign military operations, with their services ranging from consulting and risk assessment to training and combat. As a result of numerous high-profile incidents involving PMCs, such as Blackwater in Iraq or DynCorp in Bosnia, there has been a growing international interest in regulating private military activity. Regulatory responses came from many directions. The UN strategy is divided between the Human Rights Council's voluntary initiatives,[64] and the Working Group, who took a firm stance through the Draft International Convention on the Regulation, Oversight and Monitoring of PMSCs (Draft Convention), attempting to invoke state responsibility for all PMSCs registered on their territory. It also produced a number of comprehensive legally binding and voluntary guidelines aimed at enhancing the responsibility of transnational businesses to respect human rights, including prevention, mitigation, and remediation. In the meantime, the industry introduced self-regulatory bodies that certify PMCs and provide guidelines in order to drive the standards of their services internationally. Amongst such are the American Society for Industrial Security International,[65] the International Organisation for Standardisation (ISO/PAS 28007:2012)[66] providing guidelines for Private Maritime Security Companies supplying privately contracted armed security personnel on board ships, the Organisation for Economic Co-operation and Development (OECD) Guidelines for Multinational Enterprises[67] and the International Code of Conduct for Private Security Providers. The outcome of such active regulatory responses to private military conduct is a complex network of binding and voluntary provisions that all claim to regulate private military space. What complicates this picture further is the domestic jurisdiction invoked by the corporate nature of PMCs, therefore introducing contracts, company law, and tort law into the mix.

Regulation

The term 'regulation' can mean a variety of controls with different degrees of enforcement and state intervention. A common understanding of regulation is tied up with the concept of 'command and control', whereby the state uses legal rules that are often backed by criminal sanctions.[68] According to Andrees, Nasri, and Swiniarski, regulation can be statutory, i.e. legally binding, in which case it is ordained and enforced by a judicial body or government authority. It can also be voluntary, whereby the measures adopted by the industry actors serve as guiding principles and behavioural standards.[69] The OECD, for example, defines regulation as the "imposition of rules by government, backed by the use of penalties that are intended specifically to modify the economic behaviour of individuals and firms in the private sector".[70] Prices, output, rate of return, disclosure of information, standards, and ownership ceilings, or in other words, all mechanisms of social control affecting all aspects of behaviour, can all be considered as regulatory instruments.[71]

Regulation can be broadly differentiated by the level of state involvement, with the conservative approach rooted in free market principles, the liberal approach seeking a balance between regulatory and criminal sanctions, and, finally, the radical approach relying predominantly on the punitive nature of criminal justice.[72] As a critique of a centred prosecutorial theory, David Garland develops a more comprehensive approach to regulation. To address and mitigate criminal activity holistically, the 'responsibilisation' approach seeks to incorporate a wide range of civil society instruments and institutions, including the private sector.[73]

A purely state-centred definition of regulation[74] does not reflect current industry influences, which are prominent in the PMC field. By embracing a wider range of regulatory techniques, a decentred approach emphasises social responsibility rather than the punitive nature of criminalisation.[75] It can help raise and maintain industry standards and drive ethical behaviour amongst PMCs and their employees. The decentred approach is characterised by five key notions: complexity, fragmentation, interdependencies, ungovernability, and the rejection of a clear distinction between public and private.[76] Together all these notions more accurately describe current regulatory needs, whereby the state no longer holds a monopoly of force, and there are a number of new complex and interconnected actors that understand and drive industries, and the processes that govern them. These five notions create a rationalisation for a new decentred regulator who, in theory, would be much closer to the industry, and therefore more likely to understand the needs and the risks related to the regulatees.

While the contemporary security sector is no different in some ways to the proliferation of privatisation and outsourcing of numerous military functions, the lethal nature of the industry coupled with the international context of PMC presence makes the military unique. Under the current norms of IL, it is not permissible to wage a private war. Government involvement, therefore, becomes inevitable in one shape or another. Although some PMCs are hired by multinational corporations to perform non-military activities, my enquiry is concerned with the PMC engagement in international or multilateral[77] projects, whereby contractors operate in conflict or post-conflict environments of high sensitivity and are exposed to direct participation in hostilities.

A criminal justice approach, therefore, could contribute to punishing and also preventing gross violations in the realm of private security. Meanwhile, all controls that are currently in place for mercenaries and PMCs are not criminalised, with the exception of the narrow definition of mercenaries, contextualised in decolonisation. Nonetheless, the merging of the lines between public and private can be identified in 'hybrid' regulatory bodies that combine governmental and non-state actors.[78] For the private military industry, such decentred regulation can be observed in the Montreux Process and the International Code of Conduct.[79]

The purpose of regulation

When attempting to determine who should be regulated and to what end, first it is important to consider what we mean by regulation and what is its purpose.

Julia Black defines regulation as "the intentional activity of attempting to control, order or influence the behaviour of others".[80] This definition sets regulation apart from both the government operating domestic state laws, and market and social forces, by invoking the element of intentionality. As such, regulation can have multiple goals. Most generally, it aims to provide some sort of organisation, but it can also manage risk,[81] provide access to justice,[82] or strive to achieve justice.[83] My enquiry is concerned with the application and the effective exercising of the regulation, therefore focusing on a functional aspect of the definition. To unfold the key issues of this research, regulation is conceptualised as a broader mode of administering PMC activity, with 'responsibilisation' representing a more decentred approach that entails both legally binding and voluntary norms, and criminalisation, invoking criminal justice exercised through judicial systems and government authorities. As a discipline, regulation can operate across sovereign borders; it reaches both international and industry realms, forming a variety of relationships between state, law, and society.[84] Regulation can be analysed from an effectiveness perspective, whereby the gap between what a regulation sets out to do and what it does in practice is at the core of the critique. It can also be critiqued in terms of value, or whether it is aimed at the appropriate goals, and if it delivers the appropriate value of legitimacy or justice.[85] In this book, I adapt a critical approach of legal and policy reform[86] in order to assess the gap between the regulation of the private military space and the accountability that this regulation can provide in the event of gross violations by private military actors.

Building on the value-based approach, an important goal of regulation specifically concerning private security providers is to enable an appropriate use of PMCs. I side with Nigel White as he posits that "the idea of PMSCs using force may be distasteful, but if it is used in a regulated manner to protect the human rights of vulnerable people, then arguably it should not be prohibited".[87] Regulation should thus ensure an environment whereby private security resources could address the needs of the international security landscape without the risk of their acting with impunity. Effective and value-based regulation could also help PMCs to finally overcome their legally dubious and unethical reputation in the eyes of the public.

Accountability

Law and regulation fulfils its goals through enforcement, or in other words by invoking responsibility. When a PMC is involved in committing a gross violation, such as killing civilians as a result of its contracted activities, who should be responsible and in what way? Is it the contractor who fired the gun? Or perhaps the company he was recruited by, who may not have provided the appropriate training? Or should it be the state that outsourced the support of military activities to a private entity? The state is accountable to the extent of which both military conduct and human rights are viewed as primary concerns of states, rather than corporations or individuals.[88] Private military company provides the context of a professional occupation of the contractor, bringing corporate responsibility into scope. If the corporate context is removed (if, for example, a contractor acted against instruction or protocol), it then reduces the situation to an instance of one civilian killing another. This means that all three components, the contractor, the company, and the state, are crucial to establishing responsibility in PMC conduct.[89]

The use of private force prompts an interesting question about the theory and practice of state responsibility and, most importantly, relevant international regulation and how it applies. According Hannah Tonkin, the fundamental principle of state responsibility is that a state is only responsible for its *own* acts rather than all acts.[90] The rationale for this construct prevents the state from performing as the guarantor of all acts in its territory, or acts of its nationals abroad.[91] What differentiates the relationship between the state and PMCs from using the services of any other corporation is the potential resort to power on the international level, and human rights violations in the context of post-conflict reconstruction, humanitarian intervention, peacekeeping, etc.

There are very strict norms in IHL and Customary IL concerning intervention and the use of force by states.[92] Due to the governmental nature of PMC activity, a number of regulatory mechanisms have been developed to establish state responsibility, whereby the conduct of the private party is assignable to the state. Amongst such mechanisms are the Articles on Responsibility of States for Internationally Wrongful Acts (ILC Articles) adopted by the International Law Commission in 2001. Together with the Commentaries, the ILC Articles outline the conditions for attribution of private conduct to the state. There are also industry-specific regulatory bodies, such as the Montreux Document and the Draft Convention on the Regulation, Oversight, and Monitoring of PMSCs that outline the obligation of states who hire, host, and domicile PMCs. Additionally, the UN "Protect, Respect and Remedy" Framework sets out the guiding principles for states, as well as businesses, to ensure human rights values are promoted and followed. Finally, the relationship between the state, as client, and the PMC, as provider of services, is administered by contractual terms that both parties agree to. Contract law adds an extra layer of surveillance and legal enforcement, as its jurisdiction applies when one of the parties is found to be in breach of contractual terms. I explore the effectiveness of state responsibility as a mode of regulation of PMC conduct in *Chapter 5*, considering the tensions between the historic formulation of norms on mercenarism, evolving international legal responses to the use of private force, and the equalising dimension of contract law that puts the state and the PMC in a horizontal client-provider relationship.

Like states whose acts have an international dimension and a corresponding body of international laws that attempt to regulate such action, international individual responsibility has been solidified through international criminal law as a result of post-Second World War tribunals. While only states and international organisations are recognised as subjects of IL, individuals possess international legal personality under the Rome Statute of the International Criminal Court (ICC), which outlines their responsibility for the commission of core international crimes, namely genocide, crimes against humanity, crime of aggression, and war crimes.[93] In order for a PMC employee or director to be held liable for aiding or abetting a crime under the Rome Statute, it is necessary to prove the knowledge and the intent of the accused, demonstrating that the assistance was provided "for the purpose of facilitating the commission of the crime".[94]

Furthermore, Article 21 of the Draft Convention establishes the rules on individual criminal responsibility by exercising its jurisdiction over individuals through the domestic laws of state parties.[95] On a national level, contractors are also subject to domestic criminal laws just like any civilians. However, domestic criminal law is often limited by territoriality, whereby its jurisdiction does not extend beyond the national borders of the state. While individual responsibility can be invoked internationally, the status of private military contractors (that differ to that of a mercenary) poses certain limitations to the practical applicability of such regulation. For example, during the Coalition Provisional Authority administration in Iraq, hiring state had granted PMC contractors legal immunity from local criminal legal system of the state where they performed their services. To overcome these issues, in 2000 the United States Congress passed the Military Extraterritorial Jurisdiction Act, that gave federal courts jurisdiction over felonies committed by persons "employed by or accompanying the armed forces" overseas. Similarly, according to the UK 2006 Armed Forces Act, PMC contractors working for the UK Armed Forces are subject to Service discipline. I discuss individual responsibility and the challenges associated with assigning it to PMC contractors in *Chapter 5*.

Finally, there are numerous regulatory bodies that make provisions for corporate responsibility; some are international, some domestic, some binding, others self-regulating and voluntary. Corporate liability can be of a criminal (domestic criminal justice system) or social nature (in tort law) and is considered in depth in relation to PMCs in *Chapters 6* and *7*. With the rise of PMCs, mercenaries made a transition from bands of freelancers or 'dogs of war' into properly incorporated legal entities that operate under legitimate contracts across the world. Notwithstanding the ascribed legal personality that companies have acquired, the account of rationality and autonomy tends to exclude corporations from the legal realm based on the assumption that they are not persons in a metaphysical sense.[96] Historically, corporate liability developed in a different way to that of states or individuals. Unlike individuals and states, who can be tried at the ICC (and the ad hoc Tribunals) and the International Court of Justice respectively, legal persons cannot be held criminally liable on an international level. While there is no strong norm of international criminal responsibility for the corporation, the African Court of Justice and Human Rights is an emerging precedent to that end. As of May 2014, it became the first international court to recognise and criminalise corporate liability for international crimes.[97]

Conclusion

To conclude, the choice of a critical approach enables this research to consider a wide range of different configurations of state, military power, policy, and law. What separates private force from illegitimate or criminal acts is the (potential) recognition of the former as a legitimate tool chosen by the state, and the latter as a violation of its laws. For instance, while piracy and privateering are effectively the same type of activity, piracy was considered a heinous crime, while privateering was legitimised state commission.[98] It is therefore crucial to understand the narrative of legitimacy when analysing the use and regulation of different types of military power. Legitimacy does not simply arise from a widespread behaviour; it derives from normative behaviour and a sense of obligation. The importance of legitimacy is thus not purely theoretical; it transpires into norms and has the ability to drive policy.

The following chapter engages with the notion of private force as a long-existent phenomenon that is deeply entrenched in governmental, political, and economic structures, all of which should be considered when formulating current and future regulatory mechanism.

Notes

1 Cropley and Lewis (2015); Arduino (2015).
2 McFate (2014, p. 9).
3 Kinsey (2004, pp. 155–173).
4 Avant (2005, p. 22); see literature on mercenaries: Percy (2007a); Mockler (1969); Thompson (1994); Armstrong (2008); Singer (2004); McFate (2014); Axelrod, 2014; Chesterman and Lehnard (2007).
5 OAU Convention for the Elimination of Mercenaries in Africa, O.A.U. Doc. CM/433/Rev. L. Annex 1, 1972, Article 1: "Under the OAU Convention a 'mercenary' is classified as anyone who, not a national of the state against which his actions are directed, is employed, enrols or links himself willingly to a person, group or organization whose aim is: (a) to overthrow by force of arms or by any other means the government of that Member State of the Organization of African Unity; (b) to undermine the independence, territorial integrity or normal working of the institutions of the said State; (c) to block by any means the activities of any liberation movement recognized by the Organization of African Unity."
6 The Protocol Additional to the Geneva Conventions of 12 August 1949, relating to the Protection of Victims of International Armed Conflicts, Protocol I, Article 47, June 1977; some countries, including the United States, do not support the Protocol.
7 International Convention against the Recruitment, Use, Financing and Training of Mercenaries, 4 December 1989; A/RES/44/34.
8 UN Mercenary Convention, Article 1, para. 1.
9 UN Mercenary Convention, Article 1, para. 2.
10 A/70/330, Summary, p. 2.
11 A/70/330, Art. 87.
12 The Montreux Document, Art. 26 (b), p. 14.
13 ICoC, para. 51, p. 50.
14 In his book *Law's Impunity*, Hin-Yan Liu argues that although PMCs share historical lineages with mercenaries, they are fundamentally different due to their corporate legal identity.
15 A/HRC/24/45, UN General Assembly, Human Rights Council; 24th session: "Annual report of the Working Group on the use of mercenaries as a means of violating human rights and impeding the exercise of the right of peoples to self-determination", July 2013, p. 3.
16 Nikitin, A.: A/HRC/10/14 paras 40–41.
17 The Montreux Document, p. 40.
18 A/HRC/24/45, para. 11, pp. 4–5.

19 Federal Department of Foreign Affairs, Section for International Humanitarian Law.
20 The Montreux Document on pertinent international legal obligations and good practices for states related to operations of private military and security companies during armed conflict, ICRC, Montreux, 2008, p. 31.
21 The Montreux Document, Preface, Art. 9 (a), p. 9.
22 ICoC, p. 5.
23 ICoC, p. 18.
24 ICoC, *supra*, Preamble.
25 O'Brien (2007, p. 34).
26 Barkawi (2010, p. 47).
27 Thomson (1990 p. 23).
28 Report of the Committee of Privy Counsellors appointed to inquire into the recruitment of mercenaries, Cmnd. 6569, (1976, p. 2).
29 Taulbee (1985, p. 353).
30 Global Witness (2005, p. 12).
31 Global Witness (2005, p. 18).
32 McCulloch (2000).
33 Global Witness (2005, p. 4).
34 Neocleous (2015, p. 30); Linebaugh and Rediker (2000, pp. 162–163).
35 Kontorovich and Art (2010, p. 251).
36 Linebaugh and Rediker (2000, p. 156).
37 Linebaugh and Rediker (2000, p. 159).
38 Paige (2013, p. 140).
39 *United States v. Hutchings* 26 F.Cas. (Brunn.Coll.C) 440 (Circuit Court, District Virginia, 1817).
40 Rubin (1988, pp. 159–160).
41 Linebaugh and Rediker (2000, p. 161).
42 Liu (2015, p. 181).
43 Pattison (2010a, pp. 425–447); Tesón (2011 pp. 192–212); Pattison (2010b, pp. 1–31); Alexandra, Baker and Caparini (2008).
44 Rose (1999, p. 9).
45 Hampson (1991, pp. 5–6).
46 Geuss (2001, p. 44).
47 Mandel (2002, p. 33).
48 See, for example, Scahill (2007); Armstrong (2008); Young Pelton (2006).
49 Liu (2015, p. 192).
50 Liu (2015, p. 183).
51 Singer (2004).
52 Schreier and Caparini (2005, pp. 39–41).
53 McFate (2014, p. 14).
54 Defunct in 1998.
55 The company closed on 16 April 2014.
56 McFate (2014, pp. 14–17), specifically Table 2.1.
57 The Montreux Document, Preface, Art. 9 (a), p. 9.
58 Source: CENTCOM 2 Quarter FY 2011 Contractor Census Report; Troop data from Joint Chiefs of Staff, "Boots on the Ground" January report to Congress.
59 McFate (2014, p. 23).
60 See for example: Dickinson (2005, pp. 137–237); Dolovich (2005, pp. 437–546); Metzger (2003, pp. 1367–1502).
61 See Pattison (2014; 2010b, pp. 1–31); Tesón (2011, pp. 192–212); Percy (2007a; Percy 2007b).
62 McFate (2014, p. 38).
63 Ostensen (2011).
64 Guiding Principles on Business and Human Rights (2011).

65 Founded in 1955, now focusing on security sector; see: https://www.asisonline.org/About-ASIS/Who-We-Are/Pages/default.aspx.
66 ISO membership comprises 163 national standards bodies.
67 OECD.
68 Black (2002, p. 2).
69 Andrees, Nasri and Swiniarski (2015, p. 8).
70 See: https://stats.oecd.org/glossary/detail.asp?ID=3295.
71 Baldwin, Scott and Hood (1998, p. 3).
72 Clarke (2000); Simpson (2002).
73 Garland (2001); Ward and Fouladvand (2018).
74 Ogus (1994); also one of the definitions outlined by Baldwin, Scott and Hood (1998).
75 Black (2002, p. 4).
76 Black (2002).
77 Such as UN peacekeeping operations, for example.
78 Black (2002, p. 8).
79 There is a similar debate on accountability and the regulation of police forces, however, policing is outside the scope of my research. Some of the literature covering this debate: Jones, Newburn and Smith (1994); Bayley (2006); Zedner (2006, pp. 78–96); Baldwin (1987, pp. 97–114); Campbell (2014, pp. 26–27); Harkin (2015, pp. 730–746); Friedman and Ponomarenko (2015, pp. 1827–1905).
80 Black (2002, p. 25).
81 Black (2002, p. 10).
82 Parker (1999).
83 Ayres and Braithwaite (1992, chapter 3).
84 Black (2002, p. 26).
85 Black (2002, p. 28).
86 Dorsett and McVeigh (2012, p. 20).
87 White (2012, p. 20).
88 Ruggie (2011), Principle 6 State-Business Nexus; Commentary, p. 8.
89 Core literature on individual, corporate and state responsibility: Rome Statute of the International Criminal Court; Eser (2002); International Law Commission: *Responsibility of States for Internationally Wrongful Acts 2001*; The United Nations "Protect, Respect and Remedy" Framework; The UN Guiding Principles on Business and Human Rights; Draft International Convention on the Regulation, Oversight and Monitoring of Private Military and Security Companies, 13 July 2009; Wells (2001); White (2011, pp. 133–151); Pinto and Evans (2008).
90 Tonkin (2011, p. 56).
91 Tonkin (2011).
92 Henderson (2010); Gray (2000); Declaration on the Inadmissibility of Intervention in the Domestic Affairs of States and the Protection of their Independence and Sovereignty, G.A. Res. 2131, U.N. GAOR, 20th Sess., Supp. No. 14, U.N. Doc.A/6014 (1965); Convention Respecting the Rights and Duties of Neutral Powers and Persons in Case of War on Land (Hague Convention No. V), 18 October 1907; Implementation of the Declaration on the Granting of Independence to Colonial Countries and Peoples, General Assembly Resolution 2465, 23rd Session, 1968; Declaration on Principles of International Law concerning Friendly Relations and Cooperation among States in accordance with the Charter of the United Nations, G.A. Res. 2625, U.N. GAOR 25th Sess., Supp. No. 18, U.N. Doc. A/8018 (1970).
93 Art. 25 Statute of the International Criminal Court UN Doc./A.CONF.183.9*, 2187 UNTS 1998, p. 90.
94 Rome Statute, Part 3, Article 25 (3) (c).
95 The Draft Convention, Article 21.
96 Wells (2001, p. 65).

97 Draft Protocol on Amendments to the Protocol on the Statute of the African Court of Justice and Human Rights, May 15, 2014, STC/Legal/Min/7(I) Rev. 1, Art. 46C; see also Decision on the Draft Legal Instruments, Doc. Assembly/AU/8(XXIII), at 1 in African Union, Decisions, Declarations And Resolution, Assembly/AU/Dec.517-545(XXIII).

98 Kontorovich (2004, p. 187).

References

"Guiding Principles on Business and Human Rights. Implementing the United Nations 'Protect, Respect and Remedy' Framework, UN Human Rights Office of the High Commissioner", New York and Geneva, 2011.

A/70/330.

A/HRC/10/14.

A/HRC/24/45, UN General Assembly, Human Rights Council; 24th session: "Annual Report of the Working Group on the Use of Mercenaries as a means of Violating Human Rights and Impeding the Exercise of the Right of Peoples to Self-Determination", July 2013.

Alexandra, A., Baker D.-P. and Caparini, M. (eds): *Private Military and Security Companies: Ethics, Policies, and Civil-Military Relations*, Routledge Military Studies, New York, 2008.

Andrees, B., Nasri, A. and Swiniarski, P.: "Regulating Labour Recruitment to Prevent Human Trafficking and to Foster Fair Migration: Models, Challenges and Opportunities", 2015, *International Labour Organization*, pp. 1–95.

Arduino, A.: *Security Privatisation with Chinese Characteristics. The Role of Chinese Private Security Corporations in Protecting Chinese Outbound Investments and Citizens*, Policy Report, S. Rajaratnam School of International Studies, June 2015.

Armstrong, S.: *War PLC: The Rise of the New Corporate Mercenary*, Faber & Faber Limited, London, 2008.

Avant, D.: *The Market for Force: The Consequences of Privatising Security*, CUP, Cambridge, 2005.

Axelrod, A.: *Mercenaries: A Guide to Private Armies and Private Military Companies*, Sage, London, 2014.

Ayres, I. and Braithwaite, J.: *Responsive Regulation: Transcending the Deregulation Debate*, OUP, Oxford, 1992.

Baldwin, R.: "Why Accountability?", 1987, Vol. 27 (1), *British Journal of Criminology*, pp. 97–114.

Baldwin, R., Scott, C. and Hood, C.: *A Reader on Regulation*, OUP, Oxford, 1998.

Barkawi, T.: "State and Armed Force in International Context" in Colas, A. and Mabee, B. (eds): *Mercenaries, Pirates, Bandits and Empires: Private Violence in Historical Context*, Hurst & Company, London, 2010.

Bayley, D.: *Changing the Guard: Developing Democratic Police Abroad*, OUP, Oxford, 2006.

Black, J.: "Critical Reflections on Regulation", 2002, Vol. 27, *Australian Journal of Legal Philosophy*, pp. 1–36.

Campbell, E.: "The People, Policing and Power", 2014, Vol. 95 (1), *Criminal Justice Matters*, pp. 26–27.

CENTCOM 2 Quarter FY 2011 Contractor Census Report; Troop data from Joint Chiefs of Staff, "Boots on the Ground" January Report to Congress.

Chesterman, S. and Lehnard, C. (eds): *From Mercenaries to Market: The Rise and Regulation of Private Military Companies*, OUP, Oxford, 2007.

Clarke, M.: *Regulation: The Social Control of Business between Law and Politics*, Macmillan, Basingstoke and London, 2000.

Convention Respecting the Rights and Duties of Neutral Powers and Persons in Case of War on Land (Hague Convention No V), 18 October 1907.

Cropley, E. and Lewis, D.: "Nigeria Drafts in Foreign Mercenaries to Take on Boko Haram", 12 March 2015, Reuters, available at: http://uk.reuters.com/article/uk-nigeria-violence-mercenaries-idUKKBN0M80VT20150312.

Decision on the Draft Legal Instruments, Doc. Assembly/AU/8(XXIII), at 1 in African Union, Decisions, Declarations and Resolution, Assembly/AU/Dec.517–545(XXIII), availableat:www.au.int/en/sites/default/files/decisions/9661-assembly_au_dec_517_-_545_xxiii_e.pdf.

Declaration on Principles of International Law Concerning Friendly Relations and Cooperation among States in Accordance with the Charter of the United Nations, G.A. Res. 2625, U.N. GAOR 25th Sess., Supp. No. 18, U.N. Doc. A/8018 (1970).

Declaration on the Inadmissibility of Intervention in the Domestic Affairs of States and the Protection of their Independence and Sovereignty, G.A. Res. 2131, U.N. GAOR, 20th Sess., Supp. No. 14, U.N. Doc.A/6014 (1965).

Dickinson, L. A.: "Government for Hire: Privatizing Foreign Affairs and the Problem of Accountability under International Law", 2005, Vol. 45 (1), *William and Mary Law Review*, pp. 137–237.

Dolovich, S.: "State Punishment and Private Prisons", 2005, Vol. 55 (3), *Duke Law Journal*, pp. 437–546.

Dorsett, S. and McVeigh, S.: *Jurisdiction*, Routledge, Abingdon, 2012.

Draft International Convention on the Regulation, Oversight and Monitoring of Private Military and Security Companies, 13 July 2009.

Draft Protocol on Amendments to the Protocol on the Statute of the African Court of Justice and Human Rights, May 15, 2014, STC/Legal/Min/7(I) Rev. 1.

Eser, A.: "Individual Criminal Responsibility" in Cassese, A., Gaeta, P. and Jones, J. (eds): *The Rome Statute of the International Criminal Court: A Commentary*, OUP, Oxford, 2002.

Federal Department of Foreign Affairs, Section for International Humanitarian Law, available at www.eda.admin.ch/psc.

Friedman, B. and Ponomarenko, M.: "Democratic Policing", 2015, Vol. 90 (6), *New York University Law Review*, pp. 1827–1905.

Garland, D.: *The Culture of Control: Crime and Social Order in Contemporary Society*, OUP, Oxford, 2001.

Geuss, R.: *History and Illusion in Politics*, CUP, Cambridge, 2001.

Global Witness: "Paying for Protection: The Freeport Mine and the Indonesian Security Forces, A Report by Global Witness", July 2005.

Gray, C.: *International Law and the Use of Force*, OUP, Oxford, 2000.

Hampson, F.: "Mercenaries: Diagnosis before Prescription", 1991, Vol. 22, *Netherlands Yearbook of International Law*, pp. 3–38.

Harkin, D.: "Simmel, the Police Form and the Limits of Democratic Policing", 2015, Vol. 55 (4), *British Journal of Criminology*, pp. 730–746.

Henderson, C.: The Persistent Advocate and the Use of Force: The Impact of the United States upon the Jus ad Bellum in the Post-Cold War Era, The Ashgate International Law Series, Routledge, Abingdon, 2010.

Implementation of the Declaration on the Granting of Independence to Colonial Countries and Peoples, General Assembly Resolution 2465, 23rd Session, 1968.

International Convention against the Recruitment, Use, Financing and Training of Mercenaries, 4 December 1989; A/RES/44/34 available at www.un.org/documents/ga/res/44/a44r034.htm.

International Law Commission: *Responsibility of States for Internationally Wrongful Acts 2001.*

International Organisation for Standardisation, available at: www.iso.org/iso/home/about.htm.

Jones, T., Newburn, T. and Smith, D. J.: *Democracy and Policing*, Policy Studies Institute, London, 1994.

Kinsey, M. A.: Transparency in Government Procurement: An International Consensus?", 2004, Vol. 34 (1), *Public Contract Law Journal*, pp. 155–173.

Kontorovich, E.: "The Piracy Fallacy: Modern Universal Jurisdiction's Hollow Foundation", 2004, Vol. 45 (1), *Harvard International Law Journal*, pp. 183–239.

Kontorovich, E. and Art, S.: "An Empirical Examination of Universal Jurisdiction for Piracy", 2010, Faculty Working Papers, Paper 38, Vol. 98 (1), *California Law Review*, pp. 243–276.

Linebaugh, P. and Rediker, M.: *The Many-Headed Hydra. Sailors, Slaves, Commoners, and the Hidden History of the Revolutionary Atlantic*, Beacon Press, Boston, 2000.

Liu, H.-Y.: *Law's Impunity: Responsibility and the Modern Private Military Company*, Hart Publishing, Oxford, 2015.

Mandel, R.: *Armies without States: The Privatisation of Security*, Lynne Rienner Publishers, London, 2002.

McCulloch, L.: "Trifungsi: The Role of the Indonesian Military in Business", paper delivered to the International Conference on Soldiers in Business, Jakarta, 17–19 October 2000.

McFate, S.: *The Modern Mercenary: Private Armies and What They Mean for the World Order*, OUP, Oxford, 2014.

Metzger, G. E.: "Privatization as Delegation", 2003, Vol. 103 (6), *Columbia Law Review*, pp. 1367–1502.

Mockler, A.: *Mercenaries*, Macdonald and Company, London, 1969.

Neocleous, M.: "The Universal Adversary Will Attack: Pigs, Pirates, Zombies, Satan and the Class War", 2015, Vol. 8 (1), *Critical Studies on Terrorism*, pp. 15–31.

O'Brien, K.: "What Should and What Should Not Be Regulated?" in Chesterman, S. and Lehnard, C. (eds): *From Mercenaries to Market: The Rise and Regulation of Private Military Companies*, OUP, Oxford, 2007.

OAU Convention for the Elimination of Mercenaries in Africa, O.A.U. Doc. CM/433/Rev. L. Annex 1, 1972.

Ogus, A.: *Regulation: Legal Form and Economic Theory*, Clarendon Press, Oxford, 1994.

Organisation for Economic Cooperation and Development, available at: www.oecd.org/corporate/mne/.

Ostensen, A. G.: "UN Use of Private Military and Security Companies: Practices and Policies", The Geneva Centre for the Democratic Control of Armed Forces, SSR Paper 3, 2011, available at: www.dcaf.ch/Publications/UN-Use-of-Private-Military-and-Security-Companies-Practices-and-Policies.

Paige, T.: "Piracy and Universal Jurisdiction", 2013, Vol. 12, *Macquarie Law Journal*, pp. 131–154.

Parker, C.: *Just Lawyers: Regulation and Access to Justice*, OUP, Oxford, 1999.

Pattison, J.: "Deeper Objections to the Privatisation of Military Force", 2010a, Vol. 18 (4), *The Journal of Political Philosophy*, pp. 425–447.

Pattison, J.: "Outsourcing the Responsibility to Protect: Humanitarian Intervention and Private Military and Security Companies", 2010b, Vol. 2 (1), *International Theory*, pp. 1–31.

Pattison, J.: *The Morality of Private War: The Challenge of Private Military and Security Companies*, OUP, Oxford, 2014.

Percy, S.: *Mercenaries: The History of a Norm in International Relations*, OUP, Oxford, 2007a.

Percy, S.: "Morality and Regulation" in Chesterman, S. and Lehnard, C. (eds): *From Mercenaries to Market: The Rise and Regulation of Private Military Companies*, OUP, Oxford, 2007b.

Pinto, A. and Evans, M.: *Corporate Criminal Liability*, 2nd edition, Thompson, Sweet & Maxwell, London, 2008.

Report of the Committee of Privy Counsellors Appointed to Inquire into the Recruitment of Mercenaries, Cmnd. 6569, 1976, London.

Rome Statute of the International Criminal Court, available at: legal.un.org/icc/statute/99_corr/cstatute.htmRose, N.: *Powers of Freedom: Reframing Political Thought*, CUP, Cambridge, 1999.

Rubin, A. P.: *The Law of Piracy*, US Naval War College Press, Newport, 1988.

Ruggie, J.: Report of the Special Representative of the Secretary-General on the Issue of Human Rights and Transnational Corporations and Other Business Enterprises, Guiding Principles for the Implementation of the United Nations "Protect, Respect and Remedy" Framework; Principle 6 State-Business Nexus; Commentary, 2011.

Scahill, J.: *Blackwater: The Rise of the World's Most Powerful Mercenary Army*, Serpent's Tail, London, 2007.

Schreier, F. and Caparini, M.: *Privatising Security: Law, Practice and Governance of Private Military and Security Companies*, Geneva, 2005, pp. 39–41, available at: www.dcaf.ch.

Simpson, S.: *Corporate Crime, Law, and Social Control*, CUP, Cambridge, 2002.

Singer, P. W.: *Corporate Warriors: The Rise of the Privatized Military Industry*, Cornell University Press, 2004.

Statute of the International Criminal Court UN Doc./A.CONF.183.9*, 2187 UNTS 1998.

Taulbee, J. L.: "Myths, Mercenaries and Contemporary International Law", 1985, Vol. 15, *California Western International Law Journal*, pp. 339–363.

Tesón, F.: "Humanitarian Intervention: Loose Ends", 2011, Vol. 10 (3), *Journal of Military Ethics*, pp. 192–212.

The International Code of Conduct for Private Security Service Providers, Geneva Academy, August 2013, available at: www.geneva-academy.ch/docs/publications/briefing4_web_final.pdf.

The Montreux Document on Private Military and Security Companies, 17 September 2008, available at: www.eda.admin.ch/eda/en/home/topics/intla/humlaw/pse/psechi.html.

The Protocol Additional to the Geneva Conventions of 12 August 1949, relating to the Protection of Victims of International Armed Conflicts, Protocol I, Article 47, June 1977.

The UN Guiding Principles on Business and Human Rights; Draft International Convention on the Regulation, Oversight and Monitoring of Private Military and Security Companies, 13 July 2009.

The United Nations: "Protect, Respect and Remedy" Framework, available at: www.business-humanrights.org/sites/default/files/reports-and-materials/Ruggie-protect-respect-remedy-framework.pdf.

Thompson, J. E.: *Mercenaries, Pirates and Sovereigns: State-Building and Extraterritorial Violence in Early Modern Europe*, Princeton University Press, Chichester, 1994.

Thomson, J. E.: "State Practices, International Norms, and the Decline of Mercenarism", 1990, Vol. 34 (1), *International Studies Quarterly*, pp. 23–47.

Tonkin, H.: *State Control over Private Military and Security Companies in Armed Conflict*, CUP, Cambridge, 2011.

United States v. Hutchings 26 F.Cas. (Brunn.Coll.C) 440 (Circuit Court, District Virginia, 1817).

Ward, T. and Fouladvand, S.: "Human Trafficking, Victims' Rights and Fair Trials", 2018, Vol 82 (2), *The Journal of Criminal Law*, pp. 138–155.

Wells, C.: *Corporations and Criminal Responsibility*, OUP, Oxford, 2001.

White, N. D.: "The Privatisation of Military and Security Functions and Human Rights: Comments on the UN Working Group's Draft Convention", 2011, Vol. 11 (1), *Human Rights Law Review*, pp. 133–151.

White, N. D.: "Regulatory Initiatives at the International Level" in Bakker, C. and Sossai, M. (eds): *Multilevel Regulation of Military and Security Contractors: The Interplay between International, European, and Domestic Norms*, Hart Publishing, Oxford, 2012.

Young Pelton, R.: *Licensed to Kill: Privatising the War on Terror*, Three Rivers Press, New York, 2006.

Zedner, L.: "Policing Before and After the Police", 2006, Vol. 46 (1), *British Journal of Criminology*, pp. 78–96.

2 Private forces in different forms of governance

Historical typologies

While contemporary definitions of mercenaries were formulated as a reaction to experiences of the Cold War and the wars of national liberation, a large body of historical evidence defends and even welcomes private military force. For centuries, states relied heavily on external military support to sustain power, expand territories, and extend their rule. Typically linked to the concept of modern nation-states,[1] sovereignty and the subject of its decline are often explored in international relations (IR) and IL literature from the standpoint of modernity.[2] By decoupling the notion of sovereignty from the modern nation-state, different expressions of private and irregular force emerge in contrasting forms of governance, namely feudalism, absolutism, Italian city-republics, the early nation-state of Revolutionary France, and the outsourced government of the British Empire, run by the East India Company (EIC). In the absence of crystallised international laws, state practice of using a particular type of military force is examined as a proxy for state regulation.

The shifts in the use and regulation of mercenaries can be observed in the changing modes of governance, from Machiavellian republicanism, to growing centralisation and the professional armies of absolute monarchies. Similar republican and later national visions are endorsed in Revolutionary and republican France where foreign soldiers were gradually ruled out as the antithesis of the republic and the national army. While a norm in Western nation-states, this was contrasted with the imperial practice of the EIC and its use of foreign colonial troops overseas. Selected examples demonstrate contrasting approaches to mercenaries that existed in the same historical period but that were distinct in terms of types of governance. Although not considered states in the modern sense, different forms of governance from the fourteenth century onwards each relied on characteristic military power and distinct sources of legitimacy. Analysed through the concepts of power and legitimacy, these typologies help us to track lineages of state-military relations up to the present day, drawing attention to the differing ways in which violence was normatively organised. Throughout modern history, foreign forces of one kind or another have been deployed by the great ruling powers.[3] Tracing various forms of private military forces through the lens of shifting conflict paradigms demonstrates a political predisposition towards regulation. Historical patterns of the use of private force illustrate different normative stances in favour and against mercenaries, depending on a particular form of governance. Such a method of historical typology is crucial for analysing the effectiveness and applicability of contemporary international legal attempts to regulate PMCs as it informs the regulation beyond the black letter of law providing insights into the mechanisms and levers of power and legitimacy that have been used by different forms of governance. In the period between the fourteenth and nineteenth centuries, we observe considerable differences in sovereign and organisational structures. Bringing together these patterns of governance allows us to trace normative approaches to public and private military power.

Feudalism and absolutism

Feudalism in Europe emerged from the disintegration of an empire, forming a 'civilisation' but not a world-system.[4] Described by Tilly as *patrimonialism*,[5] this historical stage stretched up to the fifteenth century in Europe and, arguably, some of its elements merged into successive forms of governance. The Christian Church and feudal order were the two pillars of medieval society that extended through to the era of absolutism. I do not intend to provide a full historical account of feudalism; instead, I suggest some ideas that characterise the feudal order and contextualise early modern use of mercenaries.

In the feudal form of governance, fourteenth-century knights and princes prioritised continuous conquests over the stability of the territories they possessed and the population within these territories. These rulers sought legitimacy for their authority from the Church,[6] while their lords supplied the military power, leaving them with little sway over governmental processes. From an economic standpoint, the governmental construct of Western feudalism, according to Wallenstein, was a nodal system of increasing population and productivity, whereby landowners controlled the surplus and the legal system.[7] In the absence of a money-based economy, centralised defence, or administration mechanisms, political fragmentation was undoubtedly a prominent feature of feudal society.[8] The feudal military system was based predominantly on private agreements,[9] while the only 'legitimate' wars could be fought to defend and expand Christendom against the pagans, or to remedy injustice.[10] The main actors of feudal warfare were tribes, feudal levies, urban militias, and similar customary forces.[11] The prohibition of arbitrary war drastically reduced the authority of the rulers, leaving them dependent on local private military forces. Ultimately, the idea of Christian unity did not coincide with the reality of territorial fragmentation and the continuous conflicts between those striving for control of tiny strips of territory.

Power and legitimacy derived from the lord-vassal nexus. According to Montesquieu, the essence of feudalism lay in the custom of vassalage, to which the fief was entirely subordinate, used as a form of pay for loyal service.[12] While a vassal's primary duty was military service,[13] the feudal lord provided his vassals with material maintenance and protection both on the field of arms and in court.[14] The lord and the vassal who were by definition, "on different social levels", were bound together by a contract.[15] Feudal lords relied on a financially driven relationship with their vassals that carried a mercenary nature. What distinguishes this relationship from the twenty-first-century freedom of contracts witnessed between states and PMCs is the framework of oaths that characterised feudal society.[16] The same respect for oaths was observed by knights. By accepting knighthood, all knights (even those who had not pronounced it) were bound by an oath.[17] However, the common practice of "multiple vassalage"[18] provided a certain level of choice and autonomy for the vassal to pick sides in the event of a conflict between two of his lords. Such risk inevitably weakened the military power paradigm that feudal nobility relied on.

Furthermore, military power, the judicial system, and land revenue were all concentrated in the hands of lords, making them more powerful than any other feudal institution.[19] At the same time, feudal lords had virtually no governmental instruments at their disposal to provide control over the claimed territories,[20] and the legitimacy of courts was often "restricted by private vengeance".[21] Distinct mercenary features can be observed in certain aspects of the feudal judiciary system, such as trial by battle, for instance. A practice favoured by the physically strong and also by the rich, it allowed women and clerics to offer a substitution, extending it to "any man who could afford to pay a warrior to fight in his stead, spawning a regular profession of judicial champions for hire".[22]

The example of Western Europe's absolute monarchies is the next form of governance I illustrate in order to explore state practice in relation to mercenaries. Rising from its feudal roots and characterised by the rising scale of war, absolutism resonated with an increase in state authority, leaving its footprint on sixteenth-century Europe. However, due to continuing limitation by divine and natural law, 'absolute' meant 'unsupervised' rather than 'unlimited'.[23] Although many features of the feudal mode of governance remained, finding their niche in the construction of the absolutist state, the changing nature of war set in motion further development and concentration of systems that under feudalism had been fragmented and unconsolidated.

Religion played an important role in the military history as the sixteenth century marked the first era of global war stemming from the endemic struggles between Christianity (Iberians) and Islam (Ottomans).[24] Sixteenth-century absolutism had therefore embraced an ideology whereby monarchs claimed the divine right of kings as a new means of legitimising their authority.[25] To fortify their position, monarchs used the mechanisms of bureaucratisation, the monopolisation of force, the creation of legitimacy, and the homogenisation of their population.[26] As absolutist states evolved, the source of their legitimacy was diversified beyond divine law. While firmly entrenched in one prince or a dynasty, a sovereign's power now extended to a number of new institutions within their immediate interests, allowing for a shift away from feudal political fragmentation and towards state centralisation.[27] Centralisation progressed by way of integrating smaller political units under a unified territorial area, with a consolidated legislative system and political authority to administer the new territory.[28] The concentration of power initiated numerous key processes that bridged the medieval forms of governance with a modern sovereign state. Over the course of the sixteenth and seventeenth centuries, European monarchs[29] cultivated a politically mature system of set territorial borders, slow yet steady monopolisation of military power, and its reorganisation into state armies.[30] The bureaucratic state arose from administrative enhancements in the civil and military realm, introducing tax and credit systems, ample enough to sustain and nurture the belligerent ambitions of early modern states.

Obtaining the monopoly of force in a modern sense may have been a conscious strategy to further monarchical authority or a reaction to the growing warfare demands of rising absolutism. Demilitarisation of the noble class, restrictions on the civilian right to bear arms, and a conscious reinforcement of distinct state frontiers, all played a crucial role in increasing state capacity to pacify its own population.[31] Administrative and military functions were performed by those dependent directly on the monarch, as opposed to unsubordinated, disobliging feudal lords. Suppression of the private armies in Tudor England[32] and Richelieu's efforts in France to tear down the fortresses within the state only to fortify its borders,[33] are just a few examples that supported the trend.

Having reached significant heights in warfare and weapon technology, this period merited the title of 'military revolution'.[34] Although challenged by the argument that the military reforms of the sixteenth and seventeenth centuries had their lineages in mediaeval warfare and were, hence, more evolutionary than revolutionary,[35] the strategic innovation in the military and social realms had a transformative impact. Dutch Republic's Maurice of Orange and Sweden's Gustavus Adolphus introduced the officer as the vital element of the European army.[36] The officer assumed managerial responsibilities in the conduct of a battle. Not only did this change influence the conduct of war, but it also sought to shape the social construction of the state, introducing a new and increasingly important professional class in European society.[37] Bureaucratic structures were developed to administer states' heavy monetary demands to further their military growth, recruit, and pay the troops, and to fund wars, immense in scale and resources.[38] A typical army of 60,000 men, with its 40,000 horses, consumed almost a million pounds of food per day.[39] By strengthening and developing the administrative apparatus, the state could afford more flexible access to funding in the event of having to urgently raise an army, lowering the risk of financial crises and mutiny caused by unpaid military forces.[40]

Professional armies

So, what was the role of mercenaries in the process of developing professional standing armies? Usually assembled at the start of a war and disbanded at the end or even in the process of the conflict, due to a lack of resources or subsequent mutiny, the armed forces of the sixteenth century were unable to realise their full potential in the absence of effective control by the state and the structure of a permanent army. Dependence on physical capabilities was a commonplace in sixteenth-century Europe as even the most advanced societies operated at a relatively low level of technological development.[41] Distrust amongst the lower classes over the obligation to bear arms prevented monarchs from successfully building national armies.[42] This led to the inevitable use of foreign mercenaries to conduct wars and pacify local uprisings, when the sovereigns lacked authority over their people. The absolutist state pioneered the professional army, which was largely mercenary in the sense of recruitment and pay.[43] At the same time, the military revolution inflated in scale and facilitated the rapid proliferation of warfare by introducing gunpowder, portable firearms, siege artillery, anti-siege fortifications, and other significant innovations.[44]

Using mercenaries had numerous advantages. Professional disposable military resources were commonly used to conduct wars and expand the territories of the monarchy. The army of the Dutch Republic,[45] for instance, was keen to finance mercenaries since their ruling elite was a commercial class with no military aspirations.[46] In addition, it gave the rulers the means to control the lords as the new source for supplying military force emerged, "creating an employment vacuum for the lesser nobility".[47] It also mitigated the risk of uprisings, fuelled by the population growth in Western Europe and the 'vagabondage' phenomenon. By incorporating a part of the population into their armies, rulers provided employment, simultaneously using this group to pacify the others.[48] The new armies had significant influence on the integral state structure by inverting the feudal order from one where social position determined rank, to one where rank determined social position.[49] This inversion resulted in dynastic monarchs rediscovering and adapting the core military principles of antiquity: the effectiveness in combat of trained infantry.[50]

The shift in military layout was most successfully demonstrated by the example of Swiss pikemen, free peasants from the poor forest regions in central Switzerland. Their efficiency was rooted in an ordered discipline in battle rather than in the advances of innovative weaponry. They widely exported their superior military skills and were known as one of the most popular mercenary forces in history. While these flexible, highly skilled military resources were always available to princes to help execute their military strategies at home and abroad, using foreign mercenaries drastically impeded the consolidation of state sovereignty. The main challenge was to contain and fund foreign armies without the fatal consequence of bankruptcy for the monarchy. The ever-increasing cost of war, more expensive armaments, longer periods of training, and bigger administrative staffs shook the finances of every state in Europe.[51] Therefore, incorporation of mercenary units into standing professional armies could be interpreted as a cost-saving alternative to waging wars with predominantly private military resources. Such an approach can be considered a form of regulation of mercenaries through state practice.

Italian city-republics and civilian militia

Demonstrating an opposing normative approach to mercenaries, Italian city-republics reflect a form of governance that, while sharing the same historical period, differed greatly to the governmental paradigm of absolute monarchies.

Renaissance Italy contrasted in governance and military structure to the comparatively centralised absolute monarchies of Western Europe. While the dynastic monarchies north of the Alps were growing in size and capacity, Italian city-republics found it challenging to develop beyond a 'segregated mass' into a consolidated entity.

The neo-Roman political thought of Machiavelli and his contemporaries reveals an account of the development of republicanism and the anti-mercenary norms. I draw on these insights as I analyse the sources of legitimacy that prevailed in Renaissance republics, and exploring the concept and practical application of civilian militia as a type of military power, developed and promoted throughout the fifteenth and sixteenth centuries. Amongst the differing interpretations of Machiavelli and his thought,[52] I seek to build upon the work of John Greville Agard Pocock and those historians who advocate Machiavelli's republican nature.[53] Understanding Machiavelli's republican vision is important in the context of tracing the regulation of mercenaries in different historical typologies. Unlike observing regulation and normative approaches to mercenaries in the state practice of absolute monarchies, Machiavelli's republican account offers regulation at a moral (rather than purely practical) level.

In the absence of any overarching unity,[54] multiple governing authorities, otherwise known as *signorie*,[55] emerged in Northern and Central Italy. Formally independent from the German Holy Roman Empire, they formed small independent governmental structures of city-states that prevailed in the region between the ninth and fifteenth centuries. Run by landed aristocrats, known as *signori*, this mode of governance was rooted in wealth rather than any other unifying authority, such as dynasty or the Church. Resting on force and personal fraud, the legitimacy of *signori* lacked communal support and aristocratic order or duty.[56] Despite constitutional checks and balances, wealth played an important part in Italian city-republics, serving as a key source of legitimacy and power.[57] Machiavelli condemned wealth as a source of legitimacy,[58] as he deemed it deceitful, leading to corruption and the limitation of republican popular freedom.[59] Furthermore, it encouraged the aristocracy to build their own private armies, inevitably putting the integrity of a republic at danger.[60]

Unlike the relatively consolidated monarchies north of the Alps, most Italian republics suffered from internal division within the cities, while the frequency of external warfare brought incessant crises of both military and fiscal nature.[61] Although by the end of the fourteenth century, most of Italy was governed by *signori*, the cities of Florence and Venice, retaining the status of independent city-republics, maintained their power throughout the fourteenth and fifteenth centuries.[62] While Venice was designed as a mixed government, in practice it was run by a large yet finite body of ancient families, therefore limiting the political participation of citizens.[63] Florentine republican structure was also deformed under an authoritarian reorganisation, with the political participation largely governed from above.[64] With no viable bureaucracy to administer the Papal States,[65] the fragmented structure of Italian cities was neither truly republican nor monarchical in practice.

In the absence of coherent sovereign authority, "temporary coalitions and consultative institutions played significant parts in war and extraction, but little durable state apparatus emerged on a national scale".[66] Beginning in 1434, a sixty-year-long Medici rule[67] marked the decline of *signoria* political authority, as the Florentine electoral system was replaced with that of unilateral appointment.[68] By the 1490s, the major powers of Italy – Venice, Milan, Florence, Naples, and the Papal States – had been warring with each other intermittently for decades;[69] by the 1520s, the Habsburgs and Valois were fighting their dynastic wars on Italian territory.[70] As of 1540, Milan and Lombardy had fallen under Spanish rule, France occupied much of Savoy and Piedmont, Florence had become a Medici-ruled duchy, and Naples was an appendage of the Spanish crown. Even Venice and Genoa, although maintaining their oligarchic institutions, lost their authority in the Mediterranean,[71] forcing Italian republicanism to surrender in the face of proficient centralised absolutist states.

Expressions of military power by Italian city-states also differed to those seen in the absolutist mode of governance. Dependent on commerce and manufacture,[72] cities served predominantly as market centres for local commodities, with limited warfare capacity on land and at sea.[73] Military engagements were pursued out of necessity rather than strategy and were avoided where possible in order to protect the free flow of trade.[74] In the absence of a standing army or any necessary political infrastructure to facilitate a permanent military force, the *condottieri* in Italy owned their mercenary troops, "auctioning them and switching them from side to side in local wars".[75] The military disadvantages of Italian city-states became evident in the late sixteenth century, when Spain, England, and Holland all started to send large armed vessels into the Mediterranean for trade and piracy. Unable to compete with the military capacity and scale of absolute monarchies, city-states such as Ragusa, Genoa, and Venice found their previous reliance on speed, connections, and craftiness insufficient to protect them from great commercial losses.[76] Italian leaders and troops played only a marginal part in the developments fostered by the military revolution, with the army of Venice being by far the most distinct exception.[77]

There could be various explanations as to why mercenaries did not achieve the same results in Italy as in the European absolutist states. First, we must consider that different forms of governance support different military structures. Renaissance Italy was divided into multiple city-states, severely lacking the political consolidation and infrastructural capacity required to produce a permanent army, or to effectively incorporate mercenary forces. Furthermore, both the composition and organisation of the mercenary forces were different. Unlike in absolute monarchies, Italian mercenaries, auxiliary forces, and their commanding officers were predominantly foreign, paid, and trained by their country of origin.[78] Resembling the commercial structure of modern-day private military companies, the authority over these troops lay in their homeland with the ruler who had ultimate control over them.[79]

Unlike their fourteenth-century predecessors, the mercenary soldiers of fifteenth-century Italian cities were mainly formed of Italians.[80] The *condottieri* in Italy contracted out troops under their command to city-states for use in local wars. Meanwhile the other European monarchs created mercenary corps directly under their own control, forming professional standing armies.[81] While some Italian states provided an increasingly disciplined and effective military, they did not produce a universal strengthening of the morale and collective virtue of the citizenry.[82] It is at the heart of this republican rationale that Machiavelli's perception of mercenaries was formed, placing a citizen's financial independence and genuine desire to protect the republic on the other side of the spectrum, serving as a guarantee against corruption.[83]

Civilian militia as a norm against mercenaries

Critical of the political and military practices of city-states, Niccolo Machiavelli's republican views were opposed to the fragmented Italian governance that relied on mercenaries for provision of power and whose legitimacy was rooted in wealth. In his capacity as a senior official in Florence (1498–1512), Machiavelli modelled the governance of Renaissance Italy in the period of constitutional switch between monarchies and republics upon the ideal of the Roman republic. Based on a good constitution,[84] the republican ideal of civic glory,[85] and, finally, the concept of the citizen militia, Machiavelli envisaged a republican alternative to the widespread idea of dynasty and private armies dominating the European landscape.

Leonardo Bruni was the first humanist to attempt an analysis of the Florentine republican constitution.[86] Like Machiavelli, he saw great value in the liberty and loyalty of every citizen to help promote a legitimate government, and therefore reinforce the liberty of a republic.[87] Fifteenth- and early sixteenth-century Florentine republicanism emphasised the importance of "good arms and good orders"[88] or, in other words, the relationship between military resources, available to the state, and an established system of administrative power. In line with his interpretation of Roman civic traditions,[89] Bruni considered military functions "an essential attribute of citizenship itself".[90] He deemed mercenaries dishonourable, arguing that they fought poorly as they were not part of what they fought for.[91] To Machiavelli, there was nothing more commendable than citizens defending their own state through the formation of an accountable military and active participation in the governmental system. To that end, Machiavelli advocated a military force comprised of citizens, and called for the establishment of civilian militia, which materialised in 1509.[92] Through the logic of civic glory and the urge of men to defend their own, the militia was viewed as a mechanism that transformed men into citizens.[93] Subsequent republican visions also promoted a contemporary appeal for a distinct form of public security, namely a civilian responsibility to protect.[94]

While in the rest of Europe mercenaries were a precondition of the emerging royal armies, Machiavelli's neo-communal militia was formed of regular troops.[95] Promoting an ethical argument against the use of foreign mercenaries, Machiavelli failed to see them as a valid military option for the absolutist states. However, the power of dynastic authority kept mercenary troops in check and used them successfully to their military advantage.[96] Militias, on the other hand, were lacking in training and skill; their failure in Germany[97] proved that only mercenary armies could compete in the new military landscape.[98] The nature of absolutist warfare was highly territorial, requiring a military force to travel and fight beyond the homeland borders. This was not something a civilian militia had the capacity to deliver. And, although fifteenth- and sixteenth-century Italian militias found their niche in fortifying camps, digging defensive ditches,[99] patrolling streets, and intervening in public conflicts,[100] they could not compete with the professional range, experience, and capacity of mercenary forces. Their fragmented governance made it problematic for city-republics to match the ever-growing armies of absolute monarchies; they simply crumbled under the weight of the sixteenth century's military requirements.[101] Although the recourse to civilian militias in the context of the vast absolutist armies of the period was unsuccessful, the deliberate intention to restrict the use of private force on ethical grounds was clearly defined, even if the concept was not fulfilled at the time.

The French Revolution and the nation-state

Alongside the professional army, the end of the seventeenth century also saw the principles of sovereignty and territoriality assume a new form.[102] In Western Europe, absolutism ignited the process of state consolidation, reducing the differences *within* a state and increasing the differences *amongst* them, forming distinct political communities with a growing sense of national identity.[103] Sovereignty became the entitlement to rule over a distinct territory. The emerging nation-states of the late seventeenth and early eighteenth centuries started developing structures "to claim to the monopoly of legitimate physical violence within a particular territory".[104] The territory, associated with appropriation and legitimacy,[105] became an essential defining feature for the concentration and control of power. In contrast to the position of a vassal in a feudal organisation who paid for his war equipment and provisioning, as well as the administrative and legal costs of the fief entrusted to him out of his own pocket,[106] the nation-state developed a mechanism to streamline administrative processes, and assumed responsibility and control over the organised violence that only its citizens ought to take part in.

The example of the French Revolution brings to light the changing form of governance from a monarchy to an early nation-state, with its legitimacy rooted in a more centralised popular government, and its power drawn from the people, who gradually acquired the status of citizen-soldiers. From the public-private security perspective, this distinct typology demonstrates the changes this shift instilled in military organisation with a new form of conscription that pioneered the mass citizen army – *levée en masse* – at its forefront. The normative value of this type of governance lies in the regulatory attempt to outlaw foreign soldiers, juxtaposing them against French citizens, bound together by territorial borders and national ideology.

The French Revolution, according to Bukovansky, had "accelerated the shift in the European states system from the dynastic territorial state to the nation-state as the dominant model of political legitimacy".[107] Change of authority and governmental structure was inevitable when on 17 June 1789 the Third Estate's deputies transformed themselves into a 'National Assembly' against the rule of the two senior orders. Giving the Assembly the power to devise a constitution, "they thereby announced their intention of redefining royal authority in terms of 'national consent'".[108] The idea of public opinion as a source of legitimacy challenged monarchical rule.[109] It also symbolised a loss of power for the *ancien régime*, allowing the revolutionary coalitions to fill the vacuum.[110] Centralisation emerged from within the nation as the bourgeois class united and led the people under the idea of popular sovereignty.[111] These transformations in state organisation enabled changes to military structure on a national scale. Following the Seven Years War (1754–1763), an increasing warrior sentiment convinced the bourgeoisie and the nobility of the need for a standing army which ought to become national to prevent it becoming an instrument of despotism.[112] In practical terms, this meant that the legitimacy of dynastic monarchy was (at least in theory and within the constraints of historical context) replaced with national institutions of wider popular representation. Previously dictated by wealth and class, professional military careers conflicted with the concept of equality and inclusion, promoted by the Revolution. As control of the army was transferred from the king to the Assembly, a three-year project of military reorganisation had begun.[113] By taking control of the funds and the terms of enlistment, defining the budget and duration of service, and having admission based on merit rather than class, the Assembly claimed and established its legitimacy.

The Revolutionary state apparatus used literacy and ideology to drive military conscription and promote the idea of nationalism within the army. Increased literacy improved the technological capacity and therefore the effectiveness of the army, and was conducive to the organisation of a large-scale military through training and education.[114] Literacy also made soldiers more susceptible to propaganda, which, inevitably, facilitated the spread of nationalist ideology as numerous pamphlets incited soldiers to protect citizens and to disobey their officers when ordered to oppose the people.[115] The revolts soon became frequent and eventually led to the disintegration of the Royal Army in 1790–1791. A turning point was reached in March 1791 when the contract of enlistment was no longer between two individuals, but between the conscript and the state. The change was especially momentous as it implied stepping away from the notion of the private soldier carried through military history by feudalism. Such contract of enlistment asserted the separation between private and public military forces, assigning the former an air of mistrust and archaism, and the latter political relevance and strong national principles. Foreigners were disqualified, and the principle of homogeneous national armies, without foreign units or foreign private soldiers, was retained until Napoleon's rule.[116]

The concept of citizenship embraced nationalist ideology and produced a certain kind of acceptance amongst the army recruits. All members of the state were considered members of a status-group, as citizens, sharing the requirements of collective solidarity.[117] Besides strengthening the revolutionaries with ideological power, nationalism gave the state an administrative dimension.[118] The recognition of territorial sovereignty amplified the reorganisation of the military. Nation-states were now in possession of a defined territory and population which gave natural advantage to populous states such as France and Britain by allowing them to form mass armies from their own citizens.[119] Perhaps the citizen armies did not directly arise from nationalism. However, as classes and other actors attained civil and political citizenship, the state became 'their' nation-state, an 'imagined community' to which they developed loyalties.[120]

Although the army of Louis XIV included a substantial segment of French citizens, professional armies were predominantly foreign prior to 1791 changes in enlistment.[121] Later, the transformation of the key governmental bodies produced strong national militarism,[122] leaving little room for private and foreign military recruits. Raising a citizen army in exchange for the promise of equality was critical to the processes of wartime mobilisation.[123] The war of 1792 served a unifying purpose, initiating the distinction and separation between the national and the foreign, which was perceived as a threat to the Republic. When the military was later reorganised, foreign recruits of all ranks faced radical changes. Under the admissions principles of the Legislative Assembly, foreigners were disqualified from joining the army. To ensure reliability, separate legions that also contained foreign recruits were created.[124] Because legions were mistrusted on the basis of nationality, an added level of military authority was present between the soldiers of the legions and the army general.

This air of autonomy and the uncertainty surrounding their allegiances made the legions resemble private troops more than a unified national army. Although faced with nationalist controversy, foreign military forces played an important role in the French Revolution. These were used as an instrument of war and to propagate revolutionary ideas amongst foreign populations, where mercenaries were often recruited.[125] Formed by the emigrated nobility, these served as a catalyst to popular mobilisation, forming the separation between 'native' and 'alien' while fuelling the nation's drive for self-determination.[126] This crystallisation of the notion of a national state and citizenship influenced the norm against the use of foreign mercenaries in France at end of the eighteenth century. The relationship between an early model of a nation-state and a national army provides another illustration of a unique normative approach to the use of private force, forming amongst monumental transformations in military history.

La Levée en Masse

With a military policy aimed at transforming a professional army into a national army,[127] 1793 saw the introduction of a new ideological military concept of '*levée en masse*', which dramatically altered the scale of land warfare.[128] Inspired by the Minister of War, Lazare Carnot, and orchestrated by the *sans-culottes* between 1793 and 1794, the brigade formation process was essential to republicanise the army and make its chiefs respect civil power.[129] On 23 August 1793, the Committee of Public Safety ratified the Mobilisation Decree that imposed responsibility on all citizens to protect the French state. The Decree stated:

> all Frenchmen are in permanent requisition for the services of the armies. The young men shall fight; the married men shall forge arms and transport provisions; the women shall make tents and clothes and shall serve in the hospitals; the children shall turn old lint into linen; the old men shall betake themselves to the public squares in order to arouse the courage of the warriors and preach hatred of kings and the unity of the Republic.[130]

Popular sovereignty was henceforth articulated through equality of military recruitment and was reflected in the command system of a diversified national army. Formed of the early volunteers and conscripts, the army was representative of the society as a whole.[131] All single men aged between 18 and 25 were required to join military forces, therefore expanding the French army to over one and a half million soldiers by 1794. Used as a measure of internal security, the *levée en masse* united the nation and afforded the French supremacy in combat.[132] While many scholars associate national conscription with democratic governance and republican values,[133] the army was born out of necessity and desperation, as much as ideology.[134] French republican rhetoric about the spiritual bond between nation and army was more conceptual than practical. Philip Bobbit makes a distinction between the "state-nation" of Revolutionary France, where the people of all classes are put at the service of the idea of the nation, and the much later "nation-state", where the state is put at the service of the people.[135] However, the example of Revolutionary France carries normative value. This type of military conscription was unprecedented in modern history; it also contributed to the formation of a national identity.

At the same time, the concept of citizenship and the three pillars of liberty, equality, and fraternity fostered and shaped the new mass army. A modern state with its defined territory and population provided the necessary political infrastructure to implement such numerically immense armies that it was neither necessary nor economically viable to hire mercenaries. The unifying ideology of nationalism introduced republican practices to the European political landscape. It also reinforced the importance of citizen military duty, opposing it to the immorality of mercenary forces. This particular version of modernity, with national militarism at its core, was imitated by other European powers, turning the idea of national mass army into a norm desired by many states.

The British Empire and the EIC

Diametrically opposed to the example of a nation-state is a model of an outsourced governance conveyed by the EIC for the British Empire. Contrary to the military struggles between the European dynasties or nation-states, the conflict paradigm of colonial expansion was an asymmetric encounter between a sovereign European state and what was perceived as an amorphous, 'uncivilised' entity. Given the disadvantages in technology and military organisation on the part of the non-European states, and in the absence of any legal limitations for states to wage war, seventeenth-century European empires expanded by conquering large parts of Asia and Africa.[136] European empires were better equipped to obtain collective wealth and security than others because they possessed greater "capacity and legitimacy".[137] While military and administrative power was real, imperialist legitimacy was built upon Eurocentric, orientalist projections of European sovereignty.[138] Rather than rooted in dynasty, divine laws, or republican values, the legitimacy of an empire was based on an assumed cultural superiority and military strength.

Born out of the industrialisation of war, the second British Empire was a classic example of Western imperialism with a huge and well-organised armed force at its disposal.[139] Exercising an 'informal empire' on the Indian subcontinent until 1858, it allowed its peripheral rulers to retain formal sovereignty while significantly constraining their autonomy by intimidation through military and economic power.[140] Enforcement posed no real difficulties as European military strength and organisation prevailed.[141] In the case of imperial Britain, both coercion and military superiority were combined to create ostensibly legal instruments.[142]

This section explores the governmental construct of the British Empire in India by analysing the state administration, financial, and legal paradigms that were deeply immersed in military practices, and the military power. Based on the composition of the EIC army, its role within the Empire, and its relationship with the sovereign, such a colonial army ought to be deemed a private rather than a public force. The historical example of the British EIC and its colonial army illustrates the legal gaps in the classification and organisation of military power, transcending history and highlighting the importance of PMC and mercenary regulation today. Furthermore, it mirrors some of the contemporary state behaviours in their attempts to bypass the law through outsourcing military functions to a private company.

The EIC and its accession to power

Founded in 1600, the EIC was run by a court of twenty-four directors with its key focus on competitive trade.[143] By the first half of the eighteenth century, the Company had achieved the status of a respectable commercial body, connected with London City banking and the Stock Exchange.[144] While originally the EIC had a pacifist outlook and was mainly preoccupied with commerce,[145] the Anglo-French struggles of the early to mid-eighteenth century were an important factor in the Company's territorial expansion and assertion of governing power in India.[146]

With the power of the Mughal dynasty[147] dominating throughout the sixteenth and seventeenth centuries, the Indian Empire was the second greatest power in the East, after China.[148] The strength and ambition of the Mughal military system reflected in the great territorial extension at the turn of the sixteenth century.[149] Whether Britain's accession to power in India was made possible by fractions in the Mughal rule,[150] Hindu-Muslim tensions,[151] or due to the emergence of a new political order in eighteenth-century India,[152] the British seized the opportunity to insert a much stronger authority, built on trade, a strong industrial, financial, military basis, and an effective organisation of local resources. The needs of Indian rulers for cash and troops met British ambitions to play a political role as bankers and military commanders.[153]

When in 1757 Robert Clive[154] brought Bengal, Bihar, and Orissa under the protectorate of the Company, its servants were granted possession of vast territories, authority over about twenty million people, as well as access to three million pound sterling in revenues.[155] In the south, the British occupation created a new state, whereas in Bengal, the Company operated within an existing state, dealing directly with the local government.[156] Local customs were respected as the EIC focused on economic rather than cultural domination. Just like the Indian states, the British Empire in India was built on the taxation levied on the cultivators of the land.[157] A dynamic private sector bound the Indians and the British through active trade and the voluntary subordination of wealthy Indian merchants to the Europeans in exchange for security and stable commerce. The Company achieved its sovereign status by penetrating beneath the surface and building up its strength not on commerce alone. It used the local resources – popular, administrative, and military – to establish its rule and, thereafter, to expand it while retaining formal control of the territory.[158]

Legitimacy had to be established in order for the EIC to claim power over the new territories; it materialised following the India Act of 1784[159] introducing the rule of the law in the English Presidencies. After becoming administrators of Indian law, the British presided over courts in which issues of rights to land and distribution of revenue were decided.[160] The EIC also held control over military resources which were not under the direct rule of the British Empire. They were privately managed, locally sourced, and funded by the profits of the Company: taxes raised through Indian administrative systems or bribes received directly from Indian aristocrats.[161] However, in military and administrative practice, just like in trade, local traditions had to be respected if the Company was to stand a chance of establishing its authority. The common denominator amongst administrative, financial, and legal functions was the ever-growing role and presence of the military apparatus, rooted at the core of the state and the society.[162]

The army of the EIC

The eighteenth century marked a shift in the Great Power struggles, from European issues to markets and territories that ranged across the globe.[163] Administration of vast overseas territories was highly expensive and deeply impractical, unless "use was made, wherever possible, of existing political structures and resources".[164] In order to save costs and minimise the use of British soldiers, the EIC chose to obtain its military manpower from local sources.[165] The indigenous population, although lacking the training and unity of a professional army, came at a much lower cost than British soldiers. Following the French, who piloted sepoy[166] conscription, the British raised their own local forces, grouping them into battalions in Bengal and Madras by the late 1750s.[167] Unlike the French, who used coercion as a method of enlistment, the British offered voluntary service, which was an accepted norm by this time for free-born Britons.[168] For the sepoys, paid voluntary service was a more attractive alternative to the French compulsory conscription. To make the enlistment contract between the soldier and the Company more lasting, as well as to attract recruits and to purchase their quiescence during service, British policymakers deployed material incentives.[169]

Until the European invasions, Indian military culture was predominantly feudal in nature, with private mercenaries serving a different warlord based on pay and opportunity. French and British imperialists introduced a very effective mechanism that gave the sepoys a military framework and a sense of job security, while simultaneously ensuring a constant supply of military manpower. This European pseudo-standing army created a real sentiment of fraternity by offering the sepoys discipline, uniforms, and a regular pay that also guaranteed their loyalty to the Company. Furthermore, the use of more advanced firearms made the sepoys stronger and more effective than any local opposition.[170] Equality ended there, as no sepoy, however long his service tenure, could ever rise above the rank of 'native officer'.[171] In addition to the Royal Navy, which had long been an inherent source of power, the Company's forces in India added a significant new element to Britain's military capacity, a major land-based army,[172] making it a source of British imperial expansion.[173] The size of the sepoy infantry force, and the Company's ability to mobilise a flow of resources, were key to its subsequent military success.[174]

While gradually becoming the central infrastructure of the British Indian state, and an unparalleled regional military force, the army of the EIC had a complex constitution, full of contradiction and inequality. The British Army in India predominantly consisted of volunteers who were not citizens.[175] While expected to fight and die for the Empire, they did not qualify as citizens in the French revolutionary or modern sense of that term.[176] The army was composed of at least three different elements: the centralised monarchical army, the national army, and the mercenary army.[177] Although controlled by a national command, John Company's European forces consisted largely of non-nationals. Even those sepoys recruited locally were not necessarily subjects of the British Empire. For example, starting from 1820s, the region of Oudh[178] was an important source for the recruitment of Indian sepoys; however, it did not become part of British India until 1856.[179]

At this time, while most armies and some navies still contained elements of international 'service' and mercenary nobility,[180] standing armies were beginning to prevail across European nation-states and empires. However, there was one more extraordinary element to the EIC army which puts in question its status as a public military force. In 1781, the EIC hired two Hanoverian regiments.[181] These German auxiliary troops were hired out by a prince to the British, amongst other imperial powers, under a subsidy treaty stipulating the number of troops, the term of service, the geographical area in which they were to be deployed, and the missions they could be used for, in return for financial and political benefits.[182] The presence of auxiliary troops, although regulated, brings another mercenary dimension to the composition of the Company's army.[183] After the official transfer of India's political authority to Queen Victoria on 2 August 1858[184] and the dissolution of the Company in 1874 by an Act of Parliament,[185] the Company's European regiments, including the battalions raised during the Great Mutiny,[186] were transferred to the British Army. The local units, with all ranks predominantly taken by Indians, were consolidated into an Indian Army under the power of the Queen.[187] The main change, driven by the transfer of authority, was a separation between government and the military, subordinating the latter to the former.[188] While this change had gradually taken place, the army remained a dominant consideration of future imperial policy.

Was the army of the EIC private or public?

Though at home the British military had moved away from the use of foreign, private, or irregular forces, the EIC army was often referred to as mercenary. Formed of colonial subjects and two German auxiliary regiments, the enlisted soldiers fought for pay, and not to selflessly defend the Raj.[189] The concepts of mercenaries and a colonial army were purposefully separated by the layers of imperial and orientalist logic to manage British public opinion at home whilst successfully pursuing colonial goals abroad. A similar approach had often been deployed by states in the twentieth and twenty-first centuries by using mercenaries and PMCs, respectively, as part of their foreign policy. In addition to the existing types of military, mercenaries, and citizen armies, the logic of imperialism included a new, legally undefined military force: imperial troops.[190] Whether perceived as a subset of public armed forces, controlled by the sovereign,[191] or a private force outsourced by the Empire, either choice opens a debate on accountability and the ownership of colonial military power. Given that the empire had broadened the scope of its power to incorporate new territories and the resources that came with it, the quasi-state-owned colonial troops could be perceived to have existed under imperial rule and the extended sovereign capacity of the hegemon.

However, in practice, accountability and effective control would lie with the Company for two key reasons. First, India was ruled directly by a small number of the Company's servants, who were heavily reliant on the local political and administrative structures and a locally raised Indian army. Second, it was controlled indirectly, through Indian princes, treaties, troops, and resident advisers (the source of *de facto* authority). In effect, until sovereign power was officially transferred to the Crown in 1858 after the Great Mutiny, the British Indian army, alongside the administration of British India itself, was fully governed by a mercantile company. It was a classic case of 'sub-imperialism', whereby local interests dominated over metropolitan ones.[192] The source of authority was determined by men actually in India, as opposed to Company directors in London or, even less so, in Parliament. And while Parliament repeatedly insisted that the state had a right "to interpose its authority" on the Company,[193] it could not achieve the same level of influence.

Furthermore, the legal status of the Company's possessions had not been clarified, and while numerous assertions of the state's right to Indian revenues had been made by ministers, these had not been supported in law or statute.[194] In the absence of clear regulation concerning the use of colonial troops, the line between public and private tends to be blurred. The example of the EIC army is a testament to this ongoing issue. The areas where charter companies took on military functions fell outside the established order of the European state system.[195] Therefore, while the Western hemisphere was consciously building national armies and moving away from mercenaries, colonial troops could easily be deployed due to an existent legal loophole.

Normative approaches to mercenaries

Machiavelli's perception of mercenaries was defined by the questions of ethics, morality, and republicanism. Juxtaposing an army fighting for their own country and a mercenary who is hired to further someone else's political interests, Machiavelli deemed soldiers for hire useless, lacking commitment, and a motive strong enough to make them faithful and devoted.[196] It is important to draw a distinction in Machiavelli's perception of mercenaries, as he seems to reject the use of foreign mercenaries on the one hand, and applaud the structural integrity of sixteenth-century English armed forces on the other.

It is understood that the 'foreign' aspect of mercenaries is not concerned with the composition of the troops, as at the time it would be irrelevant in the absence of national borders and the contemporary notion of citizenship. Instead, it relates to the origin of the troops supplied to a king, whether they were locally sourced or sent from abroad. What Machiavelli seems to object to is the cross-border trading of military force as commodity, which demoralises the value of the state and endangers citizen security. 'Good laws' needed to lay ground for 'good armies',[197] and so Machiavelli's response to military corruption came in the shape of civilian militia, based on the citizen's right and responsibility to protect their own state, and the privilege they have of doing so.[198] Contrasting the widely deployed military strategies of Western Europe, Machiavelli's militia was an ideological attempt not fit for its time and, most importantly, for the international state system at the time. Only the horizontal growth of the government could foster an environment favourable to conceive and propel the establishment of a permanent standing army. The difference with the military development of progressive absolutist states, such as Holland or Sweden, was their capacity to train and sustain their own officers, rendering the commanding layer of the army if not 'national', at least domestic.

By the end of the sixteenth century, the majority of armies and navies of Western Europe had become royal. This was effectively the first step to them becoming national. Keeping an army embodied all year round, as opposed to disbanding for the winter, laid the foundations for the modern standing army. However, the roots of this trend were military and financial, rather than political or constitutional; the shift towards standing armies was a tactical choice.[199] Nonetheless, this change brought states and their rulers one step closer to realising the importance of a permanent state army. Although Ralston implies there were elements of abnegation and even selflessness in the way an organised infantry force operated,[200] there appears to be little evidence to suggest that absolutist states eschewed the use of mercenaries for ethical reasons. Monarchs were quite reluctant to arm civilians due to fear of uprisings, intentionally demilitarising the nobility in the effort to subordinate rivals and achieve a greater degree of centralisation.

In seventeenth-century Europe, the shifting conflict paradigm was described in the context of the rapid expansion in the scale of war, while the rise of the modern state was marked by a change in military organisation. Instead of using ad hoc mercenaries, the majority of European states gradually integrated them into their own professional armies. Military expansion began to overshadow the forces and the weaponry available to any private local competitors.[201] Practicing military skill as a mass discipline eradicated the need for narrow specialisation, such as English longbow-men, Swiss pikemen, or Spanish men-at-arms.[202] The increasing amplitude of war, powered by the absolutist state, directed the armed forces towards mass production by increasing the military productivity of a state. It reshaped the state structure by establishing an administrative system within a more centralised state apparatus.

While in the context of absolutism, foreign and mercenary soldiers were more positively associated with the professional army, the foreign soldiers of Revolutionary France, and later the French republican army were perceived as a threat to the republic and an unwelcome trespasser on the preserves of the national army. The new legitimating principle was the "people" or the "nation".[203] Revolutionary mobilisation introduced the trend of the mass citizen army and accelerated the decline of foreign and mercenary troops. Revolutionary France retained some existing normative angles, previously observed in republican thought; it also introduced new ones, making a comprehensive statement against the use of mercenaries. The common ground that prevails both in Machiavellian thought and in revolutionary pamphlets, also featuring in the American Revolution,[204] was the element of the citizen-soldier that was borrowed from antiquity in an attempt to revive the power of the ancient Roman army. The idea of soldiers who are first and foremost citizens, participating in projects of national significance, contributing to the development of the infrastructure, and raising the moral value of military status, was actively promoted in Servan's *Le Soldat-Citoyen*.[205] At the same time, Rousseau praised citizen armies while consistently denouncing professional and mercenary armies.[206] According to Rousseau's *Social Contract*,[207] every citizen should be a soldier by duty, and not by trade. Other professional officers, such as Compte de Guibert, shared the idea of a national army, condemning the armies composed of mercenaries, foreigners, and vagabonds.[208]

Another norm, previously seen in Machiavelli's republican aspirations, was the idea of a citizen militia as a measure against mercenarism. Unlike in fifteenth-century

Italian cities which predominantly relied on foreign mercenaries, the militia was an established concept in France. Some officers, like the Chevalier de Pommelles, studied ways to develop the militia into a system of conscription, while the bourgeoisie considered the transformation of the militia into a national army as "the best guarantee for the community as a whole against the 'mercenary' menace".[209] The rising nation-state with its "revitalised concept of citizen warfare"[210] created a new set of anti-mercenary norms. Key changes to military organisation, such as relative democratisation in terms of pay and admission by merit, were born out of the struggle for control of the army by the changing revolutionary leaders.[211] It must be said that these changes, although significant for their time, were not universal, and the army was far from democratised. Although born from popular, street-level agitation, the French Revolution was essentially a bourgeois revolution. Despite the ideology of popular sovereignty, the citizen army was still officered by the middle classes. Nevertheless, with the crystallisation of territorial sovereignty, the national citizen army started to become the new norm. In the meantime, legions that contained foreign recruits and were more autonomous in their structure were seen as the antithesis of the Republic.

The rise of new forms of governance created a new set of anti-mercenary norms. The normative approach to mercenaries and foreign troops following the French Revolution was different to the economic limitations posed by absolutism, and not fully in line with the purely republican ideology promoted by Machiavelli. Not only were mercenaries imposing on already stretched state budgets and undermining the moral value of citizen-soldiers, but they were now opposing a notion of territorial sovereignty that did not exist in Italian city-republics or any other previous form of government. With the crystallisation of the concept of the nation-state, standing armies flourished and grew in strength and size. The new political relationship between citizens and the state meant that citizens were perceived as representatives of their home country.

As citizen armies became the new norm, states also began to pass neutrality laws, which prohibited their citizens' enlistment in foreign armies. The overseas empires followed a different normative logic to Westphalian Europe. In the latter half of the nineteenth century, the great powers preferred to reserve the national population for domestic use, as the main military focus on the continent turned to building mass national armies.[212] According to Barkawi, this combination of the institution of neutrality and the essentials of nation-state building meant that mercenarism declined as an institution.[213] At the same time, colonial armies fostered the spread of the empires and made their existence possible, providing a lucrative, effective, and accessible substitute for foreign mercenaries. According to Owens, the incorporation of imperial soldiers into armies and private trading companies is explained by the normative shift away from mercenaries and private armies.[214] A similar argument is promoted by Percy,[215] although the example of the EIC's army illustrates a different side to this trend, rooted in a specific mode of governance.

In a time when "war and the military were central to state leadership and foreign policy",[216] the British Empire was outsourcing administrative and military authority to a trading organisation. One possible explanation lies in the limited knowledge the British Parliament had of India and its population. Meanwhile, EIC servants understood and did not interfere in the local culture, granting the Company its prevalent authority. To a great extent, the EIC had a firm hold on local infrastructure, building connections that were fruitful for themselves as well as the Empire. Hence, at first, there was no advantage in disturbing the successful management of affairs. Another explanation can be found in the negative perception of colonialism and the government's desire to further distance imperial expansion from domestic affairs.[217] The belligerent and subjugating image of the Second British Empire went against the norms of liberty and law, established in the Metropole. The structure of imperial governance was handled at arm's length. By creating a buffer of supposed legitimacy between 'virtuous' Britain and the 'backward' colonial regime, it removed direct responsibility from the Crown.

To compare the two modes of governance further, power in imperial Britain was not centralised and rationalised in the manner of the post-Revolutionary France; instead, it was diffused and conflicted. Even at the height of imperialism, England was liberal in its approach to conscription, unlike the French monarchy. The constant conflict between Parliament and the Indian administrators, who were often censured for despotism, highlights the lack of true centralisation of power and legitimacy across the British Empire. It was a combination of competing authorities, unresolved conflict, and innovation. In India, there was no central police force, no central administration of the military, no constitution, nor obedient judiciary.

As demonstrated in the EIC example, power, right up until the mid-nineteenth century, was scattered across the Empire rather than concentrated in any central state. Eighteenth-century imperialism presented an element of 'extra-territorial' sovereignty, which significantly increased the EIC's military and economic power on the Indian subcontinent as well as in Europe. The sepoy army was at the core of British imperial expansion as it helped to establish and secure Britain's dominance of the rich and lucrative Indian subcontinent. Later, under the direct rule of the Crown, it featured prominently in both World Wars, successfully fighting for the Empire. A legal and normative paradox, this is simply one historical example that demonstrates states' methods of removing responsibility in the pursuit of their sovereign needs through alternative means.

Conclusion

Different governmental formations resorted to different types of military forces, forming broad historical patterns. The overall conclusion that can be drawn from the typologies discussed in this chapter is that more centralised states that consolidate their administrative and legal apparatuses are more likely to also be in greater control of the army, and where possible incorporate or eliminate any private or irregular soldiers. In Western absolute monarchies, mercenaries were a means to an end; their military skills were used to fortify the army, incorporating professional soldiers into the core regiments. Nation-states also shared the anti-mercenary stance, often invoking the republican ideals of antiquity, as voiced by Machiavelli.

On the other hand, the context of colonial history alludes to a broader geopolitical conditionality that played a significant role in the new military configuration. This conditionality arises from the availability of disposable cost-effective colonial resources. In addition, the brutal and legally dubious nature of colonialism makes it problematic to consider the move away from mercenaries to be a norm, driven by ethics and republican values in the case of overseas empires.

Some historical accounts[218] view the use of colonial armies as the sovereign's choice of military power. While Britain may have ceased hiring private mercenary companies for its own national army after the Crimean War (1853–1856),[219] it fielded hundreds of thousands of foreign soldiers before and after 1858 in the form of colonial armies and auxiliary troops.[220] In reality, there may not have been a conscious shift away from the use of mercenary or private forces; the lack of regulation and the novelty of colonial armies were a lucrative ground for raising a cost-effective mass army through the legitimate use of non-national forces. British colonialism in India provided the context for a new, unclassified type of military force. Thompson calls it 'extraterritorial violence',[221] referring to foreign military manpower, as well as the existence of private military forces of various kinds, such as those employed by the great trading companies of the early period of European expansion.

While the institutionalisation of the national army created a strong rationale against the use of mercenaries and foreign legions, colonial encounters introduced European powers to a brand-new pool of unclassified military resources. Neither mercenary nor national, these forces formed an integral part of colonial armies, raising questions about their legitimacy and highlighting the disparity between public and private in the military context. Moreover, the outsourcing of military functions to a private body is a tactic states continue to use to this day in order to economise, or to evade responsibility, thus transforming the EIC "from an historical curiosity into a highly relevant case study".[222]

Notes

1 The Peace of Westphalia (1648).
2 See MacCormick (1999); Brown (2010); Magnuson (2010, pp. 255–312).
3 Kiernan (1998, p. 16).
4 Wallerstein (1974, pp. 17–18). Background reading on feudalism: Ganshof (1964); Coulborn and Strayer (1956); Strayer (1970).
5 Tilly (1990, p. 29).
6 Held et al. (1999, p. 35).
7 Wallerstein (1974, p. 18).
8 Fischer (1992, p. 444). Fischer outlines three orders in the feudal society: the *oratores*, or clergy, providing the community with divine grace; the *bellatores*, or knights; and the *laboratores*, or peasants, who procured economic sustenance.
9 Brown (1974, p. 1073).
10 The just war doctrine, Fischer (1992, p. 436).
11 Tilly (1990, p. 29).
12 According to Montesquieu, quoted in Stephenson (1941, p. 789).
13 Bloch (1962, p. 220).
14 Fischer (1992, p. 448).

15 Bloch (1962, p. 227).
16 Bloch (1962, p. 237).
17 Bloch (1962, p. 317).
18 Fischer (1992, p. 449).
19 Barendse (2003, p. 511).
20 Held et al. (1999, p. 34).
21 Bloch (1962, p. 360).
22 Bloch (1962, pp. 456–457).
23 See Hartung and Mousnier; Wallerstein (1974, p. 144).
24 Housley (1992).
25 Wallerstein (1974, p. 144).
26 Wallerstein (1974, p. 136).
27 Genicot (1966, p. 700).
28 Held et al. (1999, p. 36).
29 Louis XI in France, Henry VII in England, and Ferdinand of Aragon and Isabella of Castile in Spain.
30 These developments have not been coherent across Western Europe. This is a general summary of the features of absolutism, and different forms of government are called out and analysed to demonstrate key distinctions.
31 Pocock (1975, p. 386).
32 Stone (1967, pp. 199–272).
33 Tilly (1990, p. 69).
34 The concept was first formulated by Michael Roberts and focuses on the changing nature of war and its relationship to the state in the age of military expansion. See Roberts (1967, p. 199). For further background on military revolution, see the following accounts: Parker (1988); Black (1991); Parker (1976, pp. 195–214).
35 Black (2000, p. 57).
36 Ralston (1990, p. 8).
37 Ralston (1990).
38 Held et al. (1999, p. 107); Ralston (1990, pp. 8–9).
39 Tilly (1990, p. 81).
40 Ralston (1990, p. 9).
41 Black (2000, p. 25).
42 Roberts (1967, p. 200).
43 Kiernan (1957, p. 78).
44 Roberts (1967, p. 199); McNeil (1982).
45 The Dutch Republic was the first in Europe to establish an armed force on a more lasting basis, towards the end of the sixteenth century.
46 Ralston (1990, pp. 6–7).
47 Wallerstein (1974, p. 143).
48 Wallerstein (1974, pp. 139–143).
49 Feld (1977, p. 20).
50 Ralston (1990, p. 3).
51 Roberts (1967, pp. 206–207).
52 Barber (1994, pp. 403–422); Grant (1999, 671–674); Colish (1971, pp. 323–350); Newell (1987, pp. 612–634); Flanagan (1972, pp. 127–156).
53 Pocock (1975); Baron (1961, pp. 217–253); Colish (1999, pp. 597–616); Bock (1990); Skinner (2004).
54 After the end of Episcopal rule, when the Empire collapsed and the Church lost its overarching authority.
55 By the 1280s, the *signoria* had become the normal constitutional form over the entire northern plain, signalling the start of victory of tyranny over republicanism; see Waley (1989, pp. 166–170).

56 Anderson (1974, p. 162).
57 Kent (1978, p. 608).
58 See also the dialogue of Lorenzo and Niccoli about the sources of nobility; from Bracciolini, P.: *De Nobilitate*, referenced in Skinner (2004, p. 134).
59 Pocock (1975, p. 157); Skinner (2004, p. 167).
60 Skinner (2004, p. 175).
61 Waley (1989, p. 165).
62 Venice was governed by the principles of Machiavelli's "good constitution". It distinguished a Doge (a monarch), a Senate (the aristocracy), and a Consiglio Maggiore (democracy). See: Skinner (2004, pp. 5, 126); Machiavelli (1994a, "The Discourses", p. 91); Pocock (1975, pp. 83–113).
63 Pocock (1975, p. 100). The idealisation of Venetian mixed government was later known as the "Venetian myth". On the "Venetian myth" and its application by Florentine aristocracy, see: Grubb (1986, pp. 43–94); Robey and Law (1975, pp. 3–59); Rubinstein (1968).
64 Rubinstein (1968, p. 13).
65 Anderson (1974, p. 146).
66 Tilly (1990, p. 21).
67 On the Medici regime, see Brinton (1925); Kent (1978).
68 Kent (1978, pp. 14–16).
69 Tilly (1990, p. 77).
70 Tilly (1990, p. 78).
71 Tilly (1990, p. 78).
72 Held et al. (1999, p. 35); Tilly (1990, p. 21).
73 Anderson (1974, p. 153).
74 Mallett and Hale (1984, pp. 8–9).
75 Anderson (1974, p. 161).
76 Tilly (1990, p. 64).
77 Mallett and Hale (1984, p. 4).
78 One of the most infamous mercenary groups was the White Company, led by Sir John Hawkwood, see: https://www.britannica.com/biography/John-Hawkwood; Machiavelli elaborates extensively on the ill qualities of mercenaries in Chapter Twelve of *The Prince*, pp. 38–42.
79 Machiavelli (1994, "The Discourses", pp. 183).
80 Kiernan (1957, p. 71).
81 Anderson (1974, p. 161).
82 Mallett (1990, p. 177).
83 Shalhope (1986, p. 127).
84 Machiavelli (1994a, p. 89); Rubinstein (1990, p. 6).
85 Skinner (2004, p. 149).
86 Skinner (2004, p. 5); see also: Bruni (2005).
87 Skinner (2004, p. 131); Machiavelli (1994a, "The Discourses", p. 123).
88 Silvano (1990, p. 58).
89 See Bruni: The Militia and Funeral Oration.
90 Pocock (1975, p. 89).
91 Pocock (1975, p. 89).
92 Najemy (1990, p. 112).
93 Pocock (1975, pp. 292–293).
94 Baron (1961, pp. 218–219); Levi-Malvano (2009). Giannotti advocated for equality under one public authority and condemned private affiliations; see Pocock (1975, p. 291) (*Archivio Storico Italiano*, 1891, ser. 5, vol. 8, Sanesi, G. R. (ed.): *Un discorso sconosciuto di Donato Giannotti intorno alla milizia*, p. 17).
95 Oman (1937).

96 Anderson (1974, p. 168).
97 Roberts discusses the tendency towards the use of citizen militias in many German States: Saxony, Bavaria, Brandenburg, etc.
98 Roberts (1967, p. 199).
99 Silvano (1990, p. 178).
100 Tilly (1990, p. 55).
101 Tilly (1990, p. 65).
102 Held (2005, p. 37).
103 Tilly (1975, p. 19).
104 Weber (2004, p. 33).
105 Held (2005, p. 37).
106 Weber (2004, p. 36).
107 Bukovansky (2002, p. 165).
108 Jenkins (1990, p. 16). This shift was more symbolic than universal, as the nation-state at the period was neither democratic in the contemporary sense, nor had fully rid itself of the class relationships of the *ancien régime*.
109 Bukovansky (2002, pp. 182–183); Jenkins (1990, p. 19).
110 Jenkins (1990, p. 166).
111 IR literature takes a more refined approach to popular and national sovereignty and often distinguishes between the two. See: Barkin and Cronin (1994, pp. 107–130); Hall (1998); Buchheit (1978); Hobsbawm (1990).
112 Bertaud (1988, p. 40).
113 This covers the period between 1789 and 1792; Bertaud (1988, pp. 44–58).
114 Posen (1993, p. 121).
115 Bertaud (1988, pp. 22–26).
116 Posen (1993, p. 100).
117 Wallerstein (1974, p. 145).
118 Feld (1977, p. 21).
119 Tilly (1990, p. 65).
120 Mann (1993, p. 74).
121 In the context of eighteenth-century politics, notions of foreign and mercenary soldiers were interchangeable.
122 Schama (2004, p. 858).
123 Bukovansky (2002, p. 209).
124 Bertaud (1988, pp. 74–80).
125 Bertaud (1988, p. 74).
126 Jenkins (1990, p. 21).
127 Bertaud (1988, p. 39).
128 Fitzsimonds and Van Tol (1994, p. 25).
129 Bertaud (1988, p. 89).
130 Mobilisation Decree, Article 1; Parliamentary Archives 1787–1860.
131 Posen (1993, p. 94).
132 Lytle (1958, p. 331).
133 Rothenberg (1989, pp. 983); see also Posen and Bertaud.
134 Forrest (2004, p. 112).
135 Bobbit (2002).
136 Anghie (1999, p. 51).
137 Avant (2005, p. 24).
138 On legal orientalism and European cultural prejudice: Ruskola (2002 pp. 179–234); Gadamer (2004); Nunn (1997, pp. 323–372); Cohn (1996); see also: Omissi (1994, p. 2); Mann (2012, p. 33).
139 Held et al. (1999, p. 94).
140 Mann (2012, p. 18).
141 Anghie (1999, p. 33); Omissi (1994, p. 3).

142 Anghie (1999, p. 41).
143 In the sixteenth and seventeenth century of European expansion trade took precedence over the territorial imperative which prevailed during the 'New Imperialism' of the nineteenth century. See Black (2000, p. 32).
144 Fieldhouse (1966, p. 140). General literature on the EIC: Philips (1961); Gardner (1971); Bowen (2006); Keay (1993).
145 Ferro (1997, p. 55).
146 Fieldhouse (1966, pp. 166–167).
147 Also known as Mogul.
148 Fieldhouse (1966, p. 162).
149 Black (2000, p. 54).
150 Fieldhouse (1966, p. 162).
151 Spear (1961, p. 186).
152 Marshall (1998, p. 493); Fieldhouse (1966, p. 163).
153 Marshall (1998, p. 497), see also Marshall 1968.
154 Also known as Clive of India, a British officer who established military and political supremacy of the EIC in Bengal.
155 Marshall (1998, p. 492); Washbrook (1999, p. 399).
156 Spear (1961, p. 194).
157 Marshall (1998, p. 504).
158 Fieldhouse (1966, p. 164).
159 Implemented in India after 1786 by the reforming Governor-General Lord Cornwallis; Ray (1998, pp. 520–521).
160 Marshall (1998, p. 504).
161 Indians who hired Company troops had to pay the Company, and reward the officers privately.
162 From the mid-1820s, the government of India maintained "sixteen European regiments of the line as well as a permanent standing army of 170 sepoy regiments, totalling 235,000 men." Washbrook (1999, p. 402).
163 Kennedy (1989, p. 195).
164 Held et al. (1999, p. 41).
165 Kiernan (1998, p. 16).
166 From the Persian *sipahi*, 'soldier', Omissi (1994, p. 3).
167 Omissi (1994).
168 Kiernan (1998, p. 16).
169 Omissi (1994, p. 48).
170 Spear (1961, p. 191).
171 Kiernan (1998, p. 26).
172 Washbrook (1999, p. 401).
173 Marshall (1998, p. 491).
174 Barua (1994, p. 600); Ray (1998, p. 517).
175 Arielli and Collins (2013, p. 5).
176 Arielli and Collins (2013, p. 7); there was no concept of a 'British Citizen' until the 1948 British Nationality Act. Until that point, both UK and colonial residents shared the same national identity as British subjects. After 1948, they all became citizens of the UK and colonies, and this wasn't differentiated until 1981.
177 Barua (1994, p. 614).
178 Also known as Awadh.
179 Arielli and Collins (2013, p. 5).
180 Mann (1993, p. 420).
181 Tzoref-Ashkenazi (2013, pp. 32–33).
182 Tzoref-Ashkenazi (2013, p. 32); see also Kiernan (1998, p. 16).
183 A large part of the Loyalist army in the North American revolution was comprised of Hanoverian and Hessian units.

184 Reid (2009, p. 12).
185 See Parliament and Empire.
186 Further literature on the Great Mutiny: Spear (1961, pp. 264–273); Callahan (2008, pp. 16–34); Gardner (1971, pp. 255–288); Naidis (1970, pp. 75–78).
187 Reid (2009, p. 13).
188 Washbrook (1999, p. 419).
189 Omissi (1994, p. 47).
190 Owens (2010, pp. 25–26).
191 Jeremy Black refers to British EIC as 'authorised non-state violence', see Black (2000, p. 203).
192 Marshall (1998, pp. 498–499).
193 Sir William Meredith, 10 May 1773, *Parliamentary History*, xvii, p. 803 in Marshall (1987, p. 114).
194 Bowen (2006, p. 537).
195 Singer, p. 35.
196 Machiavelli (1994a, "The Discourses", p. 140). As demonstrated in *Chapter 1*, motivation is a parameter that continues to dominate contemporary definitions of mercenaries.
197 Mallett (1990, p. 179).
198 Machiavelli (1994b, "The Prince", p. 46).
199 Roberts (1967, p. 201).
200 Ralston (1990, p. 3).
201 Tilly (1990, p. 69).
202 Feld (1977, p. 19).
203 Mann (1993, p. 200).
204 Literature linking the French and American Revolutions: Dull (1975); Bukovansky (2002).
205 Bertaud (1988, p. 43).
206 Gourevitch (1997, p. 294).
207 Rousseau (1947).
208 Bertaud (1988, p. 41).
209 Bertaud (1988).
210 Bukovansky (2002, p. 204).
211 Bertaud (1988, p. 83).
212 Thompson (1994, p. 96).
213 Barkawi (2010, p. 38).
214 Owens (2010, p. 27).
215 Percy (2007, pp. 121–122).
216 Mann (1993, p. 413).
217 Armitage (2000, p. 3).
218 Fieldhouse (1966); Kiernan (1998); White and MacLeod (2008).
219 Percy (2007, p. 148).
220 Barkawi (2010, p. 40); Black (2000, p. 203).
221 Thompson (1994, p. 37).
222 *The Economist* (2011).

References

Anderson, P.: *Lineages of the Absolutist State*, NLB, London, 1974.

Anghie, A.: "Finding the Peripheries: Sovereignty and Colonialism in Nineteenth-Century International Law", 1999, Vol. 40 (1), *Harvard International Law Journal*, pp. 1–80.

Arielli, N. & Collins, B. (eds): *Transnational Soldiers: Foreign Military Enlistment in the Modern Era*, Palgrave Macmillan, Basingstoke, 2013.

Armitage, D.: *The Ideological Origins of the British Empire*, CUP, Cambridge, 2000.

Avant, D.: *The Market for Force: The Consequences of Privatising Security*, CUP, Cambridge, 2005.

Barber, N.: "Machiavellianism and Altruism: Effect of Relatedness of Target Person on Machiavellian and Helping Attitudes", 1994, Vol. 55 (1), *Psychological Reports*, pp. 403–422.

Barendse, R. J.: "The Feudal Mutation: Military and Economic Transformations of the Ethnosphere in the Tenth to Thirteenth Centuries", 2003, Vol. 14 (4), *Journal of World History*, pp. 503–529.

Barkawi, T.: "State and Armed Force in International Context" in Colas, A. and Mabee, B. (eds): *Mercenaries, Pirates, Bandits and Empires: Private Violence in Historical Context*, Hurst & Company, London, 2010.

Barkin, S. J. and Cronin, B.: "Changing Norms and the Rules of Sovereignty", *International Organization*, 1994, Vol. 48 (1), pp. 107–130.

Baron, H.: "Machiavelli: The Republican Citizen and the Author of 'the Prince'", 1961, Vol. 76 (299), *The English Historical Review*, pp. 217–253.

Barua, P.: "Military Developments in India, 1750–1850", 1994, Vol. 58 (4), *The Journal of Military History*, pp. 599–616.

Bertaud, J. P.: *The Army of the French Revolution: From Citizen-Soldiers to Instrument of Power*, Princeton University Press, Guilford, 1988.

Black, J.: *A Military Revolution? Military Change and European Society, 1550–1800*, Humanities Press, Atlantic Highlands, 1991.

Black, J.: *War and the World. Military Power and the Fate of Continents 1450–2000*, Yale University Press, London, 2000.

Bloch, M.: *Feudal Society*, 2nd edition, Routledge, Abingdon, 1962.

Bobbit, P.: *The Shield of Achilles: War, Peace and the Course of History*, Penguin Books, London, 2002.

Bock, G., Skinner, Q. and Viroli, M. (eds): *Machiavelli and Republicanism*, CUP, Cambridge, 1990.

Bowen, H. V.: *The Business of Empire: The East India Company and Imperial Britain, 1756–1833*, CUP, Cambridge, 2006.

Brinton, S.: *The Golden Age of the Medici (Cosimo, Piero, Lorenzo de' Medici) 1434–1494*, Methuen & Co., London, 1925.

Brown, E. A. R.: "The Tyranny of a Construct: Feudalism and Historians of Medieval Europe", 1974, Vol. 79 (4), *The American Historical Review*, pp. 1063–1088.

Brown, W.: *Walled States, Waning Sovereignty*, Zone Books, New York, 2010.

Bruni, L. (translation and introduction by Scheepers, A.): *In Praise of Florence: The Panegyric of the City of Florence and an Introduction to Leonardo Bruni's Civil Humanism*, Olive Press, Amsterdam, 2005.

Buchheit, L.: *Secession: The Legitimacy of Self-Determination*, Yale University Press, New Haven, 1978.

Bukovansky, M.: *Legitimacy and Power Politics: The American and French Revolutions in International Political Culture*, Princeton University Press, Woodstock, 2002.

Callahan, R.: "The Great Sepoy Mutiny" in Marston, D. P. and Sundaram, C. S. (eds): *A Military History of India and South Asia: From the East India Company to the Nuclear Era*, Indiana University Press, Bloomington, 2008.

Cohn, B. S.: *Colonialism and Its Forms of Knowledge: The British in India*, Princeton University Press, Princeton, 1996.

Colish, M. L.: "Republicanism, Religion, and Machiavelli's Savonarolan Moment", 1999, Vol. 60, *Journal of the History of Ideas*, pp. 597–616.

Colish, M. L.: "The Idea of Liberty in Machiavelli", 1971, Vol. 32, *Journal of the History of Ideas*, pp. 323–350.

Coulborn, R. and Strayer, J. R.: *Feudalism in History*, Princeton University Press, Princeton, 1956.

Dull, J. R.: *The French Navy and American Independence: A Study of Arms and Diplomacy, 1774–1787*, Princeton University Press, Princeton, 1975.

Feld, M.: *The Structure of Violence: Armed Forces as Social Systems*, Sage Publications, London, 1977.

Ferro, M.: *Colonization: A Global History*, Routledge, London, 1997.

Fieldhouse, D. K.: *The Colonial Empires: A Comparative Survey from the Eighteenth Century*, Weidenfeld and Nicolson, London, 1966.

Fischer, M.: "Feudal Europe, 800–1300: Communal Discourse and Conflictual Practices", 1992, Vol. 46 (2), *International Organization*, pp. 427–466.

Fitzsimonds, J. R. and Van Tol, J. M.: "Revolutions in Military Affairs", 1994, Spring Issue, *The Joint Force Quarterly*, pp. 24–31.

Flanagan, T.: "The Concept of *Fortuna* in Machiavelli" in Parel, A. (ed.): *The Political Calculus*, University of Toronto Press, Toronto, 1972, pp. 127–156.

Forrest, A.: "L'Armee de L'an II: La Levée en Masse et la Création d'un Mythe Réepublicain", 2004, Vol. 335 (1), *Annales Historiques de la Révolution Française*, pp. 111–130.

Gadamer, H. G.: *Truth and Method*, 2nd rev. edition, Continuum, London, 2004.

Ganshof, F. L.: *Feudalism*, Harper & Row, New York, 1964.

Gardner, B.: *The East India Company: A History*, Granada Publishing Limited, London, 1971.

Genicot, L.: "Crisis: From the Middle Ages to Modern Times" in Postan, M. M. (ed.): *The Cambridge Economic History of Europe from the Decline of the Roman Empire: The Agrarian Life of the Middle Ages*, CUP, Cambridge, 1966.

Gourevitch, V. (ed.): *Rousseau: The Social Contract and Other Later Political Writings*, CUP, Cambridge, 1997.

Grant, R. W.: "Hypocrisy and Integrity: Machiavelli, Rousseau, and the Ethics of Politics", 1999, Vol. 38 (3), *Dialogue: Canadian Philosophical Review*, pp. 671–674.

Grubb, J. S.: "When Myths Lose Power: Four Decades of Venetian Historiography", 1986, Vol. 58 (1), *The Journal of Modern History*, pp. 43–94.

Hall, R.: *National Collective Identity: Social Constructs and International Systems*, Columbia University Press, New York, 1998.

Held, D.: "At the global crossroads: The end of the Washington Consensus and the Rise of Global Social Democracy?" 2005, Vol. 2 (1), *Globalizations*, pp. 95–113.

Held, D. et al. (eds): *Global Transformations: Politics, Economics and Culture*, Polity, Cambridge, 1999.

Hobsbawm, E. J.: *Nations and Nationalism since 1780*, CUP, Cambridge, 1990.

Housley, N.: *The Later Crusades 1274–1580. From Lyons to Alcazar*, OUP, Oxford, 1992.

Parliament and Empire: *East India Company and Raj 1785–1858*, available at: www.parliament.uk/about/living-heritage/evolutionofparliament/legislativescrutiny/parliament-and-empire/parliament-and-the-american-colonies-before-1765/east-india-company-and-raj-1785-1858/.

Jenkins, B.: *Nationalism in France: Class and Nation since 1789*, Routledge, London, 1990.

Keay, J.: *The Honourable Company. A History of the English East India Company*, Harper Collins, London, 1993.

Kennedy, P.: *The Rise and Fall of the Great Powers: Economic Change and Military Conflict from 1500 to 2000*, Fontana Press, London, 1989.

Kent, G.: *The Rise of the Medici: Faction in Florence, 1426–1434*, OUP, Oxford, 1978.

Kiernan, V. G.: "Foreign Mercenaries and Absolute Monarchy", 1957, Vol. 11, *Past and Present*, pp. 66–86.

Kiernan, V. G.: *Colonial Empires and Armies, 1815–1960*, Sutton Publishing Ltd, Stroud, 1998.

Levi-Malvano, E.: *Montesquieu et Machiavelli*, Biblio Bazaar, Paris, 2009.

Lytle, S.: "Robespierre, Danton, and the Levée en Masse", 1958, Vol. 30 (4), *The Journal of Modern History*, pp. 325–337.

MacCormick, N.: *Questioning Sovereignty: Law, State, and Nation in the European Commonwealth*, OUP, Oxford, 1999.

Machiavelli, N.: "The Discourses" in Machiavelli, N. (ed. Wootton, D.): *Selected Political Writings*, Hackett Publishing Company Inc., Cambridge, 1994a.

Machiavelli, N.: "The Prince" in Machiavelli, N. (ed. Wootton, D.): *Selected Political Writings*, Hackett Publishing Company Inc., Cambridge, 1994b.

Magnuson, W.: "The Responsibility to Protect and the Decline of Sovereignty: Free Speech Protection under International Law", 2010, Vol. 43 (2), *Vanderbilt Journal of Transnational Law*, pp. 255–312.

Mallett, M. E. and Hale, J. R.: *The Military Organisation of a Renaissance State: Venice C. 1400 To 1617*, CUP, Cambridge, 1984.

Mallett, M.: "The Theory and Practice of Warfare in Machiavelli's Republic" in Bock, G., Skinner, Q. and Viroli, M. (eds): *Machiavelli and Republicanism*, CUP, Cambridge, 1990.

Mann, M.: *The Sources of Social Power, Vol. II The Rise of Classes and Nation-States, 1760–1914*, CUP, Cambridge, 1993

Mann, M.: *The Sources of Social Power, Vol. III Global Empires and Revolutions, 1890–1945*, CUP, Cambridge, 2012

Marshall, P. J.: "Empire and Authority in the Later Eighteenth Century", 1987, Vol. 15 (2), *The Journal of Imperial and Commonwealth History*, pp. 105–122

Marshall, P. J.: *Problems of Empire: Britain and India 1757–1813*, George Allen and Unwin Limited, London, 1968.

Marshall, P. J. (ed.): *The Oxford History of the British Empire: The Eighteenth Century*, OUP, Oxford, 1998.

McNeil, W. H.: *Pursuit of Power: Technology, Armed Force and Society Since A.D. 1000*, University of Chicago Press, Chicago, 1982.

Mobilisation Decree, Article 1; Parliamentary Archives 1787–1860.

Naidis, M.: *The Second British Empire 1783–1965: A Short History*, Addison-Wesley Publishing Company, London, 1970.

Najemy, J.: "Machiavelli's service to the Republic" in Bock, G., Skinner, Q. and Viroli, M. (eds): *Machiavelli and Republicanism*, CUP, Cambridge, 1990.

Newell, W. R.: "How Original is Machiavelli? A Consideration of Skinner's Interpretation of Virtue and Fortune", 1987, Vol. 15, *Political Theory*, pp. 612–634.

Nunn, K.: "Law as a Eurocentric Enterprise", 1997, Vol. 15, *Law and Inequality*, pp. 323–372.

Oman, C.: *A History of the Art of War in the Sixteenth Century*, Dutton, New York, 1937.

Omissi, D.: *The Sepoy and the Raj: The Indian Army, 1860–1940*, Macmillan Press Limited, London, 1994

Owens, P.: "Distinctions, Distinctions: 'Public' and 'Private' Force?" in Colas, A. and Mabee, B. (eds): *Mercenaries, Pirates, Bandits and Empires: Private Violence in Historical Context*, Hurst & Company, London, 2010.

Parker, G.: "The 'Military Revolution,' 1560–1660 – a Myth?", 1976, Vol. 48 (2), *The Journal of Modern History*, pp. 195–214.

Parker, G.: *The Military Revolution: Military Innovation and the Rise of the West 1500–1800*, CUP, Cambridge, 1988.

Percy, S.: *Mercenaries: The History of a Norm in International Relations*, OUP, Oxford, 2007.

Philips, C. H.: *The East India Company 1784–1834*, Manchester University Press, Manchester, 1961.

Pocock, J. G. A.: *The Machiavellian Moment: Florentine Political Thought and the Atlantic Republican Tradition*, Princeton University Press, Princeton, 1975.

Posen, B. R.: "Nationalism, the Mass Army, and Military Power", 1993, Vol. 18, (2), *International Security*, pp. 80–124.

Ralston, D. B.: *Importing the European Army: The Introduction of European Military Techniques and Institutions into the Extra-European World, 1600–1914*, University of Chicago Press, London, 1990.

Ray, R. K.: "Indian Society and the Establishment of British Supremacy, 1765–1818" in Marshall, P. J. (ed.): *The Oxford History of the British Empire: The Eighteenth Century*, OUP, Oxford, 1998.

Reid, S.: *Armies of the East India Company 1750–1850*, Osprey Publishing, Oxford, 2009.

Roberts, M.: "The Military Revolution 1560–1660" in *Essays in Swedish History*, Weidenfeld and Nicholson, London, 1967.

Robey, D. and Law, J.: "The Venetian Myth and the *De Republica Veneta* of Pier Paolo Vergerio", 1975, Vol. 15, *Rinascimento*, pp. 3–59.

Rothenberg, G. E.: "Soldiers and the Revolution: The French Army, Society, and the State, 1788–99", 1989, Vol. 32 (4), *The Historical Journal*, pp. 981–995.

Rousseau, J. J.: *The Social Contract*, Hafner Press, New York, 1947.

Rubinstein, N.: "Machiavelli and Florentine Republican Experience" in Bock, G., Skinner, Q. and Viroli, M. (eds): *Machiavelli and Republicanism*, CUP, Cambridge, 1990.

Rubinstein, N.: "The Venetian Constitution in Florentine Political Thought" in Rubinstein, N. (ed.): *Florentine Studies: Politics and Society in Renaissance Florence*, Faber & Faber, London, 1968.

Ruskola, T.: "Legal Orientalism", 2002, Vol. 101 (1), *Michigan Law Review*, pp. 179–234.

Schama, S.: *Citizens: A Chronicle in the French Revolution*, Penguin Books, London, 2004.

Shalhope, R. E: "The Armed Citizen in the Early Republic", 1986, Vol. 49, *Law and Contemporary Problems*, pp. 125–141.

Silvano, G.: "Florentine Republicanism in the Early Sixteenth Century" in Bock, G., Skinner, Q. and Viroli, M. (eds): *Machiavelli and Republicanism*, CUP, Cambridge, 1990.

Singer, P. W.: *Corporate Warriors: The Rise of the Privatized Military Industry*, Cornell University Press, 2004.

Skinner, Q.: *Visions of Politics: Volume II: Renaissance Virtues*, CUP, Cambridge, 2004.

Spear, P.: *India: A Modern History*, University of Michigan Press, New York, 1961.

Stephenson, C.: "The Origin and Significance of Feudalism", 1941, Vol. 46 (4), *The American Historical Review*, pp. 788–812.

Stone, L.: *The Crisis of Aristocracy, 1558–1641*, OUP, Oxford, 1967.

Strayer, J. R.: *On the Medieval Origins of the Modern State*, Princeton University Press, Princeton, 1970.

The Economist, 17 December 2011, available at: www.economist.com/node/21541753.

Thompson, J. E.: *Mercenaries, Pirates and Sovereigns: State-Building and Extraterritorial Violence in Early Modern Europe*, Princeton University Press, Chichester, 1994.

Tilly, C.: *Coercion, Capital, and European States, AD 990–1990*, Basil Blackwell, Oxford, 1990.

Tilly, C.: *The Formation of National States in Western Europe*, Princeton University Press, Princeton, 1975.

Tzoref-Ashkenazi, C.: "German Auxiliary Troops in British and Dutch East India Companies" in Arielli, N. and Collins, B. (eds): *Transnational Soldiers: Foreign Military Enlistment in the Modern Era*, Palgrave Macmillan, Basingstoke, 2013.

Waley, D. P.: *Italian City-Republics*, Pearson, Harlow, 1989.

Wallerstein, I.: *The Modern World-System I: Capitalist Agriculture and the Origins of the European World-Economy in the Sixteenth Century*, Academic Press, London, 1974.

Washbrook, D. A.: "India, 1818–1860: The Two Faces of Colonialism" in Porter, A. (ed.): *The Oxford History of the British Empire: The Nineteenth Century*, OUP, Oxford, 1999.

Weber, M.: "Politics as a Vocation" in *The Vocation Lectures*, Hackett Publishing Company, Cambridge, 2004.

3 Mercenaries of the twentieth century and state responsibility

The first half of the twentieth century saw the pinnacle of the centralisation of military power and economic resources within states and a significant drop in mercenary activity. Enabled by developments in infrastructure and logistics, the two World Wars (1914–1918 and 1939–1945) introduced the notion of 'total war', a term describing extreme mobilisation and targeting of national economies and populations.[1] While the First World War was orchestrated by the elite, it was executed by the masses[2]; first drawing the numbers from volunteers and, by 1916, through conscription to compensate for a decline in volunteering.[3] The science and technology behind total warfare were key, and states were happy to invest in these new progressive and lethal developments.[4] Submarines, fighter planes, artillery shells, and tanks all contributed to the totality of the Great War. A mature level of industrialisation meant that around sixty million men were mobilised into the armed forces and kept in the field all year round,[5] leaving little opportunity or need for mercenary forces.[6]

In a similar way, the total nature of the Second World War, with peoples, technology, and all imaginable resources centralised in the hands of the state, left almost no room for mercenary units. Citizenship and national allegiance played an important role, further emphasising the norm against the use of private military forces, while existing colonial troops served to close any military gaps across empires. The scope and scale of these wars eliminated any opening for mercenaries, with the exception of small groups of dispersed private soldiers,[7] as states obtained a monopoly on violence and refused to share it with the private sector. According to Tilly, "the [build-up] of big navies and expensive, nationally-recruited standing armies, furthermore, entailed the disarmament of civilian populations, which reduced the prevalence of small-scale private warfare".[8] The Gurkhas were the closest thing to a mercenary force experienced during the Second World War period.[9] In contemporary international legal terms, Gurkhas would not fall under the mercenary category, as they were always recruited as members of the armed forces of a party to a conflict.[10] Nonetheless, a quarter of a million professional Gurkha soldiers served in the Second World War in almost all theatres.[11] The American Volunteer Group, more widely known as the 'Flying Tigers', were a three-unit force of fighter pilots who were contracted to fight with the Chinese against the Japanese during the Second

World War.[12] This private military force had a short lifespan of only two years, before being officially disbanded in July 1942. Some soldiers later returned to serve in the military for the remainder of the war.[13]

The rise of international legal norms

It was not only state practice and socio-political behaviours of the beginning of the twentieth century that shaped the outlook on private and irregular force. Besides the drastic changes in the global political layout and major military advances brought about by the World Wars and imperial expansion, the end of the 'long nineteenth century' marked the start of the universalisation of international law (IL).[14] The international legal system that emerged in its current form at the beginning of the twentieth century built its foundation upon the rules of sovereign equality of states and against imperialist violations. From the late nineteenth century and until 1945, international regulation of mercenaries was conducted largely through the development of the law of neutrality.[15] Although no definition of mercenaries was formulated at the time, two provisions relating to the recruitment and procurement of mercenaries were included in the 1907 Hague Convention with Article 4 stating that "corps of combatants cannot be formed nor recruiting agencies opened on the territory of a neutral Power to assist the belligerents".[16]

Having rejected a German proposal for a total ban on the service of foreigners in national militaries, the European colonial powers opted merely to require neutral states to prevent commercial recruiting on their territory.[17] The International Committee of the Red Cross emphasised that neutral states have the right "to stand apart from and not be adversely affected by the conflict" and duties of "non-participation and impartiality".[18] The provisions were very clear in drawing the line on state responsibility; a state was not required to regulate its nationals if they wished to offer their military services to a third-party state during a conflict and was, therefore, not accountable for individual outsourcing of mercenaries.[19]

Non-intervention as an international legal norm

Another building block of the Westphalian tradition is the principles of non-intervention and the sovereign equality of states.[20] Largely focused on diplomacy, as opposed to coercion, these principles are believed to form the core of accepted international conduct. The Montevideo Convention of 1933 fortified the definition of a state as an actor of IL with a permanent population, a defined territory, a government, and the capacity to enter into relations with other states.[21] Furthermore, Article 8 of the Convention affirmed that "no state has the right to intervene in the internal or external affairs of another".[22] As a consequence of the two World Wars, the laws of neutrality lost much of their former importance and were superseded by the League of Nations and the United Nations, prohibiting the resort to war.[23] In addition, lessons were learned that urged the international community to outlaw extreme use of force in favour of the growing interdependence and cooperation of states, rather than reliance on the raw balance of power.[24]

Since 1957, about thirty-five UN Resolutions have been adopted by the GA with a particular focus on intervention and interference.[25] The UN GA Declaration on the Inadmissibility of Intervention (1965)[26] advocated by Latin American countries and the Soviet bloc, and the Friendly Relations Declaration (1970),[27] reinforced the principle of non-intervention and the inadmissibility of foreign troops by invitation of a government. The latter half of the twentieth century saw a number of significant regulatory endeavours in the realm of non-intervention. It was declared as one of the principles guiding relations between states in the 1975 Helsinki Final Act of the Conference on Security and Co-operation in Europe.[28] The 1976 Declaration on Non-interference[29] was wider than the Friendly Relations Declaration, as it denounced any form of interference, overt or covert, including the use of mercenary forces.[30] The Declaration also laid out a clearer exception for acts committed in pursuance of the right of self-determination.[31]

Supported by the non-aligned states and the Soviet bloc, the 1981 Declaration on the Inadmissibility of Intervention and Interference in the Internal Affairs of States was adopted by 102 votes to 22. It attempted to define the scope of intervention in more detail than previous resolutions, counterintuitively representing a very broad concept of non-interference that is not in line with the accepted understanding of reality of customary IL.[32] The increased efforts of codification in this area, deriving from different sources of law, is an indication of the efforts by the international community to reinforce and solidify the norm of non-intervention, covering a variety of scopes and avenues. State practice, however, indicates that the principle of non-intervention does not prohibit certain limited operations of foreign troops at the invitation of a government. In other cases, state practice demonstrated, although covertly, an illegitimate intervention by invitation of the opposition.

The end of the Second World War brought significant demilitarisation which, in theory, ought to signify a post-war pacifist outlook. The US Army land and air forces began partial demobilisation of its approximately 8,290,000 soldiers on 12 May 1945[33] and by the end of 1948 had trimmed the army to about one-sixteenth of its original size.[34] Since 1945, the 'Long Peace' resulted in a significant reduction of war between the Western states. It did, however, also see a significant rise of military activity throughout the rest of the world.[35]

Decolonisation and proxy warfare

Historically, the concept of sovereignty has been closely associated not only with the state, but also with the practice of imperial expansion.[36] Arguably, little changed immediately after the end of the Second World War with the overseas empires coexisting together with nation-states.[37] Decolonisation, illustrated here through a number of contained examples, provides the historical and political context of state behaviour that either directly encouraged the immediate use, or created a plausible environment for the long-term spread of private military forces. One such example derives from the struggle between the newly decolonised states, their former empires, and the two superpowers.

Arising from the end of the nineteenth century and reinforced by Article 2(4) of the UN Charter, which prohibited states from resorting to threat or use of force in their international relations, the principle of non-intervention largely prevailed until the 1960s. However, the military context of the Cold War shifted conflicts to the Global South,[38] reintroducing mercenaries and irregular troops into military conduct. The processes of decolonisation and the wars of national liberation shaped the issue in two ways; first, by internalising the nature of the conflict and second, by creating a strong demand for mercenaries. Large-scale international wars were superseded by 'border actions',[39] though these were no less vicious or brutal. National tensions meant that civil wars became more frequent, as two or more parties within the same state acquired military capacity in order to pursue state power.[40] Aggressive nationalism, seen throughout the Second World War, lived on as a consequence of the war, even more so than its cause.[41]

The lack of strong national armies created demand for military force, which often meant welcoming foreign involvement. Furthermore, the end of the Second World War gave rise to a world order ideologically divided between the Soviet Union and the US. This, in turn, marked another shift in conflict paradigm with the overwhelming majority of wars between 1945 and 1990 conducted by proxy rather than directly between the two superpowers. While proxy wars can be understood as an "international conflict between two foreign powers, fought out on the soil of a third country",[42] less state-centric views do not exclude the role of non-state actors, such as insurgent groups, and broadens the term beyond ideological motivation.[43] The underlying principle of *indirect* engagement, whereby State A uses proxies in State B to conduct 'subversive operations' on its behalf,[44] was crucial in the context of the nuclear arms race to ensure that a 'hot war' between the two superpowers could be avoided.[45]

Regardless of the extent of authority allowed for local governing groups, colonies were run by European imperialists. Force, rather than consent, was at the root of colonial administration.[46] The main transfers of power from colonial to indigenous rule took place during the first two decades of the Cold War, varying from simple and quick withdrawals in some cases, to prolonged bloody wars of liberation, as a general rule. Nationalism in the new emerging states was ideological, strong, and dynamic, unrestrained by any local administrative or industrial mechanisms. Often deriving from poverty and intensified by the colonial past, radicalisation was an inherent part of the post-colonial 'Third World'. Since empires regularly attempted to retain some of their key investments even after decolonisation, especially in the exploitation of raw materials, the new nations understood the importance of state building and prioritised its implementation.[47]

Institutions and procedures, inherited from the colonial era, prevailed in the new states after independence, often with a functioning indigenous administrative system that predated the empire, such as in India or in Nigeria.[48] Despite these governmental legacies, the former colonies found themselves in a hollow, often corrupt shell of a state, striving to recuperate decades of political and economic development. Having fought their way out from empire, they were left to be constantly looking over their shoulder in the fear of colonial return or internal disintegration due to corruption and ethnic tensions. The imposition of a Western-dominated state system with its European-style armies and constitutions to the Global South encouraged and fuelled the spread of violence, authoritarian regimes, and military autonomy.[49] Decolonisation, in the broader rhetoric of the Cold War, therefore, contributed to the militarisation of the Global South not only strategically, by treating the newly emerging territories as the battlefield of the two superpowers, but also tactically, by establishing the supply of weapons and manpower from the West to the rest of the world. Military enablement was especially prominent in those countries that supplied valuable commodities such as oil.[50]

Former colonies transitioned from imperial rule into a world ideologically partitioned by two new dominating superpowers. Both the US and the Soviets were actively pursuing newly liberated states through a different kind of imperialism. While not claiming the territories, they managed to dictate many aspects of state governance with a very limited, and often forced, choice of either communism or capitalism. States on the receiving end were often fighting wars of national liberation. Embedded in the wider context of the Cold War, different factions of emerging governments were tactically used as proxies by the Soviet Union and the US. Prevalent for over half a century, this mode of warfare played a crucial role in the militarisation of the Global South and, ultimately, the re-emergence of private military forces in the international arena.

Although proxy warfare did not rely solely on private military groups, it followed the same transactional model for demand and supply of military power, characteristic of mercenarism. Only in this scenario, the financial incentive was replaced or supplemented with political alliance and a very loose concept of protection. This increased the risks associated with managing the relationship between the benefactor and the proxy, a relationship that once again resembles that of a hiring state and a contracting party. The aid to Third-World countries was provided with strings attached, often creating an environment where the recipient had little authority.[51]

Numerous Central Intelligence Agency (CIA)-organised operations that included the financing, training, and provision of mercenary troops raise questions of legitimacy in outsourced nation-building[52] and demonstrate the increasing mercenary presence in the military landscape of the Cold War. While political reasons for frequent intervention were rooted in assumed responsibility for global world order,[53] the legal arguments only went as far as 'self-defence' and 'intervention by invitation', since ideology had not been ratified as a valid motive for intervention. For the duration of the Cold War, American foreign policy was based on pre-emptive interventions in the Global South on ideological grounds against Soviet Union-influenced left-wing movements, and vice versa. On the one hand, the provision of armaments and military advisers made it easier for the superpowers to distance themselves from some types of limited war. On the other hand, the development of permanent military alliances and of military bases in affiliated territories made it much more likely for states to get involved if their allies came under attack.[54] All these aspects fuelled global belligerency, unfolding extreme militarism across Latin America, the Middle East, Africa, and Asia.

Decline of non-interventionism

While decolonisation marked the liberation of new sovereign states from imperial rule, relentless interventions during the Cold War put the relevance of international rules on the use of force into question. Intervention on political grounds contributed to the decline of sovereignty and, most importantly, shaped the response of IL to these interventions. The formation of NATO in 1950 ensured continued joint defence preparation, while the presence of foreign troops on the ground reduced each country's military freedom, something that would have been considered an intolerable infringement of state sovereignty a decade earlier.[55] To those states whose road to independence passed through a 'battlefield', both the US and the Soviet Union were providing vitally important military aid. It was partially through economic and political dominance and partially by invitation that the framework of the Cold War led to the decline of the concepts of non-interventionism and territorial sovereignty.

At the 1962 UN Committee on Colonial Peoples, the representative for Mali raised a serious concern about the connection between military activities and colonialism, considering the presence of military bases "an impediment to the process of decolonisation" and noting that the "use of force was an inevitable consequence of a military presence".[56] While the legal norms of non-intervention were reinforced in numerous UN Resolutions and multilateral treaties, state practice was demonstrating a different trend. Until the Second World War, the legality of supplying certain types of armaments to belligerents was still sometimes questioned, and it was frequently argued that such sales would almost automatically involve the supplier in the conflict.[57] However, during the Cold War and thereafter, the Americans and the Soviets supplied the Global South with military training, weapons, and often auxiliary forces, changing the normative approach to military assistance and intervention.[58]

Most commonly, interventions were provoked when the two competing policies were pursued in the same state, triggering indirect US and Soviet involvement through proxies. Such foreign policy frameworks, albeit almost always covert, set a precedent for the use of private forces. Moreover, this gradually reintroduced mercenary and private military groups into the security landscape. The Cold War introduced a significant limitation to the principle of state sovereignty, namely the practice of intervention by invitation or consent. Chapter V of the International Law Commission (ILC) describes eight different circumstances that can be considered as precluding the wrongfulness of state intervention.[59]

Consent, covered in Article 20, is arguably the most relevant condition for post-1945 interventions, as it reflects the conflict paradigm of proxy warfare. According to Article 20, valid state consent precludes the wrongfulness of an act by another state.[60] While such codification did not allow for unlimited state intervention, it marked the weakening of the norm of non-intervention, opening it up to political interpretation.[61] The waning notion of territorial sovereignty laid the premise for indirect state intervention and 'arms-length' politics, allowing the superpowers to establish an interventionist policy with a global reach.[62] Mercenaries became the most widely used tool for covert operations in proxy warfare. Their return had a particularly negative impact in the wars of national liberation, signalling the need for an international legal response to regulate these forces that were often perceived as a sign of neo-colonialism by the newly liberated nations.

Mercenary forces in the Congo and Angola

Starting from the early 1960s, mercenaries were a prominent tool of Congolese internal policy.[63] One of the first and most notorious instances of mercenary deployment was by Moïse Tshombe's secessionist government in the province of Katanga.[64] During the Congolese Civil War, the CIA established an army in the Congo to back pro-Western leaders Cyrille Adoula and Joseph-Desiré Mobutu. On 24 November 1964, 500 Belgian paratroopers were airlifted into the city, diverting from a much more extensive US-backed military operation against the rebels, executed by European mercenaries and Cuban pilots who were funded and organised by the CIA.[65] George Godley, the US ambassador to the Democratic Republic of the Congo and later ambassador to Laos, spoke openly about US involvement in the 'nation-building' of Congo, which included dependency on Western mercenaries to pacify the population.[66] The Mobutu dictatorship was reinstated under the pretext of modernisation and elimination of future insurgency.[67]

The Mobutu government had also been known to hire mercenaries to suppress further revolts in Katanga.[68] When the Congo was renamed Zaire between 1971 and 1997, about 300 Chinese instructors served with the National Front for the Liberation of Angola and were joined by fifty contracted military personnel from Romania and North Korea.[69] The purpose and use of mercenaries in the Congo stretched from supporting secessionist movements, to being hired by the government to combat extremist groups, to opposing the government itself.[70] The short few decades of Congolese independence were mutilated by various mercenary groups, hired by conflicting political factions, intervening and shaping state politics.

In 1975, after years of bloody fighting and civil unrest in Angola, Portugal finally let go of its last African colony. The transition to a new government was to take place on 11 November 1976 with three political factions competing for control of the country. These were the pro-communist Popular Movement for the Liberation of Angola (MPLA), and two pro-Western organisations, Holden

Roberto's National Front for the Liberation of Angola (FNLA) and Jonas Savimbi's National Union for the Total Independence of Angola (UNITA). Beyond the ideological rivalry with the Soviet Union, Angola had little importance to questions of US national security, and its economic significance did not exceed the small amounts of petroleum extracted from the Cabindan fields and the coffee export to the American markets.[71] However, not only did the Soviet and US governments operate on Angolan territory through mercenary troops, UNITA troops were trained and led by South African and Portuguese military teams, as well as various mercenary groups.[72]

In September 1976, the first South African training camp was operational inside Angola.[73] Over three months, the CIA was allocated almost $50 million in total to be used to train, equip, and transport anti-MPLA troops.[74] The bulk of the money was spent on arms and on paying French and South African mercenaries to help organise the Angolan troops, especially those of the FNLA.[75] While 10,000 organised Cuban regular army troops were fighting on the MPLA side, mercenaries were instrumental in the military performance of the FNLA and UNITA. The CIA recruited twenty Frenchmen to work directly with Bob Denard,[76] famous for his mercenary activity in the Congo, and 300 Portuguese mercenaries. While the Portuguese were already being recruited in small numbers by the FNLA, Colonel Castro, and Captain Bento,[77] the latter had never materialised for Operation Savannah.[78] The third mercenary force, involving around 160 British and American venturers, was organised and financed by Holden Roberto, allegedly also from CIA funds.[79] The lack of sponsors and of cooperation from Congress ironically turned out to be a winning combination that limited the scope of escalation in Angola, therefore preventing another Vietnam.[80] It did, however, introduce an unregulated market for force, exacerbating the security problems in the region.

These are only a few examples; others include Nationalist Chinese troops in Burma,[81] Sumatran Rebels in Indonesia,[82] Khamba horsemen,[83] the Cuban Bay of Pigs Invasion Force,[84] Meo tribesmen of *L'Armee Clandestine*,[85] the Ukrainian Insurgent Army,[86] the Afghan Mujaheedin,[87] El Salvador death squads,[88] the Haitian National Intelligence Service,[89] and so on. Both sides had relentlessly raised, trained, and sponsored third-party military troops, which were often radical and contentious, to pursue their political goals, disregarding the sovereign borders and political integrity of the 'Third World' states they operated in.

International legal response to the use of irregular forces

Anti-mercenary norms

Given the central and often devastating role that soldiers of fortune played in the wars of national liberation in Africa associating with instability and secessionist movements,[90] it is not surprising that the push towards formulating anti-mercenary norms were particularly prominent amongst the African countries. The rise of new, independent states began to change the role of the

United Nations. The five-year conflict over the decolonisation of the Congo was a testament to the changing role of the UN from a tool of US foreign interventions into a more diverse forum, bringing together the non-aligned countries, less susceptible to American influence than before.[91] The newly decolonised states urgently turned to the UN, the Organisation of African Unity (OAU), and other multilateral treaty-negotiating fora, with the goal of developing and implementing norms to limit the use of mercenaries.[92] Commercial military activity was deemed to violate the right to self-determination, and, therefore, ought to be prohibited.

The Declaration on the Granting of Independence to Colonial Peoples of 1960[93] was the first significant GA resolution to mark the legitimacy of decolonisation. However, it made no mention of regulation of force by national liberation movements.[94] In 1965, the UN passed a Declaration on the Inadmissibility of Intervention,[95] whereby it explicitly implemented a wording appropriate for the context of the Cold War, prohibiting direct or indirect intervention, legally covering the threat of proxies.[96] Although it did not reference mercenarism, it instructed states to refrain from organising, assisting, or financing terrorist or armed activities directed towards the violent overthrow of the regime of another state.[97] The 1968 UN GA Resolution 2465 Article 8 condemned the use of mercenaries against movements for national liberation and independence, and called upon "the Governments of all countries to enact legislation declaring the recruitment, financing and training of mercenaries in their territory to be a punishable offence and prohibiting their nationals from serving as mercenaries".[98]

The 1970 resolution on the Legal Status of the Combatants fighting against colonialism[99] was a step towards a more formal codification of mercenaries. In the context of wars of national liberation, the resolution considered the use of mercenaries by colonial and racist regimes to be a criminal act, and mercenaries themselves to be criminals.[100] The resolution did not provide any further guidelines for regulation, and left this matter to the legal and political interpretation of national courts. The 1970 Friendly Relations Declaration followed similar approach, condemning intervention and emphasising state duty to refrain from organising irregular forces, including mercenaries, for incursion into the territory of another state.[101] All efforts were drawn towards regulating and outlawing mercenary activity in Africa and the rest of the Third World.

In 1972, the first definition of mercenaries was formulated in the OAU Convention, while the Diplock Report was published in 1976 following British involvement in Angola, signalling governments' awareness of the issue and the need for new legislation. The non-aligned countries repeatedly denounced foreign mercenary activities in the 'Third World' during this period. Their criticism was heard at the Diplomatic Conference on Humanitarian Law, held in Geneva from 1974 to 1977. Arguing to deprive mercenaries of any legal protection, they were able to force regulatory change, despite the objections raised by other states.[102] As a result, in 1977 Additional Protocol (AP) I was established, defining mercenaries in Article 47 and, in theory, excluding them from combatant and prisoner of war status upon capture.[103] Furthermore, since 1987 the

Commission approved a special *rapporteur* to monitor the alleged use of mercenaries in contemporary conflicts on the African continent.[104] This was a direct result of the concerns raised by the African states based on their detrimental experiences of mercenary involvement since the 1960s.

Codification of mercenaries by the OAU

> In the making of international regulations, consensus between states can only be reached "at the price of ambiguity".[105]
>
> (Christine Gray)

In 1972, the OAU ratified the Convention for the Elimination of Mercenaries in Africa, containing a definition of mercenaries based on nationality and motive. It was formulated based on the challenges that mercenaries posed for national liberation movements and the sovereign integrity of the newly established African states. Instead of focusing on monetary gain, it identified the aims of a mercenary as being to overthrow a government, undermine independence, and interfere with the liberation movements.[106] Despite a clear aversion to mercenaries and the innovative nature of the definition, the OAU Convention did not explicitly forbid the employment of mercenaries.[107] This formulation aimed to regulate foreign private recruits from Europe and South Africa, leaving non-nationals, employed by a government to defend itself from dissident groups within its own borders, outside of the legislation. This was the case of the Cuban troops that fought for the Popular Movement for the Liberation of Angola (MPLA) during the Angolan civil war.[108]

Nevertheless, the OAU Convention was binding amongst the states who are signatories to the treaty,[109] and its key purpose was to outlaw and eliminate mercenaries who, in the context of national liberation movements in post-colonial Africa, were considered a threat to sovereignty, independence, and development.[110] In contrast to the 1907 Hague Convention, the OAU Convention called for states to introduce laws forbidding their nationals from engaging in mercenary activities.[111] This provision invoked state responsibility to both prevent mercenary activity on their territory and to take extraterritorial measures to prevent their citizens from committing any of the offences defined in Article 2. It classified mercenarism and all auxiliary activities, such as training, financing, and recruitment, crimes against peace and security in Africa.[112] Unlike any previous treaties, it explicitly declared the duty of contracting states to impose sanctions for any offences that fell under Article 2 of the Convention.[113]

In 1976, triggered by significant mercenary activity in Angola, Appendix II was added to the OAU Convention. It reinforced the need for codification and expanded the definition not only to include the actors (mercenaries) but also to reinforce international legal regulation over the act of mercenarism.[114] The definition was no longer limited to foreign nationals; the crime of mercenarism could now apply to "the individual, group or association, representatives of state and the State itself" acting for personal gain, amongst other reasons listed in the original Convention.[115] Furthermore, Article 5 of the Appendix highlighted the fact that not only are offences committed by mercenaries considered a crime; being classified as a mercenary is a crime in itself.[116]

British mercenaries in Angola and the Diplock report

Significant international attention turned to mercenary activity following the trial of thirteen foreigners in Angola in 1976.[117] All were convicted of the crime of "being a mercenary", with four offenders sentenced to death, and the others to long prison sentences.[118] Published as a result of the recruitment of British mercenaries to join the armed forces of the FNLA in Angola, the Diplock Report[119] aimed to assess whether the UK had sufficient controls in place to regulate British citizen recruitment for mercenary service. The assessors had to, therefore, agree on a definition of mercenaries in order to conduct the inquiry. Dismissing 'motivation' on the basis of it being too vague and inconclusive to serve as the defining criterion, the Report proposed to identify mercenaries only by reference to what they do, and not why they do it.[120] A definition was consequently advised in line with UK national jurisdiction, classifying a mercenary as "any person who serves voluntarily and for pay in some armed force other than that of Her Majesty in the right of the United Kingdom".[121] This definition was formulated for the purpose of the enquiry, exclusively for the UK. While it could contribute to formulating a norm and a workable definition under IL, it had not evolved to acquire an international dimension and universality.

Central to the Diplock Report was the debate concerning the regulation of recruitment of mercenaries on the territory of the UK versus the enlistment of British citizens into foreign armed forces abroad. As the former could be regulated by means of national jurisdiction, the report concluded that any new penal legislation should be aimed at prohibiting the recruitment of mercenary services and advertising of such recruitment in the UK.[122] The latter, however, was deemed to fall outside of national criminal law, as the state had no means of enforcing the prohibition of citizen enlistment outside of the UK.[123] The report, therefore, proposed "the abolition of any statutory offence by a United Kingdom citizen of enlisting as a mercenary while abroad".[124] Outlining the challenges that the irregular conflict paradigms pose to national legislation, the Report concluded that the UK government had no legal authority to prevent the enlistment or recruitment of mercenaries until the status of every party to the conflict in Angola was established under IL.[125] Moreover, when the Diplock Report was published in 1976, serving as a mercenary was not considered an offence under IL.[126]

A year later, however, the norm was solidified in the Additional Protocol I to the Geneva Conventions of 1949.[127] Although it was not the first international legal effort to regulate the use of mercenaries, AP I produced the most widely accepted international definition of a mercenary. Unlike all previous definitions, the one formulated in AP I was the first geographically neutral codification of mercenaries under IL, applicable to all member states.[128] Charged with a complex task of providing a frame of reference, the definition had to be broad enough to encompass all present and future political circumstances, while also being targeted enough to limit the scope of political and ideological interpretation. Motivation and nationality were chosen as the two parameters to define mercenaries under IL. While this definition was formulated as a result of OAU codification initiatives, it made no reference to national liberation movements, or any other specific political circumstance beyond the references to 'armed conflict' and 'hostilities'. The definition was narrow in comparison to that formulated in the OAU Convention; in order to be deemed a mercenary under AP I, all six criteria must be met.[129] Moreover, AP I applies solely to situations of international armed conflict, leaving the realm of civil wars and post-conflict hostilities outside of its scope. While AP I provides the most widely accepted international definition of a mercenary, some states, such as the US, Turkey, and countries in the Middle East, have not ratified it. Instead, these are governed by the Conventions where the definition of combatant and, therefore, prisoner of war, is more inclusive.

A turning point: OAU Appendix III and the mercenary convention

The creation of provisions on mercenaries under AP I and the esteemed authority of the Geneva Conventions guided the normative approach, adding an element of universality to the issue. By doing so, it neglected to articulate the nuance so presciently captured by the OAU Convention. Proving an effective mechanism in articulating national interests of newly decolonised states, the OAU's trajectory of international regulation of mercenaries was defined by the relentless interventions into the state affairs of African countries from the 1960s onwards. By the time AP I came about, the OAU Convention had already made significant steps in outlawing mercenarism as a crime against peace and security in Africa. As a response to the ongoing struggles caused by mercenarism, it had expanded the definition of mercenaries attempting to outlaw all types of mercenary activity, regardless of the nationality, or the level of the involvement of the offenders. Hence why the addition of Appendix III in the form of the International Convention against the Activities of Mercenaries in 1980[130] could be considered a step back and a turning point that diverged the trajectory of regulation of mercenaries and PMCs today and gave rise to limitations associated with state responsibility in using private force.

Aligning with the narrow definition of mercenaries found in AP I[131] that focuses on monetary gain, direct participation in combat, and nationality,[132] it changed the narrative of recognising the act of mercenarism as a crime. Moreover, it compromised the future codification by overwriting this one legal precedent of criminalising the timeless transactional nature of mercenary activity and instead encapsulating the definition of a mercenary which was bound by the historical context of the Cold War.

The International Convention against the Recruitment, Use, Financing and Training of Mercenaries,[133] further solidified the approach and international perception of mercenaries. Known more widely as the UN Mercenary Convention, it came into force in 2001 and, to date, has been ratified by thirty-five states only.[134] Needless to say, the majority of states involved are those who suffered from mercenary activity to the detriment of their national liberation during the Cold War, while none of the permanent UN Security Council member states have so far ratified the Convention. Articles 5–15 of the Convention stipulate the terms of state responsibility relating to recruitment, use, financing, or training of mercenaries, shifting the onus onto states for codifying relevant legal procedures in their respective national jurisdictions to tackle the offences set out by the Convention. Article 1 clause 2(i) broadened the definition of mercenaries to include non-nationals recruited to overthrow a "Government or otherwise undermining the constitutional order of a State; or undermine the territorial integrity of a State". While the definition of mercenaries was largely based on AP I, it now extended to "armed conflict"[135] and also to "any other situation",[136] providing a useful and timely application to non-international armed conflict. However, its authority did not cover those states which chose not to ratify it, and the act of mercenarism remained uncodified under its auspices.

The Nicaragua case

Different normative views on the use of mercenaries were reflected in the patchy development of international treaties and customary law concerning the rising volume of private and mercenary actors after 1945. To highlight some of the ways in which international law tackled the questions of private force and state responsibility, I explore the use of the Contras in Nicaragua by the US government in the 1980s.

The US relationship with Nicaragua, and the rest of the Latin America, extends beyond the context of proxy warfare and dates back to the 1850s, when the US felt obliged to intervene directly against local resistance to foreign control in Nicaragua. The trend continued towards the end of the nineteenth century with interventions in Cuba, the Caribbean, and Central America.[137] In 1933, Nicaragua's political leader Augusto César Sandino proclaimed the country to be the centre of a new anti-US Central American movement, following his defeat to the US-sponsored regime in the twenties.[138] Therefore, even before the Cold War, Nicaragua had borne a symbolic meaning in the challenges it presented to US foreign policy which, subsequently, manifested itself through proxy warfare. In a similar vein, Nicaragua and Honduras also served as a training ground for the right-wing belligerent group, the Contras, that, in agreement with the Organisation of American States, were raised and armed by the US against the elected Guatemalan government of Jacob Arbenz in 1954.[139] The Luis Somoza Debayle government also provided training bases for American-sponsored interventions in Cuba in 1961 and supplied its own troops to join those of the US in the Dominican Republic in 1965.[140]

When the US lost an ally in Somoza to the Sandinista revolution in 1979, they turned to previously deployed tactics of economic pressure, managed subversions, and the threat of a military intervention.[141] In November 1981, President Ronald Reagan signed a top secret National Security Directive authorising the

CIA to spend $19 million to recruit and support the Contras, opponents of Nicaragua's Sandinista government.[142] In supporting the Contras, the CIA carried out several acts of sabotage without consent of Congressional intelligence committees. In response, Congress passed the Boland Amendment, prohibiting the CIA from providing aid to the Contras.

On numerous occasions Ronald Reagan, alongside the representatives of his administration, openly spoke about the ideological and political reasons for intervening in Nicaragua and supporting the Contras.[143] These statements mainly referenced international policy and not the law[144] as the US did not claim the legal right of invitation to use force to overthrow the government of Nicaragua. First of all, the use of force was carried out through proxies, and not by direct forcible intervention of the US army. Second, it was done covertly through CIA operations and, arguably, did not call for legal justification.[145] The inadmissibility of forcible intervention was solidified in Article 2 (4); and although the US covert operation qualified under IL as non-forcible support for forcible action by non-state actors,[146] it still breached the non-use of force principle.[147] While the Cold War provided the rhetoric for the regular subordination of the Third World to the superpowers,[148] this time international law had the ability and the scope to step in, resulting in the *Nicaragua case*.[149]

In April 1984, the Nicaraguan government filed a claim with the International Court of Justice (ICJ) on the basis of forcible military intervention by the US in "Nicaragua's internal affairs, in violation of Nicaragua's sovereignty, territorial integrity and political independence and of the most fundamental and universally accepted principles of international law".[150] The ICJ held that the US violated IL by supporting the Contras in their rebellion against the Nicaraguan government and by mining Nicaragua's harbours:

> the action constituted a breach of international law in that it involved injuring citizens of Nicaragua without any lawful justification, and was a serious violation of the sovereignty and territorial integrity of Nicaragua.[151]

The Court established that the US committed a *prima facie* violation,[152] meaning the evidence before trial was sufficient to prove the case unless there was substantial contradictory evidence presented during the trial.[153] As for the self-defence argument, put forward by the US representatives, the Court dismissed it on the basis that there is no such rule in customary IL that would allow a state to exercise this right based on its own assessment: "where collective self-defense is invoked, it is to be expected that the State for whose benefit this right is used will have declared itself to be the victim of an armed attack".[154] The key lesson of the *Nicaragua case* arose from the ICJ ruling on the nature of US intervention. While intervention by invitation of the state government is permissible under IL, the Court assessed that the US intervened with the purpose of assisting the opposition to forcibly remove the ruling government. Such act is forbidden as the principle of non-intervention would become obsolete if forcible assistance to rebel groups was to be permissible.[155]

The ICJ formulated an authoritative general dictum according to which "it is difficult to see what would remain of the principle of non-intervention in international law if intervention, which is already allowable at the request of the government of a State, were also to be allowed at the request of the opposition".[156] In terms of IHL, an intervention in support of the opposition would change the nature of the conflict from internal (or internationalised) to international. In other words, a foreign state who intervenes and sides with insurgents is effectively fighting the legitimate government of the host state.[157] In the context of a civil conflict, the difference between international and internal conflict occurs when the intervening state is either directly involved in the civil war or is deemed to have full control of a party to the conflict.[158] This distinction is important because there are no provisions for prisoners of war in non-international armed conflicts, and captured rebels would be subject to the domestic law of the state where the conflict is taking place.[159] The ICJ found the US government to be in breach of the principles of non-intervention and non-use of force, granting Nicaragua the sum of 370.2 million US dollars in reparations (which remains unpaid).[160]

Defining mercenaries and state responsibility in the Nicaragua case

Despite the clear ruling of the Court, two closely related points require further consideration. First is the legal status of the Contras under IL, and second is the attribution of authority to the US in relation to the Contras. To help explore these two issues, I refer back to the power and legitimacy nexus explored in the previous chapter. The notion of state responsibility has traditionally been associated with the concept of territorial sovereignty.[161] While there is no inherent justification for the state monopoly of violence, military power is typically concentrated where power and legitimacy coincide. Institutions or governance systems that embrace sovereignty are also those in possession of economic resources and, are therefore, concerned with providing security for its subjects, resources, territory, and so on, through the military means under its controls. This correlation builds an important link between the state, the military forces it controls, and the responsibility it upholds under IL. A violation of IL by a state creates responsibility in two scenarios: first, if loss or damage resulted from the act; and, second, if the delinquency can be attributed to the state.[162]

Establishing control and attribution was the central challenge to invoking state responsibility in the case of the use of the Contras by the US government. During the *Nicaragua case* proceedings, the majority of contemporary legal instruments concerning the use and regulation of mercenaries were internationally established and available to the Court. The 1977 AP I defined mercenaries, the 1974 Definition of Aggression referenced their use and affiliation to the recruiting state and, of course, the wars of liberation in Africa had provided an array of examples of the use of mercenaries by proxy. In their statements to the Court, Nicaragua described the Contras as "bands of mercenaries which have been recruited, organised, paid and commanded by the Government of the United

States".[163] On that basis, they argued that the Contras had no real autonomy from the US government, strongly advocating the need for attribution of authority.[164] In addition, numerous public statements made by the US government referred to irregular armed groups as mercenaries; however, the Court made no such distinction. The Court's judgement did not invoke the definition of mercenaries codified in AP I, even though the Contras were described exclusively in those terms by the Nicaraguan side in the case pleadings, oral arguments, and documents. The only mention of mercenaries in the ICJ judgement were in reference to the Nicaraguan claim concerning the extent of US government control and authority over the Contras, and other formulations made by Nicaragua.

Realising the importance of demonstrating the degree of control to establishing the attribution of responsibility to the US for activities of the Contras, Nicaragua had presented the Court with records of over 470 instances of US-led mercenary attacks taking place between December 1981 and November 1984.[165] These were attributed to "CIA-trained mercenaries" or "mercenary forces", and included kidnapping, assassination, torture, rape, killing of prisoners, and killing of civilians not dictated by military necessity.[166] The request for attributing responsibility to the US government was made on the basis of direct recruitment, financing, regulation, and organisation of the mercenary forces, on the strategic, tactical, and operational levels.[167] The US effective control of the Contras was also argued based on the proof that the US government repeatedly ratified and approved acts of aggression by mercenary forces against Nicaragua.[168] At the core of Nicaragua's argument was that the Contras were not acting in their own standing, instead the US government was "substantially involved" at every level of mercenary operations.[169] This terminology was taken from the 1974 GA Resolution 3314, where a specific clause related to the use of mercenaries was included in the definition of aggression.[170] While it provided legal grounds to classify US activity in Nicaragua as the use of force under Article 2 (4), at no stage in the *Nicaragua case* were the Contras defined as mercenaries by the ICJ.

All the evidence presented to the Court by Nicaragua pointed to the same conclusion: in the proxy war in Nicaragua, mercenaries were an instrument of US policy. Having examined the genesis, development, and activities of the Contra forces, in the Judgement summary of 27 June 1986 the Court confirmed that the Contras were largely financed, trained, equipped, armed, and organised by the US government.[171] Yet, the ICJ concluded that the evidence available to the Court was insufficient to demonstrate the total dependence of the Contras on the US aid, therefore leaving the Contras responsible for their own acts under international law. The Court stated that, "for the United States to be legally responsible, it would have to be proved that that State had effective control of the operations in the course of which the alleged violations were committed".[172] Although in its judgement the ICJ referred to the Friendly Relations Declaration on the matters of non-use of force and non-intervention, it omitted to mention that the Declaration also sets out three rules specifically regulating the conduct of states with regard to insurgent or terrorist groups.[173] The prohibitions are against "organising", "inciting", and "tolerating" irregular forces or armed bands, including mercenaries, for the purpose of intervention into the territory of another state.[174] Furthermore, according to the Definition of Aggression, "substantial involvement" with an armed group acting against another state makes the actions of that group attributable to the state.[175]

Though this definition had not been leveraged. Nor did the ICJ refer to the 1981 Declaration which, in Section 2, outlines the state obligation "to prevent on its territory the training, financing and recruitment of mercenaries, or the sending of such mercenaries into the territory of another State and to deny facilities, including financing, for the equipping and transit of mercenaries".[176] There was no further mention of the alleged IL violations by the Contra forces, or how these ought to be classified and regulated by the ICJ, or by domestic legal systems. The *Nicaragua case* highlighted a significant overlap between the rules on forcible intervention and customary law in Article 2(4).[177] Even though the GA resolution 2625 (XXV)[178] viewed the support for subversive or terrorist armed activities within another state as a threat or use of force, therefore breaching the principle of non-intervention and the use of force,[179] numerous incidents involving mercenary groups committing offences against Nicaraguan citizens were left out of the ICJ's judgement.

The issue here is twofold. First, the Contras were not defined as mercenaries by the Court. The lack of ICJ ruling on this matter is problematic as it removes a great degree of responsibility from the Contras themselves, leaving their legal status ambiguous. Second, it alleviates the issue of US responsibility. In other words, if the Contras were deemed mercenaries, they would inevitably have had direct connection and full financial dependency on the US government, or on the CIA who procured them. If, however, the Contras were deemed freedom fighters, they could be seen to have had a valid motive under the AP I definition to fight independently from US support. Unfortunately, this debate was not held as part of the ICJ judgement, and the issue was neglected entirely. Overall, it is clear that the regulation of mercenaries or irregular forces was not in the scope of the *Nicaragua case* from the standpoint of the Court. Missing an opportunity to formulate a norm and a legal precedent, or even to leverage legal tools available at the time of the case, the Court had subscribed to the politicisation of the issue of the use and regulation of private force, paving the way for the mercenary companies of the nineties and their commercial, more legitimate, and versatile successors of the twenty-first century.

Conclusion

Throughout the first half of the twentieth century, the world was preoccupied with global wars fought by centralised states and their national standing armies. The prevalent mode of governance that characterised states during this time was a sovereign nation-state with its typology of a centralised 'warfare' government. Fulfilling the belligerent needs of the twentieth century, the strong state provided robust military infrastructure, manpower, as well as the necessary democratic controls through the choice of products, investment, and intervention in the internal management of private arms companies.[180]

The international legal system of the twentieth century was founded upon the rules of Westphalian sovereign equality, non-intervention, and state monopoly of force, in order to promote human rights and to serve as a shield of protection against aggression and imperialist violations. However, these principles had been undermined for two centuries through imperial expansion on the part of the West. Equally, the two World Wars showed that nationalism does not only equate to citizenship, but often leads to political extremism, military conscription, and ethnic disasters. The premise of IL was not fit to serve the international system at the time and it was certainly not future-proof. The Second World War put an end to world empires and initiated the process of decolonisation, drastically changing the political landscape.

Territorial empires gave way to two opposing superpowers that created and cultivated the framework of the Cold War through cultural imperialism, "the global carrier of the social practices of 'modernity' in all its manifestations",[181] and, most prominently, through proxy warfare. While Article 2 (4) of the UN Charter established the principles of non-intervention following the end of the Second World War, IL was not focused on regulating mercenarism. Mercenaries had not been widely deployed in Europe for centuries, and the empires were still holding on to their fading authority over the colonial troops in their possession, which served as a plausible alternative to private contractors. There was no immediate legal precedent or normative state practice that would call for regulation on the subject of mercenarism. It was not until the wars of national liberation that mercenaries surfaced again, playing a major role in the belligerent activities in the Global South, with some of the most severe and contentious episodes suffered in the countries of Central Africa. Decolonisation created a geopolitical loophole for powerful states to intervene, creating states with a new type of sovereignty, the "sovereignty of absence of value".[182] The Global South has undergone a so-called liberal democratic 'formatting', leaving them with the postmodern sovereignty of globalisation and empire.

The IL of the twentieth century was largely politicised.[183] Treaties were considered the strongest binding mechanism for recognition and compliance with IL by the states. In essence, the nature of such IL is purely state-centric, as these are bilateral or multilateral agreements between states and states only. Treaty law, such as UN resolutions and International Conventions, and case law, such as court rulings, were frequently disregarded by states and deemed purely arbitrary. The outcome of the *Nicaragua case* was a testament to that. Although the ICJ clearly classified US intervention and the use of proxies in Nicaragua as illegitimate activities that undermine state sovereignty, the Court's judicial procedure could not enforce the participation of both parties. Furthermore, following the US withdrawal from the case, the ICJ ruling, based on unilateral input, was not a strong enough authority to enforce the paying of US compensation to the government of Nicaragua.

Another major challenge that twentieth-century IL faced was the lack of universality in its relevance and applicability. While responding to anti-mercenary movements, it also provided an easy opt-out mechanism for states. While AP

I was the legal response that African states were actively campaigning for, two challenges arise from the codification of mercenaries and their prisoner of war status in the AP I. The definition of mercenaries was so specific that it omitted a range of irregular military actors, and, therefore, failed to provide comprehensive regulation. The original definition of mercenaries agreed by the OAU Convention was situational and political, limited by the regional specificity of the issue of mercenarism. While it cannot be used to define mercenaries universally across geographies and different forms of conflict, it was arguably more valuable, as it attempted to criminalise the act of mercenarism which was ultimately overridden by the addition of Appendix III. The *Nicaragua case* exhibited the weaknesses of IL, which fell subject to the political interpretation of a more powerful state.[184] The ICJ statement, according to which "intervention is allowable at the request of the government",[185] marked a departure from the stance taken in the 1960s and 1970s regarding state intervention and the use of foreign troops, stretching the norm on non-intervention further and weakening the sovereign integrity of states. Finally, the wording of the UN Mercenary Convention, alongside other international legal efforts, clearly aimed to cater for the post-colonial misuse of mercenaries. However, its ability to regulate the use of private military actors today comes into question. With UN efforts to regulate mercenaries applicable only to situations of international armed conflict or national liberation movements, and the act of mercenarism not being criminalised, twentieth-century international law has left some significant gaps unfilled, and the question of the legality of mercenaries unanswered.

Notes

1 Mann (2012, p. 153).
2 For more detail on soldier motivation, see: Audoin-Rouzeau and Becker (2000).
3 Mann (2012, p. 145).
4 Mann (2012, p. 142).
5 Mann (2012, pp. 140–141).
6 Britain and France continued to deploy huge hired armies of colonial subjects in the conflict.
7 McFate (2014, p. 20).
8 Tilly (1991, p. 38).
9 On Gurkhas, see: Cross and Gurung (2007); Birch (2013, pp. 490–492).
10 AP I, art. 47, para. 2(e).
11 See: www.ayo-gorkhali.org/en/timeline/soldiers-of-empire/1939-45-world-war-ii.
12 Toland (1963).
13 See:www.history.com/news/history-lists/6-legendary-mercenary-armies-from-history.
14 Anghie (1999, p. 1).
15 Kinsey (2008, p. 3).
16 Convention (V) respecting the Rights and Duties of Neutral Powers and Persons in Case of War on Land. The Hague, 18 October 1907; Chapter I: The Rights and Duties of Neutral Powers, Art. 4.
17 Convention Respecting the Rights and Duties of Neutral Powers and Persons in Case of War on Land (Hague Convention No V), 18 October 1907, 1 Bevans 654–658, Art. 4.
18 The Law of Armed Conflict. Neutrality.

19 The Law of Armed Conflict. Neutrality, Art. 6.
20 Holsti (1988, p. 81); Funston (2000, p. 1).
21 Montevideo Convention on the Rights and Duties of States.
22 Montevideo Convention on the Rights and Duties of States, Art. 8.
23 Convention (V) respecting the Rights and Duties of Neutral Powers and Persons in Case of War on Land. The Hague, 18 October 1907.
24 Held et al. (1999, p. 62).
25 Held et al. (1999, p. 350).
26 See: Declaration on the Inadmissibility of Intervention in the Domestic Affairs of States and the Protection of their Independence and Sovereignty (1966, pp. 662–664); Paul (1996, pp. 103–119); Levin (1966, pp. 21–25).
27 See: Rosenstock (1971, pp. 713–735); Sahovic (1972); Arangio-Ruiz (1972, pp. 419–742); Keller (2008).
28 1975 Helsinki Final Act, Art. 1 (a), Principle VI Non-intervention in internal affairs.
29 UNGA 92; A/RES/31/91.
30 A/RES/31/91, 31/91, Art. 3.
31 A/RES/31/91, 31/92, Art. 2; Jamnejad and Wood (2009, p. 355).
32 Jamnejad and Wood (2009, p. 355).
33 Sparrow (1984, p. 21).
34 McCormick (1998, p. 10).
35 Tilly (1991, p. 38).
36 Duncanson (2006, p. 57).
37 Mann (2012, p. 165).
38 The term 'Third World' will be used in this chapter when referring to the Global South in the context of the Cold War.
39 Gray (2000, p. 51).
40 Tilly (1991, p. 39).
41 Mann (2012, p. 165).
42 Deutsch (1964).
43 Mumford (2013, p. 40).
44 Mumford (2013).
45 Towle (1981, p. 21).
46 Westad (2007, p. 76).
47 Westad (2007, p. 90).
48 Westad (2007).
49 Tilly (1991, p. 38).
50 Tilly (1991, p. 39).
51 Westad (2007, p. 96).
52 McCormick (1998, p. 120).
53 See Zubok (2009, p. 248).
54 Towle (1981, p. 21).
55 Towle (1981, p. 24).
56 Special Committee on the Situation with Regard to the Implementation of the Declaration on the Granting of Independence to Colonial Countries and Peoples, 640th Meeting, 30 September 1968, *AjAC.109jSR.640*, p. 16.
57 See: Borchard and Lage (1940).
58 Towle (1981, p. 22).
59 Also see: Draft articles on Responsibility of States for Internationally Wrongful Acts, with commentaries, 2001, Part 1: Internationally Wrongful Act of a State, pp. 32–86.
60 International Law Commission: Responsibility of States for Internationally Wrongful Acts 2001, Art. 20.
61 The opposition cannot legitimately invite a foreign state to intervene, but this rationale was frequently overlooked during the Cold War.
62 Westad (2007, p. 130).

63 Hempstone (1962); Clarke (1968); Mockler (1969, pp. 155–171).
64 Taulbee (1985, p. 341).
65 Westad (2007, p. 136).
66 Ambassador Godley to State, 30 October 1965, DDRS.
67 Westad (2007, p. 143).
68 Clarke (1968, p. 68).
69 Westad (2007, p. 227).
70 Taulbee (1985, p. 341).
71 Stockwell (1978, p. 43).
72 Marcum (1976, p. 417).
73 Westad (2007, p. 230).
74 Westad (2007, p. 228).
75 Stockwell (1978, pp. 40–57).
76 The French intelligence service introduced CIA case officers to Bob Denard, and for $500,000 cash – paid in advance – he agreed to provide twenty French mercenaries; Westad (2007, p. 228).
77 Westad (2007, p. 228).
78 Operation Savannah is considered to be the first large-scale cross-border operation into Angola by the SADF (South African Defence Force) during the so-called bush war. See: www.opssavannah.net.
79 Marcum (1976, p. 419); Stockwell (1978, pp. 223–224); Report of the Committee of Privy Counsellors appointed to inquire into the recruitment of mercenaries, Cmnd. 6569, 1976, London, p. 1.
80 Stockwell (1978, p. 217).
81 Wise and Ross (1964, pp. 84–87).
82 Conboy and Morrison (1999); Scott (1985, pp. 239–264); Wise and Ross (1964, pp. 88–94).
83 Blum (2003, pp. 21–26).
84 McCormick (1998, p. 144).
85 Blum (2003, pp. 140–144).
86 See: archive.larouchepac.com/node/29841.
87 Prados (2002, pp. 466–471).
88 LeoGrande (1998, pp. 149–284); Nairn (1984).
89 Weiner (1993).
90 Axelrod (2014, p. 187); Foreign and Commonwealth Office (2002, p. 14).
91 Westad (2007, p. 136).
92 Avant (2005, p. 201).
93 Declaration on the Granting of Independence to Colonial Countries and Peoples, Adopted by General Assembly resolution 1514 (XV) of 14 December 1960.
94 Gray (2000, p. 45).
95 Declaration on the Inadmissibility of Intervention in the Domestic Affairs of States and the Protection of their Independence and Sovereignty, G.A. Res. 2131, U.N. GAOR, 20th Sess., Supp. No. 14, U.N. Doc.A/6014 (1965).
96 U.N. Doc.A/6014, Art. 1.
97 U.N. Doc.A/6014, Art. 2.
98 Implementation of the Declaration on the Granting of Independence to Colonial Countries and Peoples, General Assembly Resolution 2465, 23rd Session, 1968, Art. 8.
99 Preceded by The General Assembly "Reaffirming the declarations made in General Assembly resolutions 2548 (XXIV) of December 1969 and 2708 (XXV) of December 1970 that the practice of using mercenaries against national liberation movements in the colonial Territories constitutes a criminal act."

100 Basic principles of the legal status of the combatants struggling against colonial and alien domination and racist régimes, General Assembly Resolution 3103, 1970, Art. 5; Taulbee (1985, p. 346).
101 Declaration on Principles of International Law concerning Friendly Relations and Cooperation among States in accordance with the Charter of the United Nations, G.A. Res. 2625, U.N. GAOR 25th Sess., Supp. No. 18, U.N. Doc. A/8018 (1970), Art. 1.
102 Towle (1981, p. 25).
103 Colonel Draper (1979, p. 7).
104 Glahn and Taulbee (2013, p. 418).
105 Gray (2000, p. 46).
106 OAU Convention for the Elimination of Mercenaries in Africa, O.A.U. Doc. CM/433/Rev. L. Annex 1, 1972, Article 1.
107 Taulbee (1985, p. 347).
108 Kinsey (2008, p. 4).
109 OAU Convention, Article 3.
110 OAU Convention, Preamble.
111 OAU Convention, Article 3 (a).
112 OAU Convention, Article 2.
113 OAU Convention, Article 5.
114 Appendix II to the OAU Convention, Draft Convention on the Prevention and Suppression of Mercenarism, Article 1, Draft produced by the International Commission of Inquiry on Mercenaries, in Luanda, Angola, June 1976.
115 Appendix II to the OAU Convention, Article 1 (a).
116 Appendix II to the OAU Convention, Article 5.
117 Taulbee (1985, p. 347).
118 Cesner and Brant (1977, p. 339).
119 Report of the Committee of Privy Counsellors appointed to inquire into the recruitment of mercenaries, Cmnd. 6569, London, August 1976.
120 Report of the Committee of Privy Counsellors appointed to inquire into the recruitment of mercenaries, Cmnd. 6569, p. 2.
121 Report of the Committee of Privy Counsellors appointed to inquire into the recruitment of mercenaries, Cmnd. 6569.
122 Report of the Committee of Privy Counsellors appointed to inquire into the recruitment of mercenaries, Cmnd. 6569, p. 12.
123 The Diplock Report, p. 3.
124 The Diplock Report, p. 11.
125 The Diplock Report, p. 10.
126 The Diplock Report, p. 3.
127 The Protocol Additional to the Geneva Conventions of 12 August 1949, and relating to the Protection of Victims of International Armed Conflicts, 8 June 1977. Also referred to as AP I, or Protocol I in the text.
128 The Protocol Additional to the Geneva Conventions of 12 August 1949, relating to the Protection of Victims of International Armed Conflicts, Protocol I, Article 47, June 1977; see also Chapter 1, p. 25
129 Taulbee (1985, p. 351).
130 Appendix III to OAU Convention, International Convention against the Activities of Mercenaries in 1980, U.N. Doe. A/35/366/Add.1 at 10–16, 1980.
131 1977 Additional Protocol I to the 1949 Geneva Conventions.
132 1977 Additional Protocol I to the 1949 Geneva Conventions, Article 1.
133 Adopted in 1989 by UN Resolution 44/34. International Convention against the Recruitment, Use, Financing and Training of Mercenaries, 4 December 1989; A/RES/44/34.

134 As of December 2016.
135 Mercenary Convention, Article 1, para. 1.
136 Mercenary Convention, Article 1, para. 2.
137 Westad (2007, p. 144).
138 Westad (2007, p. 145).
139 McCormick (1995, p. 122); See: http://listverse.com/2007/07/10/top-10-secret-armies-of-the-cia/; Westad (2007, p. 147).
140 McCormick (1995, p. 211).
141 McCormick (1995, pp. 211, 220).
142 LeoGrande (1998, pp. 285–552).
143 *Nicaragua*, pp. 41–50.
144 Gray (2000, p. 56).
145 Gray (2000, p. 75).
146 Jamnejad and Wood (2009, p. 361).
147 *Nicaragua*, para. 195.
148 Westad (2007, p. 143).
149 Otherwise known as the Case concerning military and paramilitary activities in and against Nicaragua; International Court of Justice, Pleadings, oral arguments, documents, Vol. IV, available at www.icj-cij.org/docket/files/70/9619.pdf. On the *Nicaragua case* see: Czapliński (1989, pp. 151–166); Norton Moore (1987, pp. 151–159); Highet (1987, pp. 1–56); Hargrove (1987, pp. 135–143).
150 *Nicaragua*, Application Instituting Proceedings, para. 1.
151 *Nicaragua*, Pleadings, Oral Arguments, Documents, para. 169.
152 Gray (2000, p. 56).
153 Definition of *prima facie* see: http://dictionary.law.com/default.aspx?selected=1598#ixzz405HOhe9A.
154 *Nicaragua*, para. 195.
155 Gray (2014, p. 626).
156 *Nicaragua*, para. 246; Nolte (2010).
157 Turns (2014, p. 827).
158 Shaw (2008, p. 1194).
159 Shaw (2008, p. 1196).
160 ICJ Judgement summary, 27 June 1986, XII (paras. 283–285), p. 168.
161 Taulbee (1985, p. 356).
162 Taulbee (1985, p. 357).
163 ICJ Judgement, para. 114.
164 ICJ Judgement, para. 114.
165 *Nicaragua*, pp. 136–159.
166 ICJ Judgement, para. 113.
167 Pleadings, Oral Arguments, Documents, para. 257.
168 Pleadings, Oral Arguments, Documents, paras 270–271.
169 Pleadings, Oral Arguments, Documents, para. 265.
170 Definition of Aggression, United Nations General Assembly Resolution 3314 (XXIX); A/RES/29/3314: "The sending by or on behalf of a State of armed bands, groups, irregulars or mercenaries, which carry out acts of armed force against another State of such gravity as to amount to the acts listed above, or its substantial involvement therein."
171 ICJ Judgement Summary, Section V, paras 75–125.
172 ICJ Judgement Summary.
173 Jamnejad and Wood (2009, p. 361).
174 2625 (XXV). Declaration on Principles of International Law concerning Friendly Relations and Co-operation among States in accordance with the Charter of the United Nations; A/RES/25/2625.

175 A/RES/29/3314, Art. 3 (g).
176 Declaration on the Inadmissibility of Intervention and Interference in the Internal Affairs of States, 9 December 1981; A/RES/36/103, II (g).
177 Gray (2000, p. 55).
178 A/RES/25/2625, 24 October 1970.
179 *Nicaragua*, para. 205.
180 Krahmann (2010, pp. 66–69).
181 Golding and Harris (1997, p. 51).
182 Douzinas (2007, p. 289).
183 See: Koskenniemi (2005, pp. 61–92, at p. 63).
184 When the 1965 Declaration on the Inadmissibility of Intervention was described by the US as a mere a statement of political intent, the ICJ did not contest that.
185 *Nicaragua*, para. 246.

References

1975 Helsinki Final Act, Art. 1 (a), Principle VI Non-intervention in internal affairs.

2625 (XXV). Declaration on Principles of International Law concerning Friendly Relations and Co-operation among States in accordance with the Charter of the United Nations.

A/RES/25/2625.

A/RES/29/3314.

A/RES/44/34.

Anghie, A.: "Finding the Peripheries: Sovereignty and Colonialism in Nineteenth-Century International Law", 1999, Vol. 40 (1), *Harvard International Law Journal*, pp. 1–80.

Appendix II to the OAU Convention, Draft Convention on the Prevention and Suppression of Mercenarism, Article 1, Draft produced by the International Commission of Inquiry on Mercenaries, in Luanda, Angola, June 1976.

Appendix III to OAU Convention, International Convention against the Activities of Mercenaries in 1980, U.N. Doe. A/35/366/Add.1 at 10–16, 1980.

Arangio-Ruiz, G.: "The Normative Role of the General Assembly of the United Nations and the Declaration of Principles of Friendly Relations", 1972, Vol. 137, *Collected Courses*, pp. 419–742.

Audoin-Rouzeau, S. and Becker, A.: *14–18: Understanding the Great War*, Hill & Wang, New York, 2000.

Avant, D.: *The Market for Force: The Consequences of Privatising Security*, CUP, Cambridge, 2005

Axelrod, A.: *Mercenaries: A Guide to Private Armies and Private Military Companies*, SAGE Publications, London, 2014.

Basic Principles of the Legal Status of the Combatants Struggling against Colonial and Alien Domination and Racist Régimes, General Assembly Resolution 3103, 1970, Art. 5.

Birch, G.: "Gurkha Tales: From Peace and War, 1945–2011", 2013, Vol. 44 (3), *Asian Affairs*, pp. 490–492.

Blum, W.: *Killing Hope: US Military and CIA Interventions since World War II*, Zed Books, London, 2003.

Borchard, E. and Lage, W. P.: *Neutrality for the United States*, Yale University Press, New Haven, 1940.

Case Concerning Military and Paramilitary Activities in and against Nicaragua; International Court of Justice, Pleadings, oral arguments, documents, Vol. IV, available at: http://www.icj-cij.org/docket/files/70/9619.pdf.

Cesner, R. E. and Brant, J. W.: "Law of the Mercenary: An International Dilemma", 1977, Vol. 6 (3), *Capital University Law Review*, pp. 339–370.

Clarke, S. J. G.: *The Congo Mercenary: A History and Analysis*, The South African Institute of International Affairs, Johannesburg, 1968.

Colonel Draper, G. I. A. D.: "The New Law of Armed Conflict", 1979, Vol. 124 (3), *Journal of the Royal United Services Institute*, pp. 3–11.

Conboy, K. J. and Morrison, J.: *Feet to the Fire: CIA Covert Operations in Indonesia, 1957–1958*, Naval Institute Press, Annapolis, 1999.

Convention (V) Respecting the Rights and Duties of Neutral Powers and Persons in Case of War on Land. The Hague, 18 October 1907; Chapter I: The Rights and Duties of Neutral Powers, Art. 4.

Convention (V) Respecting the Rights and Duties of Neutral Powers and Persons in Case of War on Land. The Hague, 18 October 1907, ICRC, available at: www.icrc.org/ihl/INTRO/200?OpenDocument.

Convention Respecting the Rights and Duties of Neutral Powers and Persons in Case of War on Land (Hague Convention No. V), 18 October 1907, 1 Bevans 654–658, Art. 4.

Cross, J. P. and Gurung, B.: (eds): *Gurkhas at War: Eyewitness Accounts from World War II to Iraq*, Greenbill Books, London, 2007.

Czapliński, W.: "Sources of International Law in the Nicaragua Case", 1989, Vol. 38 (1), *The International and Comparative Law Quarterly*, pp. 151–166.

Declaration on Principles of International Law concerning Friendly Relations and Cooperation among States in Accordance with the Charter of the United Nations, G.A. Res. 2625, U.N. GAOR 25th Sess., Supp. No. 18, U.N. Doc. A/8018 (1970).

Declaration on the Granting of Independence to Colonial Countries and Peoples, Adopted by General Assembly resolution 1514 (XV) of 14 December 1960.

Declaration on the Inadmissibility of Intervention and Interference in the Internal Affairs of States, 9 December 1981.

Declaration on the Inadmissibility of Intervention in the Domestic Affairs of States and the Protection of their Independence and Sovereignty, G.A. Res. 2131, U.N. GAOR, 20th Sess., Supp. No. 14, U.N. Doc.A/6014 (1965).

"Declaration on the Inadmissibility of Intervention in the Domestic Affairs of States and the Protection of their Independence and Sovereignty", 1966, Vol. 60 (3), *The American Journal of International Law*, pp. 662–664.Definition of Aggression, United Nations General Assembly Resolution 3314 (XXIX).

Deutsch, K. W.: "External Involvement in Internal War" in Eckstein, H. (ed.): *Internal War, Problems and Approaches*, New York, Free Press of Glencoe, 1964.

Douzinas, C.: *Human Rights and Empire: The Political Philosophy of Cosmopolitanism*, Routledge-Cavendish, New York, 2007.

Draft Articles on Responsibility of States for Internationally Wrongful Acts, with commentaries, 2001, Part 1: Internationally Wrongful Act of a State.

Duncanson, I.: "Law as Conversation" in *International Law and Its Others* (ed. Orford, A.), CUP, Cambridge, 2006.

Foreign and Commonwealth Office: *HC 577 Private Military Companies: Options for Regulation 2001–02*, The Stationery Office, London, 2002.

Funston, J.: *ASEAN and the Principle of Non-Intervention: Practice and Prospects*, Institute of Southeast Asian Studies, Singapore, 2000.

Glahn, G. V. and Taulbee, J. L.: *Law among Nations: An Introduction to Public International Law*, Routledge, London, 2013.

Golding, P. and Harris, P. (eds): *Beyond Cultural Imperialism: The Many Cultural Faces of Imperialism by Annabelle Sreberny-Mohammadi*, SAGE Publications, London, 1997.
Gray, C.: *International Law and the Use of Force*, OUP, Oxford, 2000.
Gray, C.: "The Use of Force and the International Legal Order" in Evans, M. D. (ed.): *International Law*, 4th edition, OUP, Oxford, 2014.
Hargrove, J. L.: "The Nicaragua Judgment and the Future of the Law of Force and Self-Defense", 1987, Vol. 81 (1), *The American Journal of International Law*, pp. 135–143.
Held, D. et al. (eds): *Global Transformations: Politics, Economics and Culture*, Polity, Cambridge, 1999.
Hempstone, G.: *Rebels, Mercenaries and Dividends: The Katanga Story*, Praeger, New York, 1962.
Highet, K.: "Evidence, the Court, and the Nicaragua Case", 1987, Vol. 81 (1), *The American Journal of International Law*, pp. 1–56.
Holsti, K. J.: *International Politics: A Framework for Analysis*, Prentice-Hall International Editions, Englewood Cliffs, 1988.
http://archive.larouchepac.com/node/29841.
http://dictionary.law.com/default.aspx?selected=1598#ixzz405HOhe9A.
http://listverse.com/2007/07/10/top-10-secret-armies-of-the-cia/.
http://www.ayo-gorkhali.org/en/timeline/soldiers-of-empire/1939-45-world-war-ii.
http://www.history.com/news/history-lists/6-legendary-mercenary-armies-from-history.
http://www.opssavannah.net.
ICJ Judgement summary, 27 June 1986.
Implementation of the Declaration on the Granting of Independence to Colonial Countries and Peoples, General Assembly Resolution 2465, 23rd Session, 1968, available at: http://daccess-dds-ny.un.org/doc/RESOLUTION/GEN/NR0/244/25/IMG/NR024425.pdf?OpenElement.
International Convention against the Recruitment, Use, Financing and Training of Mercenaries, 4 December 1989.
International Court of Justice, Pleadings, Oral Arguments, Documents, Vol. IV, available at http://www.icj-cij.org/docket/files/70/9619.pdf.
International Law Commission: Responsibility of States for Internationally Wrongful Acts 2001, Art. 20.
Interview with Ambassador Godley to State, 30 October 1965, DDRS.
Jamnejad, M. and Wood, M.: "The Principle of Non-Intervention", 2009, Vol. 22 (2), *Leiden Journal of International Law*, pp. 345–381.
Keller, H: "Friendly Relations Declaration" in Wolfrum, R. (ed.): *Max Planck Encyclopaedia of Public International Law*, Oxford Public International Law, Oxford, 2009 (online ed.), available at: opil.ouplaw.com/view/10.1093/law:epil/9780199231690/law-9780199231690-e938#law-9780199231690-e938-div1-2.
Kinsey, C.: "International Law and the Control of Mercenaries and Private Military Companies", *Cultures & Conflits* [online], English documents, available online from 26 June 2008, p. 3, 4, available at: http://conflits.revues.org/11502.
Koskenniemi, M.: "International Legislation Today: Limits and Possibilities", 2005, Vol. 23 (1), *Wisconsin International Law Journal*, pp. 61–92.
Krahmann, E.: *States, Citizens and the Privatization of Security*, CUP, Cambridge, 2010.
LeoGrande, W. M.: *Our Own Backyard: The United States in Central America, 1977–1992*, The University of North Carolina Press, London, 1998, pp. 285–552.

Levin, D.: "The Non-Interference Principle Today", 1966, Vol. 12 (11), *International Affairs*, pp. 21–25.

Mann, M.: *The Sources of Social Power, Vol. III Global Empires and Revolutions, 1890–1945*, CUP, Cambridge, 2012.

Marcum, J. A.: "Lessons of Angola", 1976, Vol. 54 (3), *Foreign Affairs*, p. 417.

McCormick, D.: *The Downsized Warrior*, New York University Press, New York, 1998.

McCormick, T. J.: *America's Half Century: United States Foreign Policy in the Cold War and After*, 2nd edition, The Johns Hopkins University Press, Baltimore, 1995.

McFate, S.: *The Modern Mercenary: Private Armies and What They Mean for the World Order*, OUP, Oxford, 2014, p. 20.

Mercenary Convention, Article 1, para. 1.

Mockler, A.: *The Mercenaries: The Men Who Fought for Profit – from the Free Companies of Feudal France to the White Adventurers in the Congo*, Macmillan, London, 1969, pp. 155–171.

Montevideo Convention on the Rights and Duties of States, Uruguay, December 26, 1933, Art. 1, available at: http://www.cfr.org/sovereignty/montevideo-convention-rights-duties-states/p15897.

Mumford, A.: "Proxy Warfare and the Future of Conflict", 2013, Vol. 158 (2), *The RUSI Journal*, pp. 40–46.

Nairn, A.: "Behind the Death Squads: An Exclusive Report on the US role in El Salvador's Official Terror", 1984, *The Progressive*, available at: http://www.historyisaweapon.com/defcon1/nairnelsalvadorbtds.html.

Nicaragua, Pleadings, Oral Arguments, Documents, Section III. Express Admissions of Responsibility on the Part of the Government of the United States.

Nolte, G.: "Intervention by Invitation", *Max Planck Encyclopedia of Public International Law*, 2010, Oxford Public International Law, available at: http://opil.ouplaw.com/view/10.1093/law:epil/9780199231690/law-9780199231690-e1702?prd=EPIL.

Norton Moore, J.: "The Nicaragua Case and the Deterioration of World Order", 1987, Vol. 81 (1), *The American Journal of International Law*, pp. 151–159.

OAU Convention for the Elimination of Mercenaries in Africa, O.A.U. Doc. CM/433/Rev. L. Annex 1, 1972.

Paul, C.: "Humanitarian Interventions and the Limits of Sovereignty", 1996, Vol. 10 (2), *Public Affairs Quarterly*, pp. 103–119.

Prados, J.: "Notes on the CIA's Secret War in Afghanistan", 2002, Vol. 89 (2), *The Journal of American History*, pp. 466–471.

Report of the Committee of Privy Counsellors Appointed to Inquire into the Recruitment of Mercenaries, Cmnd. 6569, London, August 1976.

Rosenstock, R.: "The Declaration of Principles of International Law Concerning Friendly Relations: A Survey", 1971, Vol. 65 (5), *American Journal of International Law*, pp. 713–735.

Sahovic, M. (ed.): *Principles of International Law Concerning Friendly Relations and Cooperation*, Oceana Publications, New York, 1972.

Scott, P. D.: "The United States and the Overthrow of Sukarno, 1965–1967", 1985, Vol. 58 (2), *Pacific Affairs*, pp. 239–264.

Shaw, M. N.: *International Law*, 6th edition, CUP, Cambridge, 2008.

Sparrow, J. C.: *History of Personnel Demobilization in the United States Army*, The Free Press, New York, 1984.

Special Committee on the Situation with Regard to the Implementation of the Declaration on the Granting of Independence to Colonial Countries and Peoples, 640th Meeting, 30 September 1968, *AjAC.109jSR.640.*

Stockwell, J.: *In Search of Enemies: A CIA Story*, Andre´ Deutsch, London, 1978, pp. 40–57.

Taulbee, J. L.: "Myths, Mercenaries and Contemporary International Law", 1985, Vol. 15, *California Western International Law Journal*, pp. 339–363.

The Law of Armed Conflict. Neutrality, ICRC, available at: https://www.icrc.org/eng/assets/files/other/law8_final.pdf.

The Protocol Additional to the Geneva Conventions of 12 August 1949, Relating to the Protection of Victims of International Armed Conflicts, Protocol I, Article 47, 8 June 1977.

Tilly, C.: "War and State Power", 1991, Vol. 171, *Middle East Report*, pp. 38–40.

Toland, J.: *The Flying Tigers*, Laurel Leaf Books, Random House LLC, New York, 1963.

Towle, P.: "The Strategy of War by Proxy" 1981, Vol. 126 (1), *The RUSI Journal*, pp. 21–26.

Turns, D.: "The Law of Armed Conflict" in Evans, M. D. (ed.): *International Law*, 4th edition, OUP, Oxford, 2014

UNGA 92; A/RES/31/91.

Weiner, T.: "C.I.A. Formed Haitian Unit Later Tied to Narcotics Trade", November 14, 1993, *The New York Times*, available at http://www.nytimes.com/1993/11/14/world/cia-formed-haitian-unit-later-tied-to-narcotics-trade.html?pagewanted=all.

Westad, O. A.: *The Global Cold War: Third World Interventions and the Making of Our Times*, CUP, Cambridge, 2007.

Wise, D. and Ross, T. B.: *The Invisible Government*, Random House, New York, 1964.

Zubok, V. M.: *A Failed Empire: The Soviet Union in the Cold War from Stalin to Gorbachev*, The University of North Carolina Press, Chapel Hill, 2009.

4 New wars, neoliberalism, and the rise of PMCs

Throughout the first half of the twentieth century, the world was preoccupied with global wars fought by centralised states and their national standing armies. The prevalent mode of governance that characterised states during this time was a sovereign nation-state with its typology of a centralised 'warfare' government. Fulfilling the belligerent needs of the twentieth century, the strong state provided robust military infrastructure, manpower, as well as the necessary democratic controls through the choice of products, investment, and intervention in the internal management of private arms companies.[1] The end of the Cold War brought significant demilitarisation, creating a pool of unemployed experienced military personnel, providing sufficient supply of security resources. It also marked a significant increase and spread of private military companies (PMCs) who until that point were never used overtly as part of official state policy.

Both strong and weak states were promoting privatisation and the outsourcing of security; the former did so as a result of neoliberal policies, while the latter had little choice in the absence of strong existing military structures. Whether emerging from the collapse of Yugoslavia, or engrossed in the ongoing internal wars on the African continent, politically weaker states were on the receiving end of Western neoliberal ideas. With growing internal unrest, corruption, and fragmented governance, their fragile internal conditions were exacerbated by their economic dependency on the International Monetary Fund (IMF) and the World Bank for humanitarian and economic support,[2] whose structural adjustment programs were portraying a form of economic imperialism.[3] The Washington Consensus played a similar role providing loans to indebted countries in exchange for a restructuring of their domestic economies towards neoliberal standards of privatisation, high interest rates, and reduced government spending.[4] Ethnic wars in Bosnia and Sierra Leone highlight the trend for privatisation of violence both internally and internationally.

The end of the twentieth century was characterised by, what appears to be, a sharp normative change from exclusive use of state-owned and organised military resources to a widespread commodification of security through privatisation and outsourcing. The resurgence of private security in the form of PMCs and their continuing proliferation until the present day coincided with the formulation of neoliberal principles and the subsequent policy changes in the security sector.

Neoliberalism provided the context to the mode of governance that prevailed in parts of the Western hemisphere from the 1980s. Its principles were indirectly imposed on the Global South through economic aid and various peacebuilding efforts. Most importantly, neoliberal reforms carried normative value, contributing to the changing perception of private security from categorically unacceptable at the start of the twentieth century to a plausible and even preferred solution from the 1980s onwards.

New wars and the rise of PMCs

Unlike the ambiguous use of mercenaries in covert operations during the Cold War, private civilian contractors were much more openly integrated into military structures and government policy at the turn of the twenty-first century. The presence of contractors versus military personnel grew from one to fifty in 1991, to a staggering ratio of one to ten in 2003.[5] The rise of PMCs at the end of the Cold War can be explained in different ways. Availability of resources as a result of military downsizing created a considerable supply of manpower, while the demand was driven by long-simmering conflicts, previously sustained by the logic of the Cold War and the balance of two superpowers.[6]

Lineages of private force can also be traced in the changing form of governance that derived from neoliberal ideals. Neoliberalism offered to address the presumed short-term security demands which arose from multiple military interventions in the former Yugoslavia, Somalia, Afghanistan, and Iraq with the temporary hire of private military contractors rather than an increase in professional soldiers, allowing countries like the UK to "punch above their weight".[7] In a methodological way, neoliberalism completed the full circle of types of governance, returning to a small government that resorts to nodal security. Although in the West, privatisation of military services was conducted through neoliberal policies, in the rest of the world, privatisation of violence was understood in the context of the failed state. While neoliberalism generated a new form of governmental rationality and state legitimacy,[8] the 'new wars' that emerged after 1989 created new opportunities with the changing conflict paradigm creating a demand for a different kind of security. Mary Kaldor explains the rise of the new wars in relation to external pressures of cutting government spending, and loss of revenue and legitimacy, leading to disorder and military fragmentation.[9] Incapable of raising and maintaining their own military infrastructure and fighting the new kind of wars, failing governments all over the world became keen clients of private military firms, while utilising the surplus of arms and manpower that was generated by the Cold War.[10]

A deliberate attempt to establish ethnically homogenous territories in the newly formed countries of the former Yugoslavia laid the foundations for ethnic cleansing in Bosnia-Herzegovina between 1992 and 1995.[11] The Bosnian conflict involved different types of military power.[12] As in most new wars, the types of fighting units in Bosnia included paramilitaries, parts of the national army that were no longer controlled by the state, foreign mercenaries, organised criminal groups, and, later, external peacekeeping forces.[13] Foreign mercenary groups varied from British servicemen siding with the Croats[14] to Mujahedeen soldiers supporting Bosnian forces.[15] Other mercenaries from Russia, Italy, Denmark, Sweden, Finland, and the US were also involved in the Bosnian conflict.[16]

Due to the multitude of fighting units and in the absence of a single source of authority or military command, this kind of war was run by horizontal coalitions that cooperated with one another on the basis of common projects and negotiated partnerships.[17] The new wars could, therefore, be distinguished by the complete breakdown of the state monopoly of force. Besides the internal fragmentation of security which furthered the privatisation of violence, international involvement in the Bosnian conflict also brought private military contractors to the scene under the banner of peacebuilding operations. The severity of violence in Bosnia triggered the dispatch of UN peacekeeping forces (UNPROFOR). To provide the necessary manpower, the UN Department of Peacekeeping Operations contracted several PMCs, such as DynCorp and Defense Systems Limited to carry out tasks such as crime prevention and detection, close protection, and border security duties.[18] Operation Joint Endeavour (OJE) in Bosnia, Hungary, and Croatia was the result of the Dayton Peace Accord. OJE was conveyed as part of the Logistics Civil Augmentation Program (LOGCAP)[19] initiative following two previous operations in Somalia and Haiti. The explanation for the deployment of private forces as opposed to the US military partially lied in the political past of the Cold War: until the Accord, there was no host nation support agreement between the US and the above countries due to their former association with the Soviet bloc, making LOGCAP a practical alternative for supplying combat and service support.[20] Brown & Root, now KBR, was the private engineering and procurement company that provided logistics and a wide array of other services under the LOGCAP initiative in Bosnia.[21] The LOGCAP II contract was then awarded to DynCorp International to perform peacebuilding activities in Bosnia between 1997 and 2002.[22] Unlike the other three LOGCAP initiatives, little can be found on the content of this particular programme in official US government sources. On the contrary, there has been a lot of controversy in the press surrounding the scandalous behaviour of DynCorp contractors involved in prostitution and human trafficking in Bosnia.[23]

The link to the US Army official programme was rarely explicit, and public blame and responsibility was placed mainly on the UN, which was arguably a more abstract and fluid target than the US government. Although since 1998 eight DynCorp contractors were sent back from Bosnia, they have not been charged or prosecuted.[24] Moreover, DynCorp was later selected for the LOGCAP IV contract in 2007 for a term of up to ten years, which was subsequently extended twice, in 2015 and 2016.[25] The contractor continues to support the US Army with the August 2018 contract modifications, valued at $16 million awarded to DynCorp to "continue support to logistics and materials management services and to expand support into trucking services for the U.S. Army Corp of Engineers (USACE) South Atlantic Division, Task Force Power Restoration at Aguadilla and Ponce, Puerto Rico".[26]

In Bosnian conflict, however, international involvement did not stop there. In 1993, as a legal response to severe outbreaks of aggression, the Security Council established the International Criminal Tribunal for the Former Yugoslavia (ICTY) under the authority of Chapter VII of the UN Charter.[27] While the UN and North Atlantic Treaty Organization (NATO)[28] had been operating since the end of the Second World War, they were often perceived as a legitimising vehicle for US foreign policy.[29] The ICTY and the International Criminal Court (ICC), on the other hand, were an evolving exception to this rule, since in some cases these institutions investigate and try citizens of states that have not signed and ratified the Rome Statute.[30] The ICTY addressed the issues of private violence through the mechanism of individual criminal liability. Dusko Tadic was the first accused to appear before the ICTY and was charged with grave breaches of the 1949 Geneva Conventions.[31] Tadic participated in the attack, seizure, murder, and maltreatment of Muslims and Croats both within and outside three prison camps, using military and paramilitary groups.[32] The Bosnian Serb Army acted aggressively in their attempt to establish *Republica Srpska* on Bosnian territory in January 1992.[33]

As in the case of Nicaragua, it was essential to establish the relationship and the extent of control between the Yugoslavian state and the military and paramilitary forces in order to assign responsibility. Despite finding that the armed forces of the *Republika Srpska* "were almost completely dependent on the supplies of the [Army of the FRY] VJ to carry out offensive operations", the Trial Chamber found the evidence insufficient to establish either full or effective control.[34] The case then went through the Appeals Chamber, who affirmed that

> The control required by international law may be deemed to exist when a State (or, in the context of an armed conflict, the Party to the conflict) has a role in organising, coordinating or planning the military actions of the military group, in addition to financing, training and equipping or providing operational support to that group.[35]

In the *Tadic case*, the Appeals Chamber found that there was "continuing payment of salaries, to Bosnian Serb and non-Bosnian Serb officers alike, by the government of the Federal Republic of Yugoslavia (Serbia and Montenegro)"[36] which indicates and proves control.[37] The Appeals Chamber concluded that the armed forces of the *Republika Srpska* acted under the "overall control" of and on behalf of the FRY, classifying the armed conflict in Bosnia and Herzegovina between the Bosnian Serbs and the central authorities of Bosnia and Herzegovina as an international armed conflict.[38] The link between the Federal Republic of Yugoslavia and the conduct of the Bosnian Serb forces and paramilitary groups was established by ICTY and later also by the International Court of Justice (ICJ) in the *Bosnian Genocide case*.[39] However, the ICJ rejected the test for overall control, proposed by the Appeals Chamber, deeming it unsuitable as it stretches too far the necessary connection between the conduct of a state's organs and its international responsibility.[40]

Importantly, the *Tadic case* contributed to the construction of an essential element in the criminal liability for corporations, namely joint criminal enterprise.[41] The principle of this collective liability depends on lowering the culpability threshold as one individual may be deemed liable for another's actions when operating in a group. It also changed the perception of war crimes dating back to Nuremberg, to an idea that crimes against humanity can also occur outside of international conflict.[42] While the ICTY made significant progress in establishing individual criminal responsibility, there are still questions and grey areas surrounding the attribution of authority on a state and corporate level. Similar to the *Nicaragua* case, it left some crucial questions unanswered: was the prosecution of individual war criminals a proportionate legal response to ethnic and political disasters of such scale? Were existing international legal mechanisms capable of effectively allocating blame and invoking responsibility on states and corporate actors such as PMCs? Furthermore, while there was evidence of deploying private military forces, the issue of mercenarism was not raised at the time. And, as mercenarism was not codified as an international crime under the Rome Statute, to this day the ICC does not have any special jurisdiction over private military actors.[43]

Sierra Leone was another example representative of a weak state, engrossed in ongoing internal struggles following the end of the Cold War.[44] Its army, the Republic of Sierra Leone Military Force (RSLMF), was unable to neutralise the rebels and establish security.[45] The lack of adequate training, funding, or a military organisation further exacerbated security issues and in 1995 head of state Valentine Strasser first contracted Gurkha Security Guards and later Executive Outcomes (EO) to supply training and military support.[46] However, the involvement of private military firms only aggravated the instability in the country and in the region, empowering corrupt governments through appropriation of all proceeds from mineral and oil concessions.[47] As part of the funding package to the financially struggling Sierra Leone, the IMF approved payments to EO.[48] Following the neoliberal framework of global governance, the IMF had quite naturally seen private military firms as the most fitting solution to Sierra Leone's security problems.

Between 1994 and 1998, the network of EO's shareholders and associated businesses included around 30–50 military-related and mineral companies, who worked together to facilitate EO's operations in Africa.[49] When in January 1993 EO first entered Angola on a two-month contract, they were not recruited by the Angolan government or any of its factions.[50] Instead, two British special service officers hired EO to capture and defend valuable oil tanks in the towns of Soyo and Kefekwena, controlled by UNITA forces.[51] Subsequent two-and-a-half-year contract with the Angolan government confirmed EO as a significant player in the private security field and enabled its expansion both through capital and conflict opportunity. Their subsequent contract in Sierra Leone was aimed at defeating the Revolutionary United Front (who were later trained by an Israeli company, Spearhead Ltd), which ultimately led to free elections in 1996.[52] EO's outward mercenary profile was condemned by the international community and the South African government with the Regulation of Foreign Military Assistance Act 15 (1998) putting the final nail in EO's coffin. The Act precluded any South African citizen from participating in an armed conflict, nationally or internationally; it also specifically prohibited recruitment, use, training, financing, or engaging in mercenary activity, thereby criminalising mercenarism both in South Africa and outside of its borders.[53]

When in 1997 Sandline International was involved in suppressing an armed independence movement in Papua New Guinea, it subcontracted EO to facilitate armed forces and logistics needed for the military contract.[54] Although EO has been formally dissolved and Sandline have taken over their operations in Sierra Leone, currently there are few legal mechanisms to track and prevent the subcontracting relationship between the two entities, creating an impunity construct, known as the corporate veil.[55] Most jurisdictions recognise the company law doctrine of "separate corporate personality", whereby a parent company and its subsidiaries are considered to be separate legal entities, despite the link of shareholding.[56] The doctrine was reinforced in *Prest v. Petrodel*[57] as the UK Supreme Court asserted that the "courts may only 'pierce the corporate veil' in exceptionally limited circumstances".[58] Such a construct of legal separation and limited liability allows for impunity on the part of PMCs and cannot be addressed by only invoking individual criminal responsibility of PMC employees and directors.

As the main PMC clients, states welcomed the integration of private violence into their government policy, and were not prepared to outlaw it. Normalisation of private security came from every direction. Leading powers were promoting a neoliberal form of governance; weak and failing states lacked military structures and the capacity to sustain local security; international organisations, like the IMF and the World Bank, imposed impossible loan terms on developing nations while encouraging private military assistance. Finally, PMCs rose to the challenge as they acquired legal corporate status, thereby distinguishing themselves from illegitimate gangs and 'soldiers of fortune', simultaneously enabling states to avoid traditional rules of engagement and shed some of the responsibility, which would have been inevitable when using uniformed personnel.

This shifting conflict paradigm demonstrates that wars no longer took place in the same context; from the mid-twentieth century they began to be replaced with phenomena such as proxy wars and struggles of national liberation across the Third World, leading to internal conflicts, ethnic tension, humanitarian intervention, peacekeeping operations, and post-conflict reconstruction at the turn of the century. PMCs emerged and thrived in the context of these new wars, which often allowed them to bypass traditional laws of armed international conflict.

Neoliberalism

A number of economic and political factors contributed to the shift from the model of centralised government to that of a neoliberal state. Neoliberal ideals were fundamentally opposed to state interventionism, unlike those of John

Maynard Keynes, which rose to prominence in the 1930s in response to the Great Depression.[59] Contrary to welfare capitalism, neoliberalism promised greater cost-efficiency and openness to private interests by reducing the role of government, replacing state planning with the free market mechanism, or, in other words, rolling back the state.[60] According to neoliberal theory, the state favoured strong individual private property rights, contractual obligation, and the institutions of freely functioning markets and free trade.[61] Its critics, however, interpreted neoliberalism as a doctrine in which all forms of social solidarity were to be dissolved in favour of individualism.[62] Privatisation of state owned enterprises, liberalisation of trade, and deregulation of the economy have been identified as the three key features of neoliberalism.[63]

Coupled with competition, these elements ought to "eliminate bureaucratic red tape, increase efficiency and productivity, improve quality, and reduce costs, both directly to the consumer through cheaper commodities and services and indirectly through reduction of the tax burden".[64] Inadvertently, these also contributed to the acceptance and integration of private military forces into the defence policy. For example, the deregulation of all sectors opened up new areas of unrestricted market freedoms for powerful corporate interests.[65] According to Michael Bell's[66] statement in the 1994 NATO Colloquium, privatisation enabled the British government to "pursue its policy of opening up defence procurement as fully as possible to competitive pressures".[67] Such competition in procurement, in its turn, "produced substantial economies to the defence budget".[68]

Some of the principal connections between neoliberalism and the privatisation of security derive from Milton Friedman's views on governmental power as a threat to individual freedom.[69] Friedman argued that in order to prevent the abuse of state power, first of all "the scope of government must be limited"[70] and, second, state power must be dispersed.[71] He suggested that eliminating the state monopoly on power through competition with the market would establish a balance of power. In Friedman's view an "appropriate free market arrangement [for the armed forces] is volunteer military forces; which is to say, hiring men to serve".[72] Following on from that rationale, 'rolling- back' of the warfare state opened up opportunities for the private military contractor to implement neoliberal principles in the armed forces.[73] The market was seen as an alternative to the state monopoly of force that helped to divide coercive capabilities and ensured competition among multiple companies and between public and private agents, therefore preventing centralisation of power which could endanger the rights and freedoms of citizens.[74]

The UK and the US adopted neoliberalism as a new economic orthodoxy regulating public policy at the state level in 1979.[75] Both countries were governed by leaders that truly believed in the neoliberal values of Friedrich Hayek and the Mont Pelerin Society. Ronald Reagan and Margaret Thatcher promoted numerous policies of 'rolling back the state', and their success was carried forward well beyond their time in office, even by opposition parties.[76] The UK Conservative Party leader and Prime Minister, Margaret Thatcher,[77] made neoliberalism her election programme, promising to dismantle the British warfare/welfare state.[78]

Most commonly, Thatcherism was explained as a pushback against the Keynesian consensus prompted by the rise of a set of free market ideas.[79] Fragmentation of security provision among public and private providers helped to portray Thatcher's turn to neoliberalism as the continuation of a Liberal political tradition dating back to the nineteenth century.[80] Large-scale privatisation was at the top of the political agenda, offering a way to manage the state budget and raise capital. While neoliberalism was promoted in order to generate efficiencies, a more visionary goal was to transform political culture by introducing a new mentality of extended corporate and personal responsibility, innovation, and initiative.[81] In this scenario, the new role of the government was that of a customer rather than the sole manager of the security sector.[82] Furthermore, the absence of any constitutional or legal restrictions on the outsourcing of military services in the UK facilitated the privatisation of a wide range of military functions and services.[83]

Since the rise of neoliberalism in the 1980s, Britain has pioneered the privatisation and the outsourcing of significant proportions of its national defence establishment.[84] According to the Ministry of Defence (MOD), privatisation meant the relocation of military services to private suppliers "depending on whichever is better placed to deliver required services at best value".[85] Public-private partnerships and outsourcing contracts legitimised the private sector in the procuring and financing of security, and enabled the integration of civilians into the military realm. Increasing state reliance on outsourcing amplified the private sector's presence in the supply of military services.[86] In addition to the Private Finance Initiative (PFI), the MOD sought to expand its use of private contractors under standard outsourcing agreements.

To do so, the government initiated a comprehensive review of military functions to identify what kind of military support operations could be contracted out to the private sector. In 1991 the Competing for Quality White Paper revised and built on Thatcher's market-testing programme. Its focus was not privatisation per se; it was designed to improve state efficiency by promoting competition between in-house and private bidders for service delivery.[87] The document outlined three types of services: those that were inappropriate for government and should be privatised or eliminated; those that were unsuitable for government delivery and should be outsourced; and services that were appropriate for government and should be decentralised and subjected to market-testing.[88]

Most widely outsourced to the private sector was the management of military facilities, such as navy bases, garrisons, and airfields. Even the management of the Atomic Weapons Establishment at Aldermaston was contracted out.[89] Other areas of private contracting included the MOD's defence estate programme and repairs and maintenance. Since 2004 logistic support has been a growing area for private contracting, with the MOD outsourcing the majority of logistic services to Kellogg, Brown & Root (KBR) under the Contract for Logistics Support arrangement.[90] While all of these areas of privatisation demonstrate the neoliberal trend in defence and security, the outsourcing of military training had particular significance. Large-scale PFI projects catered for private training, such as the Defence Training Review and the Military Flight Training Systems contracts, "which merged private military flight training for the army, navy and the RAF".[91] Military training brought private contractors one step closer to active participation in combat, and therefore to the core function of the military. If one can train how to fight, one can also fight. Sean McFate, an academic and a former DynCorp military contractor, analysed this fine line between military training and participation in combat in the context of peacekeeping operations. While in theory there was a clear distinction between support contractors, used for defence and training, and mercenaries, who staged offensive operations on behalf of a client, in practice "if you can do one, you can do the other".[92]

Although Thatcher pioneered the neoliberal model, the Major and Blair governments developed it further, increasing the private sector contribution to national and international defence.[93] The number of civil servants in the MOD declined by 40 per cent between 1979 and 1990 as civilian positions were the first to be cut or replaced.[94] By 2000, around £10 billion, or 45 per cent of the MOD's annual function, had been reviewed for potential private sector involvement under the *Better Quality Services* (BQS) initiative.[95] Overall, the above statistics reflect the increase of private military presence in the security sector, whereby the government had taken deliberate steps to implement this change. Affiliation of significant military individuals with PMCs was another element that contributed to a gradual normalisation of the private military industry. For example, General Sir Roger Wheeler (former UK Chief of General Staff) and Lord Inge (former field marshal of the British Army) were board members of Aegis Defence Services,[96] and Lieutenant General Sir Cedric Delves (former British Army General and NATO Deputy Commander in Chief) joined the Olive Group in 2005 as a Senior Advisor.[97]

In many ways paralleling Britain's economic endeavours, US President Ronald Reagan introduced the ideological rationale for outsourcing military functions to private firms, thereby promoting the concept of the 'small state'. The premise for outsourcing was originally laid out in 1966 when the US government introduced specific procedures for comparing public and private sector provisions of goods and services in the Office of Management and Budget (OMB) Circular A-76.[98] In order to determine what should and should not be outsourced, the A-76 outlined 'Inherently Governmental Functions' which included management and direction of the Armed Services, and activities performed exclusively by military personnel who are subject to deployment in a combat, combat support, or combat service support role.[99] Notwithstanding this definition, the A-76 process was fully set up to procure private military services. After notifying Congress and comparing bids from the military and the private sector, if a private sector bid was 10 per cent of the personnel cost or $10 million lower than the competing military bid, the private bidder was awarded the contract.[100]

Additionally, following the rise of neoliberalism in the 1980s, the extent of the DOD's acquisition of military services from private firms under the A-76 procedures nearly doubled.[101] The functions that the DOD and the A-76 process defined as commercial rather than governmental, with the exception of large-scale armed combat, ranged from depot maintenance and repair, logistics, training, to intelligence services, armed guarding, and the management of government-owned facilities.[102] Not only had the latter been considered an inherently governmental function until the mid-1990s, these have also been amongst the largest growth areas in terms of outsourcing.[103]

Furthermore, the Competition in Contracting Act 1984 and two subsequent acts in 1986 had a significant impact on military procurement through deregulation, eliminating military specifications, and requiring "the military services to use competition in contracting in increasing amounts each year".[104] The Reagan administration provided the vital political backing for neoliberal ideology through further deregulation, tax and budget cuts, as well as attacks on trade union and professional power.[105] As part of the deregulation initiatives, the Commission on Roles and Missions of the Armed Forces advocated the elimination of restrictive legislation in the United States Code, Title 10 – Armed Forces, which prohibited the contracting-out of key military occupations.[106] In 1985, ten years prior to the Commission's regulation, the LOGCAP was established. It began as a US Army-administered forum for engaging private security and military firms to support US government missions abroad.[107] Initially founded in order to outline the policies and procedures for using civilian contractors during wartime,[108] in 1992 it became a centralised mechanism for PMC procurement. What distinguished LOGCAP from any previous outsourcing endeavours was the "umbrella concept" it used to obtain a wide range of support functions under one contract.[109] The scope of LOGCAP spanned across operations in Somalia, Haiti, Rwanda, Italy, and South-West Asia, and it also provided crucial support and combat forces for peacekeeping missions in Hungary, Croatia, and Bosnia.[110]

While by 2001 it became clear that public-private cost comparisons and outsourcing were not producing the anticipated efficiencies, the programme was not abandoned.[111] In the ten years between 1996 and 2006, total spending on private military services increased by 146 per cent from $46 to $113 billion.[112] So despite Reagan's promise to roll back the state, federal spending increased as a result of growing military expenses.[113] In fact, through military spending Reagan created the largest US deficit at the time, tripling Gross Federal Debt, from $900 billion to $2.7 trillion.[114] By transforming the roles of the military and private businesses with regard to decision-making and the implementation of national defence strategies, Reagan's reforms contributed to strengthening the private military position in government policy.[115] Furthermore, through the tools of privatisation and outsourcing, neoliberalism promoted nodal or fragmented security governance, whereby the state retained only partial control over defence resources, and only in the form of a contract.

Accountability and state control

By designating civilian contractor positions in a military realm, governments legitimised the notion of private military activity. While the government accepts liability when hiring individual civilian contractors who are incorporated in the military structure of the state, the issue of responsibility arises when corporate entities are involved in supplying the contractors to the state.

As part of neoliberal doctrine, states outsourced and privatised numerous governmental functions that until the 1980s were under the direct control of the state. The work of neoliberal thinkers like Hayek and Friedman promoted the concept of a minimal state,[116] something that both Reagan and Thatcher attempted to implement. In this context, state sovereignty was willingly surrendered to the global market in favour of commodity and capital movements.[117] According to Friedrich Hayek, "private monopoly is scarcely ever complete and even more rarely of long duration or able to disregard potential competition. But a state monopoly is always a state-protected monopoly – protected against both potential competition and effective criticism".[118] Hayek and his followers viewed state monopoly as a threat to individual freedom and see the market as the instrument most fit to perform the mediating function.

In neoliberalism, "the sanctity of contracts and the individual right to freedom of action, expression, and choice must be protected". [119] Friedman argued that the state should be the arbiter of contracts and, therefore, of law. However, this gives rise to two possible risks. If the state designs and puts in place legitimising mechanisms for private forces to enter the security market, then the market becomes an instrument for the consolidation of monopoly power. Such deregulation in the security sector could generate impunity if the military function, i.e. the function of killing, is left ungoverned. Also, in reality, the state may lose its hierarchical position in the face of contract law. Unless specifically stipulated, a contract between a PMC and the state creates a horizontal relationship between two equal parties to a contract.[120] As a consequence, such a contract between a state and a PMC could immunise the state against responsibility under IL, as the state would no longer seen to be directing or controlling the private security provider.[121]

As a political framework, neoliberalism also rationalised the legitimacy of the private military contractor. Amongst a number of set criteria, Additional Protocol I defined a mercenary as any person who is motivated "essentially by the desire for private gain",[122] who was promised higher rates of pay than the uniformed soldier, and who was not a national of a party to the conflict nor a local resident. As observed in neoliberal practice, most PMCs recruit contractors based on eligibility and desired expertise, therefore removing political content from the military role performed by the contractor. The privatisation of the security sector and the outsourcing of multiple defence functions and facilities blurred the distinction between the professional soldier and the private military contractor. However, according to the neoliberal vision, this political neutrality on the part of the soldier should be viewed as an advantage in terms of democratic control and accountability.[123] Equally, a profit motivation poses no issues to neoliberalism in ensuring democratic control and contractor accountability. While military services were legally exempt from outsourcing, the growing spectre of defence support functions that could and were contracted out, starting from the 1980s and continuing to this day, did in fact create a plausible environment for PMCs to exist and to prosper.

Governance and governmentality

While the challenges associated with establishing accountability and invoking liability are discussed in more depth in the following chapters, it is important to emphasise the normalisation and legitimisation of private security that derived from the state itself. The rise of neoliberalism,[124] with its trend towards privatisation and outsourcing, contributed to the commodification of security. Central to shaping the security sector in the UK and the US from the 1980s onwards, neoliberal policies also have had a normative effect on reintroducing and integrating PMCs into the domestic and international security landscape.[125] Although the shift towards the private sector is striking when analysing the late twentieth-century security landscape in the UK and the US, it was extensively articulated through government policy and various state programmes. However, we can only truly appreciate the extent of this shift if we contrast it to the national defence structure of the rest of the twentieth century. The above examples of neoliberal states present a very important connection between the prevailing form of governance and the type of military power. A neoliberal state can be envisioned as a small, decentralised government surrounded by a broader configuration of governance and key elements in civil society.[126] Characterised by the shifting ownership of means of violence from state-centric to deferred or privatised, Neoliberalism produced a mixed military arrangement comprised of a professional national army and private contractors. As part of this shift, the state monopoly of force has also been undermined,[127] by opening up this governance model to interventions and alternative authorities, such as international regulatory bodies and PMCs.[128]

Neoliberalism completed the full circle of types of governance, exhibiting some similarities to fractured feudal sovereignty.[129] The model of a neoliberal state demonstrated the return of fragmented sovereignty and decentralisation as the dominant form of governance, indicating a direct correlation between the prevalent form of governance and the type of military force it deploys. Moreover, this correlation demonstrated a deeper explanation to the rise and proliferation of PMCs, entrenched in the form of governance. While the questions of ethics surrounding mercenary and private military actors are important, they tend to ignore a conscious governmental effort to restructure state-military relationships in one way or another. PMCs did not simply arise and operate haphazardly, pushing out professional armies. They were 'welcomed' by the governments who designed their policies in a way that allowed for private military firms to exist.

In the Western hemisphere, the spread of neoliberalism transpired through changes in government policy, but also in the discourse of legality. Building on Michel Foucault's notion of governmentality, Wendy Brown explained the transformation of practices that were formerly unacceptable or irregular to becoming normal and legalised.[130] Brown argued that the norms and principles of neoliberal rationality initiated a commodification of areas that were previously considered public, or "noneconomic".[131] Brown's and Foucault's reading of neoliberalism as a "specific and normative mode of reason" could explain the changed perceptions in the sphere of private military actors. By articulating neoliberal ideals, the US and UK governments promoted privatisation and outsourcing across all sectors, including defence and security, therefore changing the legal perception of its inherently public nature.

The exponential growth of private military activity is thus directly linked to the current globalised form of governance. Whether failing or co-dependent, states no longer uphold the same extent of sovereignty as they did throughout the majority of the twentieth century. Moreover, they are overarched by global legal and political institutions and undercut by multinational corporations, shifting states further from the Westphalian concept of a monolithic entity that comprises all governmental functions behind its sovereign borders. Power is no longer administered by states alone. While it is true that states continue to be the main owners and users of military power, the growing number of operational[132] and advocacy[133] NGOs, and the rise of transnational organisations,[134] multinational corporations,[135] and global political players such as the UN and NATO, changed the political and legal dynamic by adding new actors to the international arena. It is also important to mention terrorist organisations who not only claim authority but also change the political landscape by resorting to asymmetric warfare. They are yet another non-state actor that controls the means of power and violence, typically in parallel to a formal government.[136]

Finally, the growing presence of the private military industry today indicates that the market for force is shifting, marking a decline of the state monopoly of force. All these phenomena conceptualise 'Neomedievalism',[137] a term coined by Hedley Bull, however never realised during his time. Suggesting an alternative to the Westphalian state system, 'Neomedievalism' is characterised by technological unification of the world synonymous with globalisation,[138] the regional integration of states, the rise of transnational organisations, the disintegration of states, and the restoration of private international violence.[139] All of these elements suggest a shift in the mode of governance both within and amongst states and highlight the decline of territorial sovereignty. While some characteristics of premodern governance are visible in contemporary security developments, the medieval world, as Foucault and others have insisted, is epistemically separated from our own and recovering the complexity of meaning and understanding from this period and applying them to our own is an impossible task. So, although 'Neomedievalism' is too broad of a claim, it highlights the overlap of different jurisdictions that characterises the twenty-first-century mode of governance.

Conclusion

By acquiring an international military dimension, PMCs became relevant to IL and international armed conflict. At the same time, these companies pose a significant challenge to IL as they create a situation whereby civilians have access to direct participation in hostilities. Through outsourcing and privatisation, states have handed over a portion of inherently governmental functions to private companies, allowing PMCs and their employees to obtain a certain form of power and governance loosely resembling the strands of power and legitimacy of fifteenth-century Italy. Critical political, strategic, and economic factors of neoliberal policies, coupled with changing character of war exemplified by the 'new wars' laid the premise for the legitimisation of PMCs and aided their comeback to the international arena.

Neoliberal reforms, new wars, and the rise of PMCs marked the transition from state centrism to fragmented governance which remains prevalent in today's forms of power and legitimacy. The rise of neoliberalism was an important factor in integrating private military contractors into UK and US defence and security from the 1980s onwards. Its ideology and economic policy allowed PMCs to find and establish a growing security market that significantly accelerated following the Cold War. In the context of domestic and international security, this phenomenon is accompanied by the rise of international organisations, corporations, and various military groups, all competing for authority and legitimacy alongside sovereign states on the international arena.

The shrinking of the state in favour of the free market economy coincided with the decline of state sovereignty, as international legal organisations and multinational corporations gained increasing gravitas and regulatory powers. Finally, the newly acquired of PMCs pose numerous issues to IL: these companies are no longer mercenaries in legal terms; instead, they are registered and operating openly under a licence. However, the remit of their legitimate activities is still under question, and the liability issues remain unresolved. PMCs transformed the private military landscape of colonial troops and disreputable mercenaries into a legitimised business of civilian security, while post-Cold War demilitarisation provided the numbers to support the industry and its proliferation.

How we arrived at such a widespread and seemingly unregulated use of PMCs at the end of the twentieth century can be explained in the context of neoliberal policies. Extensive privatisation and outsourcing not only made room for private providers in the security sector; more importantly, it changed the perception of normality and the legality of private security. Of course, this statement does not apply universally, otherwise PMCs would not be facing such significant criticism. However, this change of perception was substantial and touched enough states and international institutions to allow the idea of security privatisation to enter the governmental sphere. What was unimaginable fifty years ago at the time of the World Wars has become an obvious and plausible solution.

The neoliberal doctrine, coupled with new wars, PMC corporate identity, and failure to criminalise the act of mercenarism provides the context for contemporary use and regulation of PMCs, and the subsequent challenges this poses. This context challenges the view that considers PMCs a new issue under IL, providing a more comprehensive explanation of their rise, beyond the simple demilitarisation claim. Building on this background, I now turn to the questions of accountability, codification, and the ability of existing domestic and international legislation to effectively regulate the contemporary security sector. This juxtaposition of existing norms against the use of mercenaries and the prevailing economic and governance ideology promoting privatisation and outsourcing is the starting point for my contemporary legal analysis of the use and regulation of PMCs.

Notes

1 Krahmann (2010, pp. 66–69).
2 See: Peet (2009, pp. 66–177).
3 Mann (2013, p. 167).
4 Mann (2013).
5 Avant (2004, pp. 153–157).
6 Isenberg (2007, p. 82).
7 Krahmann (2010, p. 85).
8 Brown (2015, p. 51).
9 Kaldor (2002, p. 92).
10 Kaldor (2002, p. 96).
11 On the Bosnian war and ethnic cleansing, see: Bax (2000, pp. 16–36); Bell-Fialkoff (1993, pp. 110–121); Hayden (1996, pp. 783–801); Toal and Dahlman (2011); Duffield (2014).
12 Held et al. (1999, p. 72).
13 Kaldor (2002, pp. 93–96).
14 Boggan (1993)
15 Dzidic (2016)
16 Kaldor (2002, p. 49).
17 Kaldor (2002, p. 95).
18 Ostensen (2011, p. 16).
19 Also discussed in Part 2 of this chapter below.
20 Colonel Russell (1997, p. 12).
21 See: https://kbr.com/Documents/Project%20Profiles/ProjectProfile_LOGCAPIII.pdf.
22 Franke (2010, p. 11).
23 See: Isenberg (2011); Robson (2002); Diu (2012); SFOR Contractor Involvement, Human Rights Watch.
24 Liu (2015, pp. 82–83); Barnett and Hughes (2001).
25 See: www.dyn-intl.com/news-events/press-release/dyncorp-international-selected-for-logcap-iv/; See: www.dyn-intl.com/media-center/press-releases/dyncorp-international-awarded-11-month-extension-to-continue-supporting-u-s-army-under-logcap-iv/.
26 See: www.dyn-intl.com/media-center/press-releases/dyncorp-international-awarded-logcap-iv-contract-modifications-in-puerto-rico/.
27 Craven (2014, p. 231); Cryer (2014, p. 770).
28 The UN was established in 1945 and NATO in 1949.
29 See Westad (2007); Sewell and Lucas (2011).
30 McFate (2014, p. 78); on ICC jurisdiction over citizens of non-parties see Elsea (2002, pp. 25–26).
31 ICTY Statute, International Tribunal for the Prosecution of Persons Responsible for Serious Violations of International Humanitarian Law Committed in the Territory of the Former Yugoslavia since 1991, Art. 2, p. 5.
32 Van den Hole (2004–2005, pp. 272–273).
33 Craven (2014, pp. 223–224).
34 ICTY, *The Prosecutor v. Dusko Tadić*, IT-94-1, Trial Chamber II, Judgement, 7 May 1997, para. 605.
35 *Tadic*, Case No. IT-94- I-A, Appeals Judgment, at para. 137.

36 "Opinion and Judgment", *The Prosecutor v. Duško Tadic*, Case No.: IT-94-1-T, Trial Chamber II, 7 May 1997, para. 601.
37 Case No.: IT-94-1-T, para. 150.
38 Case No.: IT-94-1-T, para. 162.
39 Crawford and Olleson 2014; for the *Bosnian Genocide* case see: Application of the Convention on the Prevention and Punishment of the Crime of Genocide (*Bosnian and Hercegovina v. Serbia and Montenegro*), Merits, Judgement, ICJ Reports 2007; from Summary of the Judgement of 26 February 2007: "It [the ICJ] first notes that, during the period under consideration, the FRY was in a position of influence, over the Bosnian Serbs who devised and implemented the genocide in Srebrenica, unlike that of any of the other States parties to the Genocide Convention owing to the strength of the political, military and financial links between the FRY on the one hand and the Republika Srpska and the VRS on the other".
40 *Bosnian Genocide*, p. 43, para. 406.
41 Simpson (2002, p. 120).
42 Schabas (2001, p. 12); Case No.: IT-94-1-T, Decision on the Defence Motion for Interlocutory Appeal on Jurisdiction, 2 October 1995.
43 Liu (2015, p. 182).
44 See: Migdal (1988); Reno (1995, pp. 65–68); Venter, 1995.
45 Avant (2005, p. 83).
46 Avant (2005, pp. 85–87); see also: Schocken (2002, pp. 43–461); Harding (1997, pp. 87–97); Howe (1998, pp. 307–331).
47 Muthien and Taylor (2002, p. 195).
48 Shearer (1998, p. 68).
49 Pech (1999, p. 84).
50 See Marcum, 1976.
51 Pech (1999, p. 85).
52 Silverstein (2000, p. 165).
53 The Regulation of Foreign Military Assistance Act 15 of 1998, Art. 2, p. 4.
54 Kaldor (2002, p. 95); Pech (1999, p. 93); see also: Shearer (1998).
55 Ottolenghi (1990, pp. 338–353).
56 Schutter (2006, p. 36).
57 Prest v. Petrodel Resources Ltd & Others (2013) UKSC 34.
58 Davies and Worthington (2016, pp. 2–8).
59 Harvey (2005, pp. 20–21).
60 Prasad (2006, p. 43); Krahmann (2010, pp. 72–73).
61 Harvey (2005, p. 64).
62 Harvey (2005, p. 23).
63 Steger and Roy (2010, p. 14).
64 Harvey (2005, p. 65).
65 Harvey (2005, p. 26).
66 Britain's Deputy Under-Secretary of State for Defence Procurement, Ministry of Defence.
67 Bell (1994).
68 Bell (1994).
69 Friedman (2002, p. 2).
70 Friedman (2002).
71 Friedman (2002, p. 3).
72 Friedman (2002, p. 36).
73 Krahmann (2010, p. 74).
74 Krahmann (2010, pp. 36, 39).
75 Harvey (2005, p. 22).
76 Prasad (2006, p. 98).
77 In Office as the Prime Minister: 4 May 1979 to 28 November 1990.

78 Macdonald (1999, p. 3).
79 Prasad (2006, p. 101); see also: Cockett (1995).
80 Krahmann (2010, p. 84).
81 Harvey (2005, p. 60).
82 Smith (1990, p. 195); Macdonald (1999, p. 6).
83 Spackman (2002, p. 285).
84 Krahmann (2010, p. 84).
85 MOD (2000).
86 More generally on contracts, see: Deakin and Walsh (1996, pp. 33–47).
87 Maude (1991, pp. 25–35).
88 HM Treasury, Competing for Quality: Buying Better Public Services, Cm 1730 (London: HMSO, 1991).
89 White (1993).
90 Krahmann (2010, p. 93).
91 Krahmann (2010, p. 94).
92 Interview with Sean McFate, see: www.theatlantic.com/international/archive/2015/03/return-of-the-mercenary/388616/.
93 Krahmann (2010, p. 86).
94 Dandeker (2000, p. 43).
95 Launched in 1998; Uttley (2005, p. 7).
96 Axelrod (2014, p. 248).
97 See: www.olivegroup.com/search.php.
98 Krahmann (2010, p. 121).
99 Circular A-76, Executive Office of the President, Office of Management and Budget, 4 August 1983, Art. 6 (e).
100 Krahmann (2010, p. 121).
101 Cohen, Defense Reform Initiative Report, p. 28.
102 Krahmann (2010, pp. 131–132); GAO, Defense Budget: Trends in Operation and Maintenance Cost and Support Services Contracting.
103 Krahmann (2010, p. 130).
104 McNaugher (1987, p. 101).
105 Harvey (2005, p. 25).
106 Commission on Roles and Missions of the Armed Forces (1995, p. ES-6).
107 Logistics Civil Augmentation Program (LOGCAP), US army, regulation 700-137, 1985.
108 Ettinger (2011, p. 753).
109 Colonel Russell (1997, p. iii).
110 Colonel Russell (1997, pp. 11–12).
111 Graves (2001, p. 51).
112 Krahmann (2010, p. 129).
113 Mann (2013, p. 150).
114 Richman (1988); Mann (2013, p. 151).
115 Krahmann (2010, pp. 135–137).
116 Hayek (2001, pp. 33–45); for more on the concept of small government, see: Friedman (2002, p. 32).
117 Harvey (2005, p. 66).
118 Hayek (2001, p. 203).
119 Harvey (2005, p. 64).
120 Liu (2015, pp. 209–210).
121 See: International Law Commission Articles on Responsibility of States for Internationally Wrongful Acts.
122 A/RES/44/34, Article 1; 1 (b), available at: www.un.org/documents/ga/res/44/a44r034.htm.
123 Krahmann (2010, p. 48).

124 Literature on neoliberalism: Hayek (2001); Friedman (2002); Chomsky (1999); Wapshott (2012); Prasad (2006); Harvey (2005).
125 Foucault (2008); Brown (2015).
126 Harvey (2005, p. 77).
127 On the concept of governance see: McCarney and Stren (2003); Dixit (2004).
128 Krahmann (2010, p. 40).
129 Pratt (2000, pp. 127–145).
130 Brown (2015, p. 47).
131 Brown (2015, p. 50).
132 e.g.: Medecins sans Frontieres, Oxfam, and the Red Cross.
133 Advocacy NGOs that hired PMCs include, but are not limited to: Save the Children, CARE, CARITAS, GOAL, IRC, and Worldvision.
134 A hundred years ago there were 1,083 NGOs, today there are more than 40,000; see: Richmond (2005, p. 20).
135 Such as ExxonMobil and Walmart.
136 For more on the new actors in the international arena see McFate (2014, pp. 77–89).
137 Neomedievalism is a metaphor loosely based on the world order of the European high Middle Ages, but it does not portend a literal return to the medieval period. It is an alternative to the Westphalian system researched by Philip Cerny, Mark Duffield, Jorg Friedrichs, Stephen Kobrin, and others.
138 This closely resembles the trade and partnership networks of fifteenth-century Italian city-states.
139 McFate (2014, p. 75).

References

A/RES/44/34.

Application of the Convention on the Prevention and Punishment of the Crime of Genocide (*Bosnian and Hercegovina v. Serbia and Montenegro*), Merits, Judgement, ICJ Reports 2007

Avant, D.: "The Privatisation of Security and Change in the Control of Force", 2004, Vol. 5, *International Studies Perspectives*, pp. 153–157.

Avant, D.: *The Market for Force: The Consequences of Privatising Security*, CUP, Cambridge, 2005.

Axelrod, A.: *Mercenaries: A Guide to Private Armies and Private Military Companies*, Sage, London, 2014.

Barnett, A. and Hughes, S.: "British Firm Accused in UN 'Sex Scandal'. International Police in Bosnia Face Prostitution Claims" 29 July 2001, *The Guardian*, available at: www.theguardian.com/world/2001/jul/29/unitednations.

Bax, M.: "Warlords, Priests and the Politics of Ethnic Cleansing: A Case-Study from Rural Bosnia Hercegovina", 2000, Vol. 23 (1), *Ethnic and Racial Studies*, pp. 16–36.

Bell, M.: "Defence Industry Privatisation: The British Case", *NATO*, Colloquium, Brussels, 29–30 June 1994 at: www.nato.int/docu/colloq/1994/eco9419.txt.

Bell-Fialkoff, A.: "A Brief History of Ethnic Cleansing", 1993, Vol. 72 (3), *Foreign Affairs*, pp. 110–121.

Boggan, S.: "Britons Flock to Fight in Bosnia: Thousands of Ex-Soldiers and 'Untrained Idiots and Psychopaths' Said to be Serving as Mercenaries with All Three Sides" 10 February 1993, *The Independent*, available at: www.independent.co.uk/news/britons-flock-to-fight-in-bosnia-thousands-of-ex-soldiers-and-untrained-idiots-and-psychopaths-said-1471991.html.

Brown, W.: *Undoing the Demos: Neoliberalism's Stealth Revolution*, Zone Books, New York, 2015.

Chomsky, N.: *Profit Over People: Neoliberalism and Global Order*, Seven Stories Press, New York, 1999.

Circular A-76, Executive Office of the President, Office of Management and Budget, 4 August 1983, Art. 6 (e).

Cockett, R.: *Thinking the Unthinkable: Think-Tanks and the Economic Counter-Revolution, 1931–1983*, Harper Collins, London, 1995.

Cohen, Defense Reform Initiative Report.

Colonel Russell, D. W.: *Understanding the Application of Army's Logistics Civil Augmentation Program (LOGCAP), U.S. Army War College*, Carlisle Barracks, Pennsylvania, 1997.

Commission on Roles and Missions of the Armed Forces, *Directions for Defense*, 1995, p. ES-6.

Craven, M.: "Statehood, Self-Determination, and Recognition" in Evans, M. D. (ed.): *International Law*, 4th edition, OUP, Oxford, 2014.

Crawford, J. and Olleson, S.: "The Character and Forms of International Responsibility" in Evans, M. D. (ed.): *International Law*, 4th edition, OUP, Oxford, 2014.

Cryer, R.: "International Criminal Law" in Evans, M. D. (ed.): *International Law*, 4th edition, OUP, Oxford, 2014.

Dandeker, C.: "The United Kingdom: The Overstretched Military", in Moskos, C. C., Williams, J. A. and Segal, D. R. (eds): *The Postmodern Military*, OUP, Oxford, 2000.

Davies, P. L. and Worthington, S. (eds): *Gower Principles of Modern Company Law: Tenth Edition*, Sweet and Maxwell, London, 2016.

Deakin, N. and Walsh, K.: "The Enabling State: The Role of Markets and Contracts", 1996, Vol. 74 (1), *Public Administration*, pp. 33–47.

Diu, N. L.: "What the UN Doesn't Want You to Know" 6 February 2012, *The Telegraph*, available at: www.telegraph.co.uk/culture/film/9041974/What-the-UN-Doesnt-Want-You-to-Know.html.

Dixit, A.: *Lawlessness and Economics: Alternative Modes of Governance*, Princeton University Press, Princeton, 2004.

Duffield, M. R.: *Global Governance and the New Wars: The Merging of Development and Security*, Zed Books, New York, 2014.

DynCorp International Awarded 11-Month Extension to Continue Supporting U.S. Army Under LOGCAP IV, available at: https://www.dyn-intl.com/media-center/press-releases/dyncorp-international-awarded-11-month-extension-to-continue-supporting-u-s-army-under-logcap-iv/.

DynCorp International Awarded LOGCAP IV Contract Modifications in Puerto Rico, available at: https://www.dyn-intl.com/media-center/press-releases/dyncorp-international-awarded-logcap-iv-contract-modifications-in-puerto-rico/.

Dzidic, D.: "Report Probes Mujahideen Killings during Bosnian War", 25 January 2016, *Balkan Investigative Reporting Network*, available at: www.balkaninsight.com/en/article/bosnian-serb-victims-still-waiting-for-mujahedin-crimes-justice-01-25-2016.

Elsea, J.: *International Criminal Court: Overview and Selected Legal Issues*, Congressional Research Service, 2002.

Ettinger, A.: "Neoliberalism and the Rise of the Private Military Industry", 2011, Vol. 66 (3), *International Journal*, pp. 743–764.

Foucault, M.: *The Birth of Biopolitics: Lectures at the College de France, 1978–1979*, Palgrave Macmillan, Basingstoke, 2008.

Franke, V.: *Security by Contractor: Outsourcing in Peace and Stability Operations*, Centre for Complex Operations, National Defense University, Washington, 2010.

Friedman, M.: *Capitalism and Freedom*, The University of Chicago Press, London, 2002.

GAO: Defense Budget: Trends in Operation and Maintenance Cost and Support Services Contracting.

Graves, R. H.: "Seeking Defense Efficiency", 2001, Vol. 36 (4), *Defense Acquisitions Review*, pp. 47–60.

Harding, J.: "The Mercenary Business: Executive Outcomes", 1997, Vol. 24 (71), *Review of African Political Economy*, pp. 87–97.

Harvey, D.: *A Brief History of Neoliberalism*, OUP, Oxford, 2005.

Hayden, R. M.: "Imagined Communities and Real Victims: Self-Determination and Ethnic Cleansing in Yugoslavia", 1996, Vol. 23 (4), *American Ethnologist*, pp. 783–801.

Hayek, F. A.: *The Road to Serfdom*, Routledge, Abingdon, 2001.

Held, D. et al. (eds): *Global Transformations: Politics, Economics and Culture*, Polity, Cambridge, 1999.

HM Treasury, Competing for Quality: Buying Better Public Services, Cm 1730 (London: HMSO, 1991).

Howe, H. M.: "Private Security Forces and African Stability: The Case of Executive Outcomes" 1998, Vol. 36 (2), *The Journal of Modern African Studies*, pp. 307–331.

www.dyn-intl.com/news-events/press-release/dyncorp-international-selected-for-logcap-iv/.

www.olivegroup.com/search.php.

https://kbr.com/Documents/Project%20Profiles/ProjectProfile_LOGCAPIII.pdf.

ICTY Statute, International Tribunal for the Prosecution of Persons Responsible for Serious Violations of International Humanitarian Law Committed in the Territory of the Former Yugoslavia since 1991.

ICTY, *The Prosecutor v. Dusko Tadić*, IT-94-1, Trial Chamber II, Judgement, 7 May 1997.

International Law Commission Articles on Responsibility of States for Internationally Wrongful Acts

Interview with Sean McFate, available at www.theatlantic.com/international/archive/2015/03/return-of-the-mercenary/388616/.

Isenberg, D.: "It's Déjà Vu for DynCorp All over Again" 25 May 2011, *Huffpost Business*, available at: www.huffingtonpost.com/david-isenberg/its-dj-vu-for-dyncorp-all_b_792394.html.

Isenberg, D.: "Private Military Companies in Iraq" in Chesterman, S. and Lehnard, C. (eds): *From Mercenaries to Market: The Rise and Regulation of Private Military Companies*, OUP, Oxford, 2007.

John Pratt makes a similar argument about the sightings of premodern penal practices; Pratt, J.: "The Return of the Wheelbarrow Men; or the Arrival of Postmodern Penality", 2000, Vol. 40 (1), *British Journal of Criminology*, pp. 127–145.

Kaldor, M.: *New and Old Wars: Organized Violence in a Global Era*, Polity Press, Cambridge, 2002.

Krahmann, E.: *States, Citizens and the Privatization of Security*, CUP, Cambridge, 2010.

Liu, H.-Y.: *Law's Impunity: Responsibility and the Modern Private Military Company*, Hart Publishing, Oxford, 2015

Logistics Civil Augmentation Program (LOGCAP), US army, regulation 700-137, 1985.

Macdonald, G.: "Reform of UK Defense Procurement and State/Industry Relationships during the 1980s and 1990s", 1999, Vol. 15 (1), *Defense Analysis*, p. 3, 6.

Mann, M.: *The Sources of Social Power, Vol. IV Globalizations, 1945–2011*, CUP, Cambridge, 2013.

Marcum, J. A.: "Lessons of Angola", 1976, Vol. 54 (3), *Foreign Affairs*, pp. 407–426.

Maude, F., the Financial Secretary to the Treasury, Hansard, HC Deb 18 November 1991 Vol. 199 cc 25–35, available at: http://hansard.millbanksystems.com/commons/1991/nov/18/competing-for-quality.

McCarney, P. and Stren, R.: Governance on the Ground: Innovations and Discontinuities in the Cities of the Developing World, Woodrow Wilson Center Press, Princeton, 2003.

McFate, S.: *The Modern Mercenary: Private Armies and what they Mean for the World Order*, OUP, Oxford, 2014.

McNaugher, T. L.: "Weapons Procurement. The Futility of Reform", 1987, Vol. 12 (2), *International Security*, pp. 63–104.

Migdal, J. S.: *Strong Societies and Weak States: State-Society Relations and State Capabilities in the Third World*, Princeton University Press, Chichester, 1988.

MOD, 'Public Private Partnerships: Changing the Way We Do Business', 2000.

Muthien, B. and Taylor, I.: "The Return of the Dogs of War? The Privatization of Security in Africa", in Hall, R. B. and Biersteker, T. J. (eds): *The Emergence of Private Authority in Global Governance*, CUP, Cambridge, 2002.

Ostensen, A. G.: "UN Use of Private Military and Security Companies: Practices and Policies", The Geneva Centre for the Democratic Control of Armed Forces, SSR Paper 3, 2011, available at: www.dcaf.ch/Publications/UN-Use-of-Private-Military-and-Security-Companies-Practices-and-Policies.

Ottolenghi, S.: "From Peeping behind the Corporate Veil, to Ignoring It Completely", 1990, Vol. 53 (3), *Modern Law Review*, pp. 338–353.

Pech, K: *Chapter 5: Executive Outcomes – A corporate conquest*, 1999, p. 84, available at: https://www.issafrica.org/pubs/Books/PeaceProfitPlunder/Chap5.pdf.

Peet, R.: *Unholy Trinity: IMF, World Bank and WTO*, 2nd edition, Zed Books, London, 2009.

Prasad, M.: *The Politics of Free Markets: The Rise of Neoliberal Economic Policies in Britain, France, Germany, & the United States*, University of Chicago Press, London, 2006.

Prest v. Petrodel Resources Ltd & Others (2013) UKSC 34.

Reno, W.: *Warlord Politics in African States*, Lynne Rienner Publishers, 1999.

Richman, S. L.: "The Sad Legacy of Ronald Reagan", 1988, Vol. 6 (10), *The Free Market*, available at: https://mises.org/library/sad-legacy-ronald-reagan-0.

Richmond, P. O.: "The Dilemmas of Subcontracting the Liberal Peace" in Richmond, P. O. and Carey, H. F. (eds): *Subcontracting Peace: The Challenges of NGO Peacebuilding*, Aldershot, Ashgate, 2005.

Robson, T.: "Bosnia: The United Nations, Human Trafficking and Prostitution" 21 August 2002, available at: https://www.wsws.org/en/articles/2002/08/bosn-a21.html.

Schabas, W. A.: *An Introduction to the International Criminal Court*, CUP, Cambridge, 2001.

Schocken, C.: "The Special Court for Sierra Leone: Overview and Recommendations", 2002, Vol. 20 (2), *Berkeley Journal of International Law*, pp. 436–461.

Schutter, O. D.: "Extraterritorial Jurisdiction as a Tool for Improving the Human Rights Accountability of Transnational Corporations", December 2006, p. 36, available at: http://198.170.85.29/Olivier-de-Schutter-report-for-SRSG-re-extraterritorial-juris diction-Dec-2006.pdf.

Sewell, B. and Lucas, S. (eds): *Challenging US Foreign Policy: America and the World in the Long Twentieth Century*, Palgrave Macmillan, London, 2011.

SFOR Contractor Involvement, Human Rights Watch, available at: https://www.hrw.org/reports/2002/bosnia/Bosnia1102-11.htm.

Shearer, D.: *Private Armies and Military Intervention*, Adelphi Paper No. 316, OUP, Oxford, 1998.

Silverstein, K.: *Private Warriors*, Verso, London, 2000.

Simpson, S.: *Corporate Crime, Law, and Social Control*, CUP, Cambridge, 2002.

Smith, R.: "Defence Procurement and the Industrial Structure in the U.K.", 1990, Vol. 8 (2), *International Journal of Industrial Organization*, pp. 185–205.

Spackman, M.: "Public-Private Partnerships: Lessons from the British Approach", 2002, Vol. 26 (3), *Economic Systems*, p. 285.

Steger, M. B. and Roy, R. K.: *Neoliberalism: A Very Short Introduction*, OUP, Oxford, 2010.

The Prosecutor v. Duško Tadic, Case No.: IT-94-1-T, Trial Chamber II, 7 May 1997.

The Regulation of Foreign Military Assistance Act 15 of 1998.

Toal, G. and Dahlman, K.: *Bosnia Remade: Ethnic Cleansing and Its Reversal*, OUP, Oxford, 2011.

Uttley, M.: *Civilian Contractors on Deployed Military Operations: United Kingdom Policy and Doctrine*, Strategic Studies Institute, September 2005.

Van den Hole, L.: "Towards a Test of the International Character of an Armed Conflict: Nicaragua and Tadic", 2004–2005, Vol. 32 (4), *Syracuse Journal of International Law and Commerce*, pp. 269–287.

Venter, A. J.: "Sierra Leone's Mercenary War for the Diamond Fields", 1995, Vol. 28 (11), *Jane's International Defence Review*, pp. 65–68.

Wapshott, N.: *Keynes. Hayek: The Clash that Defined Modern Economics*, W. W. Norton & Company, London, 2012.

Westad, O. A.: *The Global Cold War: Third World Interventions and the Making of Our Times*, CUP, Cambridge, 2007.

White, D.: "MOD Trains Its Big Guns on Commercial Target", *Financial Times*, 13 December 1993.

5 Legal mechanisms and challenges in invoking individual and state responsibility for PMCs

When a private military company (PMC) is involved in committing a gross violation, such as killing a number of civilians at the time of its contracted activities, who should be responsible and in what way? Is it the contractor who fired the gun? Or perhaps the recruiting company, that may not have provided the appropriate training? Or should it be the state that outsourced the support of military activities to a private entity? All three components, the contractor, the company, and the state are crucial to establishing responsibility in PMC conduct.[1] The role of hiring state is scrutinised, given that both military conduct and human rights are viewed as primary concerns of states, rather than corporations or individuals.[2] Furthermore, the presence of armed contractors abroad, whether deemed as combatants or civilians under Additional Protocol (AP) I, adds an interstate aspect which plays an important part in these questions. In other words, it is no longer a matter of one state's national committing an offence abroad against a foreign national. The premise of such an offence is defined by the contracted operation initiated by the client state, without which the contractors would not have found themselves in close proximity to hostilities. Equally, if the context of the PMC as a professional occupation is removed, it then reduces the situation to an instance of one civilian killing another.

There are norms and treaties that ensure that a state cannot evade its responsibility by transferring its functions to a private entity. The UN Human Rights Council has also produced a number of comprehensive voluntary guidelines aimed at enhancing the responsibility of transnational businesses to respect human rights, including prevention, mitigation, and remediation. Equally, there is a set of well-established international and domestic legal mechanisms to invoke individual criminal responsibility. The purpose of this chapter is to navigate through these bodies of law in order to identify the gaps and overlaps in the existing regulatory structure for PMCs.

Between civilians and combatants: responsibility and impunity of private contractors

Given that the practicalities of holding a state or a corporation accountable poses numerous doctrinal, procedural, and political challenges, it ought to be more straightforward to establish individual liability. Nonetheless, private military contractors constitute a 'special' type of civilian population that are often subject to various exceptions to the rules of armed conflict and even criminal law. The ability to establish and invoke individual responsibility for private contractors is hamstrung by several peculiarities of this group, namely the legitimacy of a PMC contractor as opposed to a mercenary, their status of a non-combatant, their inevitable proximity to conflict and, finally, the international dimension their activity and any subsequent crimes take. Stretching across these four strands are the immunity mechanisms that can be applied by states to PMC personnel to shield them from being held criminally accountable.

Legitimacy of private contractors

First, unlike mercenaries, private military contractors are not a priori unlawful. Instead, they operate openly under a corporate construct of a company. Instead there are a number of PMC-specific regulations that aim to address and regulate the conduct of private actors with regard to human rights and humanitarian law. As part of the UN "Protect, Respect and Remedy" Framework, a number of states have adopted a range of approaches to invoke individual liability for PMC contractors, such as direct extraterritorial legislation and enforcement, whereby criminal procedure allows for prosecutions based on the nationality of the offender beyond national borders.[3] However, besides domestic legal systems, there has been an active development on the international level, specific to PMC regulation. The Working Group (WG) on the Use of Mercenaries as a Means of Violating Human Rights and Impeding the Exercise of the Right of Peoples to Self-Determination was established in 2005. In 2009, the WG introduced a new framework of regulation in the form of the Draft Convention. The purpose of the new draft was to strengthen accountability and extraterritorial provisions, especially to address the complex environments in which PMCs operate.[4] At its 15th session, on 1 October 2010, the Human Rights Council adopted resolution 15/26, by which it decided the following:

> to establish an open-ended intergovernmental working group with the mandate to consider the possibility of elaborating an international regulatory framework, including, inter alia, the option of elaborating a legally binding instrument on the regulation, monitoring and oversight of the activities of private military and security companies, including their accountability, taking into consideration the principles, main elements and draft text as proposed by the Working Group on the use of mercenaries as a means of violating human rights and impeding the exercise of the right of peoples to self-determination.[5]

Since 2010, three more sessions have been held, and the mandate of the open-ended intergovernmental working group (IGWG) had been further extended twice in order for it to undertake and fulfil its mandate, and it is currently entering its final year with a projected close date of August 2017. Following the IG-WG's fourth session, held from 27 April to 1 May 2015, the group presented its recommendations to the Council.[6] Article 21 of the Draft Convention proposed to establish rules on individual criminal responsibility. Similarly, as it applies to legal entities, the Draft Convention exercises its jurisdiction over individuals through the domestic laws of state parties.[7] It obliges each state party to take necessary measures when:

a The offence is committed in the territory of that State.
b The offence is committed on board a vessel flying the flag of that State or an aircraft registered under the laws of that State at the time the offence is committed.
c The offence is committed by a national of that State.[8]

Although it is not explicit in the above provision, one can assume that Article 21 requires state parties to take responsibility for their nationals committing offences not only on their territory, but also abroad. This approach is distinct from the majority of domestic regulation, though it is in line with the Organisation of African Unity (OAU) Convention for the Elimination of Mercenaries.[9] The Draft Convention also suggests, although it does not strictly require, that states establish jurisdiction over the offences committed against their nationals or permanent residents,[10] while Article 23 covers obligations related to prosecution, ensuring effective remedies for victims.[11] The most valuable provision relating to individual responsibility stipulates that state parties must ensure that no immunity agreement is granted to PMCs and their contractors for violations of international human rights law.[12] The significance of this passage lies in its direct attempt to eliminate the impunity that PMCs and their personnel have enjoyed through granting of protection.[13] The same clause mentions the enforcement of international humanitarian law (IHL); however, no details are specified on how states should go about this process through the premises of domestic judicial systems.

Another significant attempt at regulation of PMCs was initiated by the Swiss Federal Department of Foreign Affairs in cooperation with the International Committee of the Red Cross in 2005. Industry and civil society actors were closely engaged in the process, which comprised five intergovernmental and four expert meetings.[14] At the fourth meeting on the 'Swiss Initiative' in September 2008, the Montreux Document was finalised and adopted by consensus of the participating governments.[15] Although lacking legally binding standing, the Montreux Document outlines obligations and responsibilities that individual PMC directors and employees ought to follow. It references contractor obligations under relevant domestic laws, and all human rights and IHL provisions imposed upon them nationally.[16] According to the Montreux Document, the personnel of PMCs are

> protected as civilians under international humanitarian law, unless they are incorporated into the regular armed forces of a State or are members of organized armed forces, groups or units under a command responsible to the State; or otherwise lose their protection as determined by international humanitarian law.[17]

To interpret this statement, unless a PMC forms part of a state's military, for either various or one specific operation, PMC contractors are classified as civilians. The Montreux Document subsequently extends IHL protection to an organised group of armed civilians recruited by a state, or a non-governmental entity. This protection is, however, revoked if the contractors are participating in hostilities.[18] The Document also offers a very vague provision on superior responsibility, referring to government officials, with no particular explanation as to what establishes their superiority over PMC employees and PMC directors.[19] Furthermore, James Cockayne suggests that this provision "sidesteps the difficult question of the nature of the knowledge and intent a superior must possess in order for his or her responsibility to be triggered",[20] as it asserts that superior responsibility arises from "effective authority" and "in accordance with the rules of international law"[21] without explicitly referencing any particular rules or laws.

Status of a non-combatant

Furthermore, private military contractors, unless directly incorporated into the armed forces, hold the status of a non-combatant. This means that in most cases, military chain of command does not apply as only "contractors manage, supervise, and give directions to their employees".[22] Therefore, commanders of the armed forces that PMCs accompany do not have direct control over contractors or their employees. However, another important aspect of individual criminal responsibility develops from the idea of superior or command responsibility,[23] arising from the laws of armed conflict and firmly entrenched in treaty law in 1977 as part of Articles 43 and 87 of AP I.[24] Under the doctrine of command responsibility, a commander, or the one performing the role and the duties of a commander, may be held liable for the conduct of his subordinates.[25] In order to deem a PMC employee or director personally liable, they must have proven *de facto* control over their subordinates, and have the material ability to prevent and punish the commission of the crime.[26]

ICC Article 28 on Responsibility of commanders and other superiors clearly stipulates criminal responsibility of "a military commander or person effectively acting as a military commander" for the crimes committed by subordinates under their effective command and control.[27] In other words, their civilian status does not shield PMC employees or directors from criminal responsibility via application of Article 28. When a contractor is entitled to give orders, their responsibility may be invoked on the basis of being a *de facto* military commander.[28] Lindsey Cameron and Vincent Chetail suggest that when performing tasks that give PMC employees or directors *de facto* control over soldiers of states whose armed forces are not fully developed, their inaction and silent by-standing in the place where crimes occur could merit engaging their responsibility.

Proximity to conflict

Even if not specifically contracted to support military operations, all PMC activities largely take place in conflict zones, or territories with a high risk of unrest. Some of the more recent examples include the surfacing of Russia's private contractors of the Wagner group and Patriot in Sudan, Central African Republic, Burundi, and Yemen.[29] Some historical examples including Bosnia and Sierra Leone were discussed in previous chapters. However, operation of private military company Blackwater in Iraq has probably been most infamous to date. On 16 September 2007, in Nisour Square in Iraq, Blackwater contractors opened fire and killed seventeen Iraqi civilians, while twenty-four were wounded. PMCs provided three types of services in Iraq: personal security for senior civilian officials, non-military site security, i.e. buildings and infrastructure, and non-military convoy security.[30] A few years prior, during the Coalition Provisional Authority (CPA) administration in Iraq (21 April 2003–28 June 2004) a legal framework was established stipulating the regulation of PMC activities. It stated that

> In accordance with international law, the CPA, Coalition Forces and the military and civil personnel accompanying them, are not subjects to local law or the jurisdiction of local courts. With regard to criminal, civil, administrative or other legal process, they will remain subject to the exclusive jurisdiction of the State contributing them to the Coalition.[31]

The reference to international law does not seem to bear any judicial or practical meaning as it was not mentioned at all during the proceedings of the Blackwater case,[32] making a clear statement about the civilian status of PMC contractors and disabling the vehicle of IHL. Following the shooting, the US government passed a bill that extended the applicability of Military Extraterritorial Jurisdiction Act (MEJA) to private contractors operating in combat zones. Originally passed by Congress in 2000, MEJA gives federal courts jurisdiction over felonies committed by persons "employed by or accompanying the armed forces" overseas.[33] By extending the MEJA jurisdiction to private contractors, the US government ensured the Blackwater employees were not tried in Iraq, where the crimes were committed, but instead remained under the authority of US courts.

In the Blackwater case, the contractors disputed the applicability of MEJA jurisdiction due to their contract with the State Department, rather than the Department of Defence (DOD). The legal wording of the MEJA creates uncertainty and potential jurisdictional gaps.[34] During the trial, Gordon England, former

Deputy Secretary of Defence, testified that at the time of the shooting, Blackwater contractors were supporting the Department of State mission only, rather than the Department of Defence.[35] This distinction is important because in 2004 Congress extended MEJA jurisdiction to cover

> the civilian employees, contractors, and employees of contractors of any Federal agency or provisional authority, and their dependents, to the extent that the employment relates to the mission of the Department of Defence overseas or to operations within territory that the United States occupies solely or jointly.[36]

According to Gordon England, there was no cooperation between the Department of State and the Department of Defence, and since Blackwater was formally contracted to the Department of State, the MEJA jurisdiction could not be applied to invoke state responsibility.[37] Ultimately, four contractors were prosecuted in the US District Court for the District of Columbia[38]; they were found guilty and were sentenced to lengthy prison terms.[39]

The principle of extraterritorial criminal jurisdiction is not exclusive to the US. In the UK, for example, according to the Armed Forces Act 2006 (UK), PMC contractors working for the UK Armed Forces are subject to service discipline. This, however, does not apply to contractors recruited abroad for UK Armed Forces missions.[40] In English law, any criminal act committed by an employee of a company would lead to a breach in contract.[41] However, this is not clear-cut in the private military industry, where the legality and criminality of contracted activities cross over. The International Criminal Court Act 2001 provided jurisdiction to prosecute core crimes, such as crimes of aggression, war crimes, genocide, and crimes against humanity,[42] committed by British nationals in or outside the UK.

Today, a number of European Union member states allow for extraterritorial legislation concerning human rights by virtue of the application of the European Convention on Human Rights (ECHR).[43] However, it does not apply outside the ECHR *espace juridique*,[44] which therefore significantly limits the scope of its jurisdiction. Also, provided that PMC-caused human rights violations are more likely to occur in conflict zones and outside the ECHR founding states' judicial remit, the exact parameters of the ECHR's extraterritorial reach would ultimately rely on individual states' jurisdiction, and individual extraterritoriality clauses.

International dimension

This leads me to the next characteristic, namely international dimension. PMCs predominantly operate abroad so if a crime is committed, customarily, a local jurisdiction would apply. In the case of PMCs, a series of strategic exceptions have been made historically, underlining the extraordinary nature of private contractors.

Where national courts lack the extraterritorial reach to prosecute offences committed by their nationals abroad, the International Criminal Court may exercise its jurisdiction. Based on the principle of complementarity, the ICC may only apply authority when national legal systems are unable or unwilling to do so. Moreover, the Rome Statute provisions relating to individual criminal responsibility do not undermine the responsibility of states under IL.[45] Although the ICC and the ad hoc tribunals are the most obvious avenues for ascribing international criminal responsibility,[46] the jurisdiction of the courts is limited to the most serious crimes of concern to the international community as a whole.[47] PMC contractors bear criminal responsibility as individuals, regardless of their status under IHL, notwithstanding cases when immunity is granted. While the applicability of war crimes provisions applies to civilians and combatants alike, a link to an armed conflict needs to be established for an offence to qualify as a war crime.[48] ICC Articles 11, 12, and 13 define more specifically the conditions for international criminal prosecution. However, it is Article 25 of the ICC that defines the parameters of individual criminal responsibility.[49] The Court has jurisdiction over natural persons only, as opposed to states or corporations, and it can ascribe criminal responsibility and be held liable for a crime within the jurisdiction of the Court.[50] Individuals can be either held directly liable for the offences they committed, or be deemed responsible for ordering, soliciting or inducing, as well as aiding, abetting, or otherwise assisting the commission of a crime.[51]

Finally, immunity mechanisms exist that can prevent domestic extraterritorial jurisdictions and the international criminal law framework from treating PMC employees in the same way as all other civilians in the event of a human rights violation in the context of international crimes. Immediately, there appears to be a conflict between the independent procedure of the ICC to try most serious international crimes, and the political influence of the Security Council and certain individual states.[52] There are currently different immunity mechanisms, such as the Forces Agreement between the UK and Afghanistan,[53] and the Article 98 agreements[54] that shield UK and US military personnel from ICC investigations.

A source of individual impunity for PMC employees has been legal immunity, provided to contractors by the hiring state.[55] In Abu Ghraib lawsuits against CACI International[56] and Titan Corporation (now L-3 Services),[57] the US federal court established that "Titan employees performed their duties under the direct command and exclusive operational control of the military".[58] Establishing the presence of military control meant that government contractor immunity was extended to Titan employees and the plaintiffs' claims could be pre-empted. While CACI employees were found to have operated under a dual chain of command, supervised by both military and company managers, the court found CACI employees to have been integrated into a military mission, and, therefore, also in possession of government contractor immunity. The District of Columbia Circuit Court of Appeals ruled in favour of the defendants on 11 September 2009. While on this occasion individual responsibility had not been established, there have been recent significant developments achieved by CACI victims through tort law; these are considered in detail as part of the corporate accountability discussion in Chapter 6.

State as a client and the main actor in international law

Why is it important to invoke state responsibility in the context of PMC conduct? First of all, the military nature of PMCs sets them apart from other companies, as their business is set up to conduct military support operations on behalf of a client. PMC clients are predominantly multinational corporations, international organisations, or states. In the case of the former, PMCs are likely to provide security for an extraction business or a company operating in a high-risk environment. However, when their clients are states or international organisations, such as the UN, PMCs are likely to be recruited to support military or peacekeeping operations abroad. Contractors would work alongside military personnel, fulfilling a number of functions from logistics to military training. This proximity to combat and the potential for direct participation in hostilities brings PMCs into a grey area of legality and closer to the realm of international armed conflict. PMCs are reliant on state contracts to ensure their presence in these areas, and therefore it is crucial to examine the extent of state responsibility in this relationship.

The second reason for state involvement is tied up in the high risk of human rights violations associated with PMC operations in conflict and tension zones. In his capacity as the Special Representative of the Secretary-General on the issue of human rights and transnational corporations, John Ruggie argued that

> states individually are the primary duty-bearers under international human rights law, and collectively they are the trustees of the international human rights regime. Therefore, the closer a business enterprise is to the State, or the more it relies on statutory authority or taxpayer support, the stronger the State's policy rationale becomes for ensuring that the enterprise respects human rights, quite apart from any legal obligations States may have in certain circumstances.[59]

On the surface, there are various sources of regulation that aim to provide a comprehensive structure for the state to administer PMC conduct, and for state responsibility to be invoked in the event of gross violations by PMCs. First of all, as the body of public international law that regulates the conduct of armed conflicts, IHL offers relevant mechanisms in holding PMCs accountable. In addition to drawing a distinction between combatants and non-combatants,[60] in 2001 the International Law Commission (ILC) adopted a complete text of the Articles on Responsibility of States for Internationally Wrongful Acts (ILC Articles), together with accompanying Commentaries. More specifically,

Articles 4, 5, 8, 9, and 11 of the ILC cover the conditions for attribution of private conduct to the state.

Furthermore, the Montreux Document and the Draft Convention on the Regulation, Oversight and Monitoring of Private Military and Security Companies are the industry-specific regulatory bodies that outline the obligations of states who hire, host, and domicile PMCs. In addition, the UN "Protect, Respect and Remedy" Framework sets out the guiding principles for states, as well as businesses, to ensure human rights values are promoted and followed. Finally, the relationship between a hiring state and the PMC is administered by a contract under which both parties are liable. If the terms of the contract are breached, the jurisdiction of contract law would apply, adding an extra layer of surveillance and legal enforcement to the realm of private forces. It is noted in the Guiding Principles that states which privatise the delivery of services should continue to ensure that companies adhere to human rights norms. Failure to do so "may entail both reputational and legal consequences for the State itself".[61] While with the proliferation of neoliberal ideas, privatisation and the outsourcing of numerous services became increasingly widespread, certain functions are still considered purely governmental. The UN WG on Mercenaries asserts that

> certain functions were inherent to the State, for which it retained ultimate responsibility regardless of whether or not it outsourced that function. Some inherent State functions might not be outsourced, namely direct participation in hostilities in armed conflict, and detention and interrogation of prisoners of war, as defined in the Geneva Convention of 12 August 1949.[62]

Despite this statement, the nature of PMC activity brings companies and their employees into conflict zones, where the risk of participation in hostilities is very high. Equally, PMCs like CACI International and Titan Corporation (now L-3 Services), were officially contracted by the US Government to conduct interrogation and translation services at military prisons in Iraq.[63]

In order to establish the effectiveness of the existing regulatory regime in establishing and invoking state responsibility with regard to use of PMCs, the following section critically examines relevant existing legal mechanism and the challenges these may face.

IHL and state responsibility for PMCs: gaps in the ILC Articles on attribution of conduct

While according to Crowe and John[64] and Cameron and Chetail[65] IHL can, to an extent, resolve the issue of individual accountability for both mercenaries and private military contractors participating in hostilities as non-combatants, it poses, in my view, two greater issues. The first is the weakening of the mechanism invoking state responsibility in situations when private contractors are deployed during an armed conflict. And the second is the absence of accountability provisions on a corporate level for PMC as a company, which is discussed in more detail in Chapter 6.

In order to fully understand the extent and limitations of regulatory frameworks concerning PMC conduct, it is first important to consider the relationship between PMCs and their primary clients, states. By the nature of their business, PMCs are service providers who operate on behalf of a client rather than independently. While PMCs do not have a political agenda, as they carry out another party's strategy, states are seen to increasingly rely on PMCs for provision of security, therefore relinquishing some of their power and control. PMCs, on the other hand, operate a market for force, keeping a firm hold on the private sources of power. This dynamic of supply and demand of security services is administered by two legal frameworks, a contract that defines the terms of agreement between a state institution and the PMC, and a set of International Law Commission Articles (ILC Articles) that outline the criteria for ascribing private conduct to the acts of a state.

According to ILC Articles, "every internationally wrongful act of a State entails the international responsibility of that State".[66] ILC Article 4 provides the basic rule of attributing the conduct of state organs to the state:

> The conduct of any State organ shall be considered an act of that State under international law, whether the organ exercises legislative, executive, judicial or any other functions, whatever position it holds in the organization of the State, and whatever its character as an organ of the central Government or of a territorial unit of the State.[67]

In this scenario, the relation to the PMC is irrelevant unless the PMC acts as a state agent, i.e. is officially incorporated into the organs of government. Amongst the examples are companies such as Sandline and Executive Outcomes whose personnel were enrolled as "Special Constables" on an assignment to Papua New Guinea.[68] As seen from the previous section, PMC employee incorporation into the military chain of command had been proposed in order to extend contractor immunity to CACI and Titan employees. However, state responsibility was not invoked, therefore spreading the legal vacuum around PMC activity and fostering impunity.

ILC Article 5 covers entities that are empowered by the state and are exercising elements of governmental authority. For a state to carry responsibility over PMC actions, the PMC must be empowered by the state to exercise governmental authority. There is little clarity on what the empowerment should look like, besides the fact that only the entities that are empowered by internal law can exercise governmental authority.[69] While a contract between a state and a PMC could be considered an instrument of domestic law, it is the element of empowerment that is crucial to attribute private conduct to the state and, therefore, establish responsibility. Without a specific empowerment clause, a contract can be reduced to a horizontal service agreement between two equal parties. Similarly,

ILC Article 8 attributes responsibility to the state for conduct carried out under its direction or control. These examples may include auxiliaries and volunteers who do not necessarily form part of the armed forces but who are authorised by the state to carry out a particular mission.[70]

When a state deprives an individual of liberty, as for example in the case of detention, it takes control over the detainee's life, rights, and conditions. The state, therefore, also yields a heightened level of responsibility to protect that individual's rights.[71] Consequently, there is a strong argument to invoke state responsibility in situations when detention and correctional facilities have been outsourced to a private company, regardless of the contract in force. Nigel White acknowledges that the principles of state responsibility are extremely abstract, and "do not concern themselves with practical means and methods of implementation and enforcement".[72] Indeed, the lack of specific parameters defining 'direction and control' makes it almost impossible to attribute PMC conduct to a state. The lack of precedent in historically significant cases like *Nicaragua* and *Tadic* reinforces states' impunity when irregular forces are used.

ILC Articles 9 and 11 prove to be even weaker mechanisms; Article 9 comes into play when the private entity is "in fact exercising elements of the governmental authority in the absence or default of the official authorities and in circumstances such as to call for the exercise of those elements of authority", and Article 11 actually requires a state to "acknowledge and adopt the conduct in question as its own".

The UN Guiding Principles explicitly state that the corporate responsibility to respect human rights exists independently of state responsibility to fulfil their human rights duties, and, most importantly, does not diminish those duties.[73] This is distinct from the question of legal liability, which remains defined largely by national law provisions in relevant jurisdictions.[74] Similarly, the International Code of Conduct for Private Security Service Providers (ICoC) "does not replace the control exercised by Competent Authorities, and does not limit or alter applicable international law or relevant national law".[75] This means that neither Human Rights law, nor the voluntary industry regulation, can enact the ILC Articles to effectively manage state responsibility in the context of private company conduct. Therefore, in practice, the ILC Articles provide a weak legal framework for establishing state responsibility over the conduct of a contracted PMC.

Overall, given the intersection with armed conflict and the international dimension that often comes along with PMC activities, IHL ought to have the resources to accommodate and regulate PMC conduct. In practice, as demonstrated by the proceeding of the Blackwater trial, the civilian status of PMC contractors disabled the vehicle of IHL, apportioning the blame on the contractors, entirely bypassing IL and leaving the hiring state free from responsibility. Furthermore, the particular legitimacy that PMCs had acquired as legal entities largely circumvents the scope of IHL, leaving the regulation to contract law and PMC-specific voluntary norms.

States as PMC clients and limitations of contract law

One of the gaps in accountability arises due to conflicting protocols governing command and control of PMCs in the armed conflict. Military companies are usually bound to the state only through contracts between the contracting entities, meaning that "commanders do not have direct control over contractors or their employees; only contractors manage, supervise, and give directions to their employees".[76] Consequently, military commanders cannot give binding instructions to employees of contractors. This, in turn, means that since states do not exercise effective control, they also are not the ones charging these individuals or entities with functions that would constitute direct participation in hostilities, and, therefore, cannot be accountable for such action.[77] Furthermore, this construct renders states unable to exercise their duty of due diligence under IHL as those obligations will probably not be achievable if the commanders on-site have limited authority over PMC contractors. By the nature of contract, the client (state) and the provider (PMC) enter into a 'horizontal' agreement, whereby both parties are equal under the construct of a contract and not one subordinate to another.

The definition of the term "direct participation in hostilities" constitutes a limitation for the use of private military companies in armed conflicts. While generally, the decisive factor is whether the conduct in question directly causes harm to the enemy, in practice the line between security or support functions and combat operations is often blurred. During the occupation of Iraq, private military contractors, while bearing military arms, were allowed to exercise pre-emptive functions like to stop, search, disarm, and detain civilians if specified in the contract, regardless of the private or public nature of the contracting entity. The prevalence of the contract over IHL is further solidified in the *US field manual* stipulating that

> the terms and conditions of the contract establish the relationship between the military (US Government) and the contractor; this relationship does not extend through the contractor supervisor to his employees. Only the contractor can directly supervise its employees. The military chain of command exercises management control through the contract.[78]

Contract law plays, therefore, an important part in PMC regulation as it is a necessary element that defines the relationship between a PMC, as a service provider, and the state as its client. I therefore here explore the role and the limitations posed by contract law in the context of state responsibility. The basic principle of modern contract law is based on the compensation of the innocent party for moneys lost due to a breach.[79] Laura Dickinson identifies contracts as the vehicle of military privatisation, and, contrary to Liu, believes that contracts should be used in order to transfer the norms of public IL into the private sector.[80] In other words, a contract between PMCs and their clients can and should be drafted in a way that reflects necessary oversight, enforcement, and conduct requirements applicable to private military contractors. According to Dickinson, contracts "could resolve any lingering ambiguities about the applicability of international human rights and humanitarian law" by incorporating specific provisions for training of the personnel, accreditation of the company, etc. Dickinson proposes to also include relevant IHL provisions applicable to governmental actors in order to define the boundaries of state responsibility at the outset.[81] However, it is important to consider the relationship that a contract constructs between the state and the private provider of security.

As a client, the state is reliant on the PMC for provision of security or, in other words, protection. Therefore the client's ability to effectively control a PMC's behaviour is hamstrung by the nature of this relationship.[82] Furthermore, when a state enters into a contract with a PMC, it arguably loses its hierarchical position of authority and becomes a private party to a contract.[83] The contract between the state and the PMC, therefore, immunises the state against responsibility under ILC Article 8 as the state is no longer seen to be directing or controlling the PMC, instead entering into a 'horizontal' agreement where both parties are equal under the construct of a contract.[84] This is a serious limitation to state responsibility imposed by the structure and the nature of contract law.

While the margins of accountability are an obvious gap, created by current IL and the way the ILC Articles are drafted, the inclusion of such a provision would automatically expose the government should a PMC commit an act of gross misconduct, a situation that existing IL is keeping obscure and undefined. Potential evasion of responsibility is arguably part of the rationale for state outsourcing to a private company instead of using uniformed troops, though Dickinson does not agree with this argument. Furthermore, her proposal does not negate the 'effective control' argument. Nor does it solve the issue of the horizontal nature of a contract, whereby both parties are equal and neither one is subordinate to the other, unless state responsibility is explicitly attributed in the contract. Since liability is defined through agreement, contract law has serious limitations, as its rule is restricted to the agreed scope between the parties to the contract, becoming a very narrow means of regulating PMCs. Therefore, in the event of non-compliance with IHL and human rights, third parties are unable to make a private claim as the contract only applies to the contracting parties: the PMC as the service provider, and the state as the client.

There are numerous exceptions to compensation: "innocent parties cannot recover punitive damages, damages for pain and suffering or attorney's fees. [...] [I]nnocent parties are almost assured of *not* being fully compensated for their losses".[85] To that end, Dickinson proposes adjusting the structure of the contract to enable third parties, affected by a PMC's activity, to enforce the terms of the agreement.[86] However, the possibility of implementing these changes is low due to the breadth of detail that will unravel, should third party claims be made possible under contract law. Although Dickinson recognises the likelihood of state objections to increased contractual regulation, she argues that the ILC Articles on State Responsibility address the gaps of privatisation.[87] She deems invalid the argument that states use PMCs to avoid accountability, because there are international legal mechanisms that can ascribe PMC conduct to the state. As demonstrated above, while these provisions exist in principle, their actual applicability is extremely narrow and requires substantial supporting evidence, that both states and companies often fail to produce.

Although contract law has obvious gaps in regulating PMCs, there is no need to rely solely on one type of regulation. Contract law should, in turn, serve as a kind of audit to keep the terms of the PMC contract in check. While contract law is not subordinate to IL by default, it can explicitly articulate the ICoC clauses concerning human rights and overall standards, which is a common practice in typical service agreements across a number of sectors.

In addition, the incomplete nature of state/PMC contracts[88] is a vehicle that enforces PMCs' position of power. Reviewed contracts[89] demonstrated a high degree of ambiguity, omitting employee training requirements and leaving scope for interpretation. By outsourcing inherently state-owned functions to PMCs, governments are therefore allocating a degree of their sovereignty. Incomplete contracts are, therefore, conceived as "hybrid forms of governance, located somewhere between sovereignty and anarchy".[90] To ensure a state's authority over the means of private violence, the contract ought to explicitly state that the client, any entity that is recruiting a PMC, is superior and, therefore, assumes overall accountability for the PMC and the actions of its employees, who is the subordinate in terms of the contract. If such provisions are not stipulated in the contract, then states and PMCs will continue to exist in an equal relationship, circumventing the ILC attribution framework and reinforcing PMCs' claims to power and legitimacy.[91]

Institutional responsibility

While this work does not elaborate in detail on institutional responsibility, it is important to mention the core principles and initiatives in this realm. In 2011, the ILC adopted a set of Articles on the Responsibility of International Organisations (ARIO), ascribing international legal personality to international organisations, thereby subjecting them to IL.[92] This meant that same rules ought to apply to international organisations hiring PMCs as they would to states.

The UN had previously deployed armed PMCs in selected duty stations as a last resort in Afghanistan, Haiti, and Somalia, "in an effort to strengthen the safety and security of its personnel and to enable the Organisation to deliver its programmes and mandates in high-risk environments".[93] The principles of the deployment and use of private security resources is outlined in the UN Policy on Armed Private Security Companies.[94] The engagement and use of such services is governed by a clear accountability and responsibility framework, and clear operational standards and oversight, stipulated in the Guidelines on the Use of Armed Security Services from Private Security Companies.[95] However, the document only articulates 'Daily and Monthly Operations Reviews', omitting to explicitly state whether or not the UN is ultimately accountable for the private forces they deploy, and who is liable in the event of a violation committed by a private contractor. White and MacLeod suggest that the absence of an equivalent attribution clause in the Draft Articles on Institutional Responsibility may present a legal loophole for private military contractors since there is no separate provision for attribution of the conduct of individuals.[96] So, in principle, institutional responsibility should apply in the same manner as state responsibility. However, if neither state nor the hiring international organisation can establish authority, command, and control, then, unless a less stringent test of attribution is used, the issue would be considered solely from the perspective of corporate responsibility.[97] Nonetheless, simply because an international organisation does not exercise full control over individual states' PMC contingents, it should not evade accountability for the overall operation and the acts or omissions of PMCs during that operation.[98]

In reality, however, the concept of effective control in IL seems to operate on a separate plane to that of structural organisation. For example, in its capacity as a US government agent, the CIA trained, financed, and organised the Contras to conduct insurgency operations. In the *Nicaragua case*, the International Court of Justice (ICJ) required the establishment of 'effective control' in order to define and attribute responsibility to the American state.[99] In the end, there was insufficient evidence to establish effective control, and, therefore, a link to the American government. Similar logic applies to the UN peacekeeping forces who, on the surface, are far less controversial in nature. These forces are supplied to the UN by member states to conduct peacekeeping operations. However, IL is constructed in such a way that it hinders the establishment of responsibility over these forces and their conduct. *A priori*, the law itself renders the use of these forces problematic, as it defers the act of establishing the accountable party. In other words, neither the UN as the ultimate 'recruiter' of the peacekeeping troops, nor the member states as their 'provider', are responsible for their conduct, unless 'effective control' can be established. In this way, IL promotes a culture of blamelessness and irresponsibility for international organisations, states, and corporations, whereby liability is established after the fact, rather than at the outset.

State-centric regulation concerning PMCs

Another method of regulating PMC activity arises from intergovernmental agreements and emerging treaties, encapsulated in the Montreux Document and Draft Convention on Private Military and Security Companies (Draft Convention). Supported by fifty-three states and three international organisations as its signatories[100] as of September 2018, the Montreux Document is not a new international treaty and it does not create any new legal obligations. Meanwhile, the draft convention, although strongly advocating criminalisation of PMC misconduct, failed to resonate with the UN member state community, leaving the WG to pursue other avenues for pursuing Human Rights agenda in the context of PMC activity. Nevertheless, it is an important regulatory specimen to be analysed. While different in scope and jurisdiction, the two regulatory efforts are aimed at states (rather than individuals or corporations) and, arguably, both represent the view that is incompatible with the increasing power and legitimacy of PMCs.

The Montreux Document

The Montreux Document on Pertinent International Legal Obligations and Good Practices for States related to Operations of Private Military and Security Companies during Armed Conflict is an intergovernmental document intended to promote respect for IHL and human rights law whenever PMCs are present in armed conflicts.[101] The Montreux Document is largely state-centric in nature. Its guidelines relate to the obligations of a 'contracting state' entering into a contract with PMCs; the 'home state' where the companies are registered; and the 'territorial state' where PMCs operate.[102] This classification is arguably an important soft legal norm that constitutes an explicit recognition by signatory states of a specific duty to protect human rights during PMC operation.[103] The Document does not create any new legal obligations either for states or PMCs, and while it provides guidelines, it is not necessarily a step towards a new treaty.[104]

Nevertheless, the Document reinforces the narrative of the ILC Articles on attribution of responsibility by affirming that "entering into contractual relations does not in itself engage the responsibility of Contracting States".[105] The four conditions[106] whereby PMC violations are considered an act of the state are also consistent with the ILC Articles, and therefore with customary IL. The Document's full title indicates its specific application 'during armed conflict'. However, White argues that PMCs are more likely to be deployed outside of an armed conflict, for example, during a post-conflict reconstruction.[107] While insisting that PMCs do not operate in a legal vacuum, the Montreux Document seeks no binding authority from participating states or non-state actors using private security services. It elaborates on different agreements (interstate, belonging to international organisations, national laws, etc.[108]) that stipulate state behaviour in relation to the PMCs.

To draw upon the historical typologies and the relationship between the form of governance and the military force,[109] the Montreux Process offers a state-oriented approach to a network-based private field of activity, rendering its regulation largely ineffective. By offering a normative framework for regulated PMC participation in an armed conflict, while at the same time lacking legal enforcement, the Document inadvertently normalises and rationalises civilian participation in hostilities. A member of the UN WG, Gomez Del

Prado believes that the ICRC stamp of approval was premature, and that the Document "recognises *de facto* this new industry and the military and security services it provides. It legitimises the services the industry provides, which still remain unregulated and unmonitored".[110] In addition, the Montreux Document contains a section labelled "PMSCs and their personnel"[111] which refers to obligations, yet it makes no mention of PMC responsibility as companies. Nevertheless, the Document contains a particular provision on superior responsibility that could develop into a valuable precedent for corporate criminal responsibility internationally. In September 2008, seventeen states (including the US, the UK, China, and South Africa) officially agreed that the idea of superior responsibility, grounded in international criminal law, has a potential role in assigning responsibility for international crimes to PMC directors and those contracting PMCs.[112] According to the Montreux Document,

> Superiors of PMSC personnel, such as: a) governmental officials, whether they are military commanders or civilian superiors, or b) directors or managers of PMSCs, may be liable for crimes under international law committed by PMSC personnel under their effective authority and control, as a result of their failure to properly exercise control over them, in accordance with the rules of international law. Superior responsibility is not engaged solely by virtue of a contract.[113]

While in its current form the Montreux Process focuses predominantly on states, it is important to recognise the opportunity it creates for international criminal responsibility for corporations.

The draft convention

Critical of the overinclusive nature of the Montreux Document and the self-regulatory profile of the Code of Conduct,[114] in 2009 the WG proposed a legally binding Draft Convention on Private Military and Security Companies (Draft Convention).[115] Unlike the Montreux Document, that allows for all services to be outsourced to PMC contractors (other than direct participation in hostilities), the Draft Convention does not allow for inherently governmental functions to be performed by anyone other than the state.[116] Inherent or "Fundamental State functions" are classified in the *Definitions* of the Draft Convention as:

> functions that a State cannot outsource or delegate to non-State actors. Among such functions, consistent with the principle of State monopoly on the use of force, are waging war and/or combat operations, taking prisoners, law-making, espionage, intelligence and police powers, especially the powers of arrest or detention, including the interrogation of detainees.[117]

Resistance from the UK and the US, as well as from the EU to ratify the Convention, however, is not surprising, considering that these states welcome private security providers. The relationship between the form of governance and the type of military power used by the state comes into play. As highlighted in the previous chapter, countries that follow neoliberal ideals of 'small government', deregulation, and privatisation are likely to outsource numerous functions and activities, including security. On the contrary, those states with greater centralisation are less lenient towards integration of PMCs as it contradicts their governmental model.

The Draft Convention is a suppression convention,[118] meaning it requires states to establish jurisdiction over 'treaty crimes' or crimes of 'international concern' committed on their territory, when extradition is not possible.[119] It does, however, offer means of international supervision in the form of a Committee on the Regulation, Oversight and Monitoring of Private Military and Security Activities (Oversight Committee).[120] Article 4 (1) on state responsibility towards PMCs states that "each State party bears responsibility for the military and security activities of PMSCs registered or operating in their jurisdiction, whether or not these entities are contracted by the State". This fundamentally contradicts the basic principle that the state is only responsible for its own actions. Furthermore, it is not in line with the attribution clauses of the ILC Articles. In theory, the Draft Convention attempts to create a firmer legal position on state responsibility.

In practice, however, it creates a vast discrepancy between existing public IL and an emerging treaty, therefore polarising the PMC regulatory space. Failure to explicitly define the parameters of secondary levels of responsibility leaves the existing gap in the rules on attribution of conduct unfilled. The protection of all human rights under state jurisdiction is the only standing legal responsibility that states are bound by in the realm of PMC regulation. This means that the Draft Convention does not, in fact, impose any additional responsibility on states using PMCs. Furthermore, the Draft Convention is old-fashioned in the sense that it does not consider contemporary governmental trends, nor the trends of globalisation and the spread of free market principles.[121]

Although an overview of the work carried out by the WG has been recently published[122] and the efforts have been taken over by the IGWG, there has been no mention of any progress on the Draft Convention in the past few years. While both the Montreux Document and the Draft Convention outline the obligations of home, host, and contracting states, neither process has reached an effective implementation of these procedures. Besides the challenge of incompatibility between the legally binding nature of the Draft Convention, the contradicting content of the evolving Montreux Process, and the self-regulating PMC industry, there is a risk of polarisation between party states.[123] Two diverging regulatory cultures are likely to progress, with PMC-welcoming states endorsing the Montreux Process, and the 'non-aligned' countries striving for a stricter, more punitive regulation.

Conclusion

The choice faced by the international community is represented by the two procedures and is informed by a deep scholarly division between the advocates of a state-oriented binding approach, and those who consider that collective self-regulation regulation and soft norms are the key to upholding industry standards and the elimination of human rights violations by the PMCs. However, most importantly, neither approach is mindful of the growing gravitas of PMCs as corporate global actors, possessing legal personality and exercising a certain extent of legitimacy through self-regulation and, possessing significant strategic, logistical, operational, and combat skills translating directly into power. Hence why the primary focus of this monograph is on corporate accountability of PMCs and understanding the scope and opportunity of existing and emerging legal tools to invoke that.

Notes

1 In the context of this chapter, the terms 'liability' and 'responsibility' are interchangeable, with 'liability' referring to legal responsibility of an actor.
2 Ruggie (2011).
3 Guiding Principles on Business and Human Rights (2011, p. 4).
4 A/HRC/30/47, Art. 33 (g), p. 10.
5 A/HRC/RES/15/26, p. 2.
6 At HRC thirtieth session.
7 Draft International Convention on the Regulation, Oversight and Monitoring of Private Military and Security Companies (Draft Convention) 2009, Article 21.
8 The Draft Convention 2009, Article 21 (1)
9 The OAU Convention called for states to introduce laws forbidding their nationals from engaging in mercenary activities. See OAU Convention for the Elimination of Mercenaries in Africa 1972, Annex 1, Article 3 (a).
10 The Draft Convention 2009, Article 21 (2).
11 The Draft Convention 2009, Article 23 (1).
12 The Draft Convention 2009, Article 23 (2).
13 On immunity mechanisms, see: Simpson (2007, p. 17).
14 Cockayne (2009, p. 402).
15 Federal Department of Foreign Affairs, Section for International Humanitarian Law.
16 The Montreux Document.
17 The Montreux Document, Section E. PMSCs and their personnel, para. 26 (b), p. 14.
18 The Montreux Document, Section E. PMSCs and their personnel, para. 25, p. 14.
19 The Montreux Document, Section F. Superior responsibility, para. 27(a), p. 15.
20 Cockayne (2009, p. 411).
21 The Montreux Document, Section F. Superior responsibility, para. 27 (b), p. 15.
22 United States Headquarters Department of the Army, *Contractors on the Battlefield, Field Manual*, paras 1–22.
23 For more on superior responsibility, see: Arnold and Triffterer (2008); Mettraux (2009); Olasolo (2009).
24 Cameron and Chetail (2013, p. 616).
25 Cameron and Chetail (2013, p. 613).

26 Case law: *Celebici* Trial Chamber Judgement 2001, paras 354, 378; *Semanza* Trial Chamber 2003, para. 402; *Kordic and Cerkez* Trial Chamber Judgement 2001, paras 414–415.
27 Rome Statute of the ICC, Art. 28 (a).
28 Cameron and Chetail (2013, pp. 605, 619). See also: *Prosecutor v. Kunarac, Kovac and Vukovic*, Trial Chamber Judgement, Case No. IT-96-23-T & IT-96-23/1-T; para. 397: "The giving of orders or the exercise of powers generally attached to a military command are strong indications that an individual is indeed a commander. But these are not the sole relevant factors", p. 132.
29 See The Defence Post; Eurasia Daily Monitor 2018.
30 Isenberg (2007, p. 84).
31 Office of the Administrator of the Coalition Provisional Authority Baghdad, Iraq; Public Notice regarding the Status of Coalition, Foreign Liaison and Contractor Personnel, 26 June 2003.
32 Stewart (2015).
33 Public Law 106-523—Nov. 22, 2000.
34 Cameron and Chetail (2013, p. 624).
35 Stewart and Gray (2014).
36 H.R. 4390 (108th): MEJA Clarification Act, 5/19/2004.
37 Stewart and Gray (2014).
38 Estate of Himoud Saed Atban, et al. v. Blackwater USA, et al., the U.S. District Court for the District of Columbia, 2007.
39 Nick Slatten was sentenced to life in prison, and the other three guards, Dustin Heard, Evan Liberty, and Paul Slough, to 30 years each.
40 Cameron and Chetail (2013, p. 625).
41 Pinto and Evans (2008, p. 23).
42 White (2016, p. 596).
43 Kirshner (2015, p. 19).
44 Ryngaert (2012, p. 59).
45 Rome Statute of the ICC, Art. 25 (4).
46 On individual criminal responsibility see: Van Sledregt (2004); Eser (2002).
47 Rome Statute of the ICC, Part 2, Article 5 (1).
48 Cameron and Chetail (2013, pp. 597–598).
49 Rome Statute of the ICC, Art. 25.
50 Rome Statute of the ICC, Art. 25 (1); (3).
51 Rome Statute of the ICC, Art. 25 (3) (a), (c).
52 According to Art. 16 of the Rome Statute, "no investigation or prosecution may be commenced or proceeded with under this Statute for a period of 12 months after the Security Council, in a resolution adopted under Chapter VII of the Charter of the United Nations, has requested the Court to that effect".
53 As part of the International Security Assistance Force.
54 See Rome Statute, Art. 98; see also the Status of Bilateral Immunity Agreements.
55 Cameron and Chetail (2013, p. 623).
56 Al Shemari et al. v. CACI et al.
57 Saleh et al. v. Titan.
58 See https://business-humanrights.org/en/abu-ghraib-lawsuits-against-caci-titan-now-1-3-0.
59 Ruggie 2011, Principle 6 State-Business Nexus; Commentary, p. 8.
60 Art. 43(2) of the Protocol Additional to the Geneva Conventions of 12 August 1949, and Relating to the Protection of Victims of International Armed Conflicts ('Additional Protocol I')
61 Guiding Principles, p. 8.
62 A/HRC/30/47, Art. 33 (a), p. 10.

63 See: https://business-humanrights.org/en/abu-ghraib-lawsuits-against-caci-titan-now-l-3-0.
64 Crowe and John (2017, pp. 16–44).
65 Cameron and Chetail (2013).
66 ILC "Report of the International Law Commission: Fifty-Third Session", Art. 1.
67 ILC "Report of the International Law Commission: Fifty-Third Session".
68 Singer (2003, p. 38).
69 ILC "Report of the International Law Commission: Fifty-Third Session", p. 94.
70 Liu (2015, p. 104).
71 A/HRC/32/39, p. 16.
72 White (2012, p. 29).
73 Ruggie 2011, Principle 12 The Corporate Responsibility to Respect Human Rights; Commentary, p. 12.
74 Ruggie (2011, p. 13).
75 The International Code of Conduct for Private Security Service Providers, Geneva Academy, August 2013, para. 14, p. 23.
76 United States Headquarters Department of the Army, *Contractors on the Battlefield, Field Manual*, paras 1–22.
77 Kees (2011, p. 206).
78 *Field Manual*, paras 1–25.
79 Bix (2012, p. 87).
80 Dickinson (2007, p. 218).
81 Dickinson (2007, p. 221).
82 Liu (2015, p. 204).
83 Liu (2015, p. 208).
84 Liu (2015, pp. 209–210).
85 Bix (2012, p. 87).
86 Dickinson (2007, p. 224).
87 Dickinson (2007, pp. 228–229).
88 Cutler (2017, pp. 259–261).
89 Cutler (2017, pp. 255–269).
90 Cutler (2017, p. 261).
91 These claims are explored in more detail in the section on PMC self-regulation.
92 Akande (2014, p. 251).
93 A/HRC/30/47, Art. 65, p. 17.
94 See UN Security Policy Manual.
95 See UN Guidelines on the Use of Armed Security Services from Private Security Companies.
96 White and MacLeod (2008, p. 976).
97 White and MacLeod (2008, p. 973).
98 White and MacLeod (2008, p. 975).
99 See *Chapter 3*.
100 See www.mdforum.ch/en/participants.
101 The Montreux Document, p. 31
102 The Montreux Document, p. 10; ICoC, p. 5.
103 Cockayne (2009, p. 406).
104 A/HRC/32/39, p. 11.
105 The Montreux Document, para. 7, p. 12.
106 These are (a) Incorporation of PMCs into state regular forces, (b) PMCs are under the direct command of the state, (c) PMCs are empowered (authorised by law), and (d) PMCs acting on the instructions of the state.
107 White (2012, p. 13).
108 The Montreux Document, p. 20, p. 24.
109 As discussed in *Chapters 2, 3*, and *4*.

110 Del Prado (2008, p. 444).
111 The Montreux Document, Section E. PMSCs and their personnel, paras 22–26, pp. 14–15.
112 Stewart (2014, p. 25).
113 The Montreux Document.
114 Introduced and discussed in Chapter 6.
115 On the criticism of the Montreux Document by the UN Working Group: White (2012, p. 17).
116 The Draft Convention 2009, Preamble, p. 3.
117 The Draft Convention 2009, Art. 2 Definitions, p. 7.
118 On suppression conventions and human rights, see: Boister (2002, p. 199).
119 Del Prado 2010, A/HRC/15/25 Art. 21 (5).
120 White (2012, p. 22).
121 Based on the analysis conducted in Chapters 2, 3, and 4.
122 Mercenarism and Private Military and Security Companies: An overview of the work carried out by the Working Group on the use of mercenaries as a means of violating human rights and impeding the exercise of the right of peoples to self-determination.
123 White (2012, p. 30).

References

A/HRC/30/47.

A/HRC/32/39.

A/HRC/RES/15/26.

Akande, D.: "International Organisations" in Evans, M. D. (ed.): *International Law: Fourth Edition*, OUP, Oxford, 2014.

Al Shemari et al. v. CACI et al.

Arnold, R. and Triffterer, O.: "Article 28. Responsibility of Commanders and other Superiors" in Triffterer, O. (ed.): *Commentary on the Rome Statute of the International Criminal Court*, 2nd edition, Hart, Munich, 2008.

Bix, B.: *Contract Law: Rules, Theory, and Context*, CUP, Cambridge, 2012.

Boister, N.: "Human Rights Protection in the Suppression Conventions", 2002, Vol. 2 (2), *Human Rights Law Review*, pp. 953–976.

Business and Human Rights Centre, Abu Ghraib lawsuits against CACI, Titan (now L-3), available at: https://business-humanrights.org/en/abu-ghraib-lawsuits-against-caci-titan-now-l-3-0.

Cameron, L. and Chetail, V.: *Private Military and Security Companies under Public International Law*, CUP, Cambridge, 2013.

Celebici Trial Chamber Judgement 2001.

Cockayne, J.: "Regulating Private Military and Security Companies: The Content, Negotiation, Weaknesses and Promise of the Montreux Document", 2009, Vol. 13 (3), *Journal of Conflict & Security Law*, pp. 401–428.

Crowe, J. and John, A.: "The Status of Private Military Security Companies in United Nations Peacekeeping Operations under the International Law of Armed Conflict", 2017, Vol. 18(1), *Melbourne Journal of International Law*, pp. 16–44.

Cutler, A. C. and Dietz, T. (eds.): *The Politics of Private Transnational Governance by Contract*, Routledge, London, 2017.

Del Prado, J. L. G.: "Private Military and Security Companies and the UN Working Group on the Use of Mercenaries", 2008, Vol. 13 (3), *Journal of Conflict & Security Law*, pp. 429–450.

Del Prado, J. L. G.: Report of the Working Group on the Use of Mercenaries as a means of Violating Human Rights and Impeding the Exercise of the Right of Peoples to Self-Determination, 2 July 2010, A/HRC/15/25 Art. 21 (5).

Dickinson, L.: "Contract as a Tool for Regulating Private Military Companies" in Chesterman, S. and Lehnard, C. (eds): *From Mercenaries to Market: The Rise and Regulation of Private Military Companies*, OUP, Oxford, 2007.

Draft International Convention on the Regulation, Oversight and Monitoring of Private Military and Security Companies, 13 July 2009.

Eser, A.: "Individual Criminal Responsibility" in Cassese, A., Gaeta, P. and Jones, J. (eds): *The Rome Statute of the International Criminal Court: A Commentary*, OUP, Oxford, 2002.

Estate of Himoud Saed Atban, et al. v. Blackwater USA, et al., the U.S. District Court for the District of Columbia, 2007.

Eurasia Daily Monitor 2018, Vol. 15 (144), available at: https://jamestown.org/program/russian-pmcs-in-yemen-kremlin-style-security-export-in-action/.

Federal Department of Foreign Affairs, Section for International Humanitarian Law, available at www.eda.admin.ch/psc.

Guiding Principles on Business and Human Rights. Implementing the United Nations "Protect, Respect and Remedy" Framework, UN Human Rights Office of the High Commissioner, New York and Geneva, 2011.

ILC "Report of the International Law Commission: Fifty-Third Session" (UNGA, 2001) A/56/10.

Isenberg, D.: "Private Military Companies in Iraq" in Chesterman, S. and Lehnard, C. (eds): *From Mercenaries to Market: The Rise and Regulation of Private Military Companies*, OUP, Oxford, 2007.

Kees, A.: "Regulation of Private Military Companies", 2011, Vol. 3 (1), *Goettingen Journal of International Law*, pp. 199–216.

Kirshner, J. A.: "A Call for the EU to Assume Jurisdiction over Extraterritorial Corporate Human Rights Abuses", 2015, Vol. 13 (1), *Northwestern Journal of International Human Rights*, pp. 1–26.

Kordic and Cerkez Trial Chamber Judgement 2001.

MEJA Clarification Act, 5/19/2004, H.R. 4390 (108th), available at: www.govtrack.us/congress/bills/108/hr4390/summary.

Liu, H.-Y.: *Law's Impunity: Responsibility and the Modern Private Military Company*, Hart Publishing, Oxford, 2015.

Mettraux, G.: *The Law of Command Responsibility*, OUP, Oxford, 2009.

Office of the Administrator of the Coalition Provisional Authority Baghdad, Iraq; Public Notice regarding the Status of Coalition, Foreign Liaison and Contractor Personnel, 26 June 2003.

Olasolo, H.: *The Criminal Responsibility of Senior Political and Military Leaders as Principals to International Crimes*, Hart, Oxford, 2009.

Pinto, A. and Evans, M.: *Corporate Criminal Liability*, 2nd edition, Thompson, Sweet & Maxwell, London, 2008.

Prosecutor v. Kunarac, Kovac and Vukovic, Trial Chamber Judgement, Case No. IT-96-23-T & IT-96-23/1-T.

Protocol Additional to the Geneva Conventions of 12 August 1949, and Relating to the Protection of Victims of International Armed Conflicts.

Public Law 106–523—Nov. 22, 2000.

Rome Statute of the International Criminal Court, available at: http://legal.un.org/icc/statute/99_corr/cstatute.htm.

Ruggie, J.: Report of the Special Representative of the Secretary-General on the Issue of Human Rights and Transnational Corporations and Other Business Enterprises, Guiding Principles for the Implementation of the United Nations "Protect, Respect and Remedy" Framework, 2011.

Ryngaert, C.: "Clarifying the Extraterritorial Application of the European Convention on Human Rights. *Al-Skeini and others v. United Kingdom* App No 55721/07 (ECtHR, 7 July 2011)", 2012, Vol. 28 (74), *Utrecht Journal of International and European Law*, pp. 57–60.

Saleh et al. v. Titan.

Semanza Trial Chamber 2003.

Simpson, G.: *Law, War and Crime: War Crimes Trials and the Reinvention of International Law*, Polity Press, Cambridge, 2007.

Singer, P.: *Corporate Warriors: The Rise of the Privatized Military Industry*, Cornell University Press, New York, 2003.

Stewart, J.: *Inside the Blackwater Trial*, Conference Paper Presented at the Institute for Global Law and Policy, Harvard Law School, June 2015.

Stewart, J. and Gray, S.: "The Blackwater Trial: Part 2 – Two Legal Issues" 27 October 2014, *Just Security*, available at: www.justsecurity.org/16807/blackwater-trial-part-2-legal-issues/.

Stewart, J. G.: "The Turn to Corporate Criminal Liability for International Crimes: Transcending the Alien Tort Statute", 2014, Vol. 47 (1), *New York University Journal of International Law and Politics*, pp. 121–206.

The Defence Post, available at: www.ecfr.eu/article/commentary_russias_hired_guns_in_africa; https://thedefensepost.com/2018/11/09/russia-neelov-wagner-expert-arrest-treason/.

The International Code of Conduct for Private Security Service Providers, Geneva Academy, August 2013, available at: www.geneva-academy.ch/docs/publications/briefing4_web_final.pdf.

The Montreux Document on Private Military and Security Companies, 17 September 2008, available at www.eda.admin.ch/eda/en/home/topics/intla/humlaw/pse/psechi.html.

The OAU Convention Called for States to Introduce Laws Forbidding their Nationals from Engaging in Mercenary Activities. OAU Convention for the Elimination of Mercenaries in Africa, O.A.U. Doc. CM/433/Rev. L., 1972.

The Status of Bilateral Immunity Agreements, available at: www.iccnow.org/documents/CICCFS_BIAstatus_current.pdf.

UN Guidelines on the Use of Armed Security Services from Private Security Companies, available at: www.ohchr.org/Documents/Issues/Mercenaries/WG/StudyPMSC/GudielinesAnnexBModelContract.pdf.

UN Security Policy Manual, available at: www.ohchr.org/Documents/Issues/Mercenaries/WG/StudyPMSC/UNSecurityPolicyManual.pdf.

United States Headquarters Department of the Army, *Contractors on the Battlefield, Field Manual*.

Van Sledregt, E.: "The Criminal Responsibility of Individuals for Violations of International Humanitarian Law", 2004, Vol. 2 (3), *Journal of International Criminal Justice*, pp. 932–936.

White, N.: "Regulatory Initiatives at the International Level" in Bakker, C. and Sossai, M. (eds): *Multilevel Regulation of Military and Security Contractors: The Interplay between International, European, and Domestic Norms*, Hart Publishing, Oxford, 2012.

White, N. and MacLeod, S.: "EU Operations and Private Military Contractors: Issues of Corporate and Institutional Responsibility", 2008, Vol. 19 (5), *European Journal of International Law*, pp. 965–988.

White. N. D.: "Regulation of the Private Military and Security Sector: Is the UK Fulfilling its Human Rights Duties?", 2016, Vol. 16 (3), *Human Rights Law Review*, pp. 585–599. www.mdforum.ch/en/participants.

6 The role of international regulation and the growing power and legitimacy of companies

The question of regulation of private military forces remains critical regardless of the century. The move from mercenaries to standing armies has been observed during Absolutism with the purpose of establishing control over mercenaries and private armies.[1] Curiously, as revealed by historical typologies, private force found a way to exist to a lesser or greater extent in different types of governance. Using different constructs, such as, for instance, the colonial army of an outsourced governance of the East India Company, or groups of mercenaries operating covertly during the Cold War, the private segment of security had always formed a part of the landscape. Today, neoliberal policies reintroduced private forces to the security landscape. This change in governance model created a market for force that runs parallel to the established system of public security regulated by states and the international humanitarian law. It is characterised by the interdependent relationship of contracts (as seen in feudalism) and fragmentation (loosely resembling the fragmented security model of condottieri in Italian city-republics). Yet, what is new about twenty-first-century private military companies is that they found its home within the corporate structures of legitimately registered companies, marking a strict separation from dubious mercenaries.

As the states and international organisations become more reliant on the private security sector for provision of security, regulations and norms evolve recognising the need for these companies to respect human rights and introduce certain standards into their conduct. Under current international law, corporate liability of private military companies (PMCs) predominantly exists in the form of voluntary, self-regulatory industry standards, such as the International Code of Conduct (ICoC), the Montreux Document, or the Human Rights driven initiatives, such as the UN guidelines aimed at implementing the corporate responsibility to respect human rights. Broadly characterised as the 'responsibilisation' approach, these voluntary norms and standards are created by the industry to invoke corporate social responsibility (CSR).[2] At the other end of the spectrum of international tools for PMC regulation, the attempts to introduce a legally binding UN Draft Convention, actively promoted by the Human Rights regime, signal a competing normative approach which aims to impose stricter controls within the current international security landscape.

This chapter explores existing and emerging international regulatory tools and mechanisms that address PMCs as corporations. It further evaluates the effectiveness of industry self-regulation, contemplating the narrative it creates for the legitimacy of international corporations in the private military sector.

The Human Rights regime: UN Guiding Principles, UN Resolution 26/9, UN Draft Convention

The Human Rights regime has arguably been the most active area of IL in developing a range of initiatives to target PMC activity and help address corporate impunity. Although the work of the Human Rights Council (HRC) and various working groups has been extensive and multifaceted, no legally binding mechanisms have been established to date.

In 2011, the UN Guiding Principles on Business and Human Rights were approved, following the HRC endorsement of the Guiding Principles in resolution 17/4. Given the focus on corporate responsibility, I examine the second pillar of the Guiding Principles, namely "the role of business enterprises as specialized organs of society performing specialized functions, required to comply with all applicable laws and to respect human rights".[3]

The Guiding Principles address the responsibilities of states and corporations and require them to respect, protect, and comply with all applicable laws to uphold human rights. They further acknowledge corporate responsibility to respect human rights and stress that it exists independently of a state's responsibility to fulfil their human rights duties, and, most importantly, does not diminish those duties.[4] They also highlight the lack of clarity in corporate law regarding the human rights requirements for companies: "laws and policies in this area should provide sufficient guidance to enable enterprises to respect human rights, with due regard to the role of existing governance structures such as corporate boards".[5] Reference to the 'governance structures' resonates with the overall argument echoed throughout this monograph, concerned with developing a regulation that would be more aware and adaptable to the changing forms of power and legitimacy not only amongst states but also corporations. Having acknowledged that the risk of human rights violations is higher in areas affected by conflict, the guidelines propose an increased state presence in the form of identifying and monitoring the risks; denying access to public support and services to a business that is found to have violated human rights; and ensuring adequate liability mechanisms are in place.[6]

Nevertheless, the premise of the Guiding Principles does not build a strong foundation for corporate liability. The guidelines do not mention an adequate vetting process that ought to be undertaken by the state prior to engaging a PMC, nor do they stipulate for human rights provisions to be explicitly incorporated into the terms of the contract. The Principles misleadingly point to the provisions of the Rome Statute of the International Criminal Court (ICC) when discussing the sources of corporate criminal liability for companies, while in fact referring to national jurisdictions.[7] As a response to the shortcomings of the Guiding Principles, the HRC established an "open-ended intergovernmental working group [IGWG] on transnational corporations and other business enterprises with respect to human rights".[8] The IGWG was launched to consider the possibility of developing an international regulatory framework, including the option of drafting a legally binding instrument on the regulation, monitoring, and oversight of private military and security companies.[9] The resolution instructs the IGWG to create a legally binding international instrument to increase corporate accountability and ensure access to remedy for victims of business-related human rights abuse. Although the resolution was passed, out of the five permanent UN member states only China and Russia were in favour its adoption. A number of delegations expressed their opinion that the Guiding Principles,

> did not get to the core of the discussion on maximum protection of human rights and access to remedies, and that a complementary international instrument was needed in order to strengthen national capabilities to ensure human rights protection in the domestic sphere.[10]

Furthermore, there was a lack of consensus as to what the main focus of the IGWG should be: the implementation of the legally binding instrument or the Guiding Principles. While the overall strategy is yet to be defined, its current form appears to have some notable gaps. The treaty is limited to gross violations, therefore not covering other types of corporate human rights abuses. With its main focus on transnational corporations, the resolution does not apply to national companies, and currently does not provide a definition of what exactly is considered a transnational organisation.[11] It is also currently not clear whether the instrument would define available remedies and access to those remedies if states fail to act on obligations, or if it would focus on establishing corporate liability, or both.[12] Importantly, the special nature of PMCs was called out by a group of NGOs during the session. Referring to corporate impunity, they argued that states and international organisations should not extend any kind of immunity to PMCs that would allow them to escape corporate liability or limit access to remedy for victims.[13] This point is particularly relevant in the light of a fundamental shift in the balance of power between corporations and states, driven in particular by the rise of new technologies that facilitate cross-border management of companies and deregulation across multiple sectors.[14]

Most recently, in September 2017, the HRC decided to establish a designated open-ended IGWG with a mandate to

> elaborate the content of an international regulatory framework, without prejudging the nature thereof, to protect human rights and ensure accountability for violations and abuses relating to the activities of private military and security companies, to be informed by the discussion document on elements for an international regulatory framework on the regulation, monitoring and oversight of the activities of private military and security companies.[15]

Although the first session of the IGWG under the new mandate was originally scheduled for 28 May to 1 June 2018, it was subsequently postponed and remains to be determined. The UN Draft Convention on Private Military and Security Companies (Draft Convention) will serve as a basis for the IGWG work on developing a regulatory framework. While briefly mentioned in the previous chapter with the reference to state responsibility, the relevance and applicability of the Draft Convention to PMCs as corporations needs to be considered in more detail.

UN Draft Convention

Originally drafted by the working group (WG) on mercenaries,[16] and now under the auspices of the Open-Ended, Intergovernmental Working Group, the Draft Convention was intended to be a binding legal mechanism, applicable to all states that are party to the treaty. Although an earlier draft of the document explicitly addressed Private Military and Security Companies (PMSCs) as corporations, these provisions have been removed, stipulating exclusively state obligations.[17] Even though Article 20 includes provisions covering corporate liability, it does not specify direct liability provisions for PMCs. Instead, it requires each state party to implement national legislation that allows the affected party to make a complaint.[18] Whether criminal, civil, or administrative,[19] the liability is to be determined at state discretion and in line with state party domestic legal principles.[20] While this provision clearly shows that the Draft Convention supports criminal corporate responsibility in principle, the lack of uniformity and reliance on domestic law is likely to create a disparate practice. This could also lead to PMCs choosing to register their company in home states that have weak or no corporate liability laws in order to continue operating in a legal vacuum. These provisions do not negate contractor individual criminal liability for committing the offences in questions.[21] Finally,

> Each State Party shall, in particular, ensure that legal persons held liable in accordance with this article are subject to effective, proportionate and dissuasive criminal or non-criminal sanctions, including fines, economic sanctions, prohibitions of further employment, obligation to provide restitution and/or compensation to the victims.[22]

This provision bears great relevance and importance, as it actually mentions tangible consequences that companies could be facing if found guilty of an offence. These are adequate, measurable, and applicable to corporations in the same way that criminal charges are applicable to individuals. This provision goes beyond a mere financial penalty and could arguably be a proportionate punishment for human rights violations. However, by instructing each state party to assume accountability for corporations and adequate jurisdiction over their actions, the Draft Convention inadvertently distances itself from identifying and placing responsibility directly on the companies. According to Nigel White, by not addressing PMCs, the Draft Convention reveals the weaknesses of IL.[23] The fact that it does not recognise companies as independent bearers of responsibility could add another barrier to the formation of international corporate liability.

Article 20 exactly mirrors the wording of Article 10 of the UN Convention against Transnational Organized Crime,[24] issued in 2004. Reference to legal persons also features in Article 31 on Prevention, as it instructs all state parties to take necessary measures to "reduce existing or future opportunities for organized criminal groups to participate in lawful markets with the proceeds of crime, through appropriate legislative, administrative or other measures".[25] Such prevention measures would include establishing public records on companies that committed an offence and temporary disqualification of company directors, also to be included in the public record.[26] Public shaming of this kind could in fact serve as an effective regulatory mechanism, potentially preventing PMCs from misconduct. As profit-driven companies, PMCs have to manage their reputational risk, as in an overflowed security market bad press can cost PMCs their business. Nonetheless, the above argument applies, and all the above-mentioned enforcement mechanisms first depend on states ratifying the treaty and, second, are subject to domestic jurisdiction concerning legal entities.

The Draft Convention remains at an early stage of its formulation, as no accord has been reached in its regard amongst the UN intergovernmental working group.[27] To envision the difficulties of obtaining consensus on the Draft Convention, it is enough to recall that, to date, only thirty-five states have ratified the 1989 International Convention against the Recruitment, Use, Financing and Training of Mercenaries, which would be a logical first step and a sign of endorsement of the WG's strategy on the part of the states. In practice, the Draft Convention is diametrically opposed to the ICoC self-regulating non-binding principles. Indeed, on the international level (or, as Claire Cutler puts it, transnational),[28] the most prominent PMC regulation emerges from the industry itself.

To sum up, the work of the UN Human Rights Council has been extensive and elaborate. The IGWG intelligently identified the gaps in corporate liability and will spearhead the efforts towards a consensus on the possible Draft Convention or an alternative binding instrument. The intensity and breadth of HRC activity supports the Special Rapporteur's claim that "the extraterritorial applicability of human rights law, and specifically human rights treaties, is crucial to the regulation of the sector".[29] However, according to James Stewart, basic notions of retributive justice stipulate that the Business and Human Rights movements cannot erase past offences "out of a laudable commitment to future compliance".[30] In other words, a former serial murderer cannot avoid responsibility by discontinuing their criminal conduct and claiming compliance. Nor should this method be extended to corporations. Equally, the liability gap that fosters the corporate veil cannot currently be mitigated by Human Rights Law. Meanwhile, the imbalance created by the horizontal nature of the contracts and states' reliance on PMCs for provision of security rationalises the self-regulation of the private security industry.

Industry-focused regulation: the ICoC, the Montreux Document and other industry bodies

Although the norms of corporate responsibility vary across states and industries, the human rights regime has been urging corporations to respect human rights in their conduct.[31] Regulating companies on human rights grounds commenced as early as the mid-1990s. Established in 1999, the UN Global Compact (GC) is a network of corporate and civil society participants, all of whom work with the freestanding Global Compact Office and a variety of UN agencies.[32] The GC was formed as a result of public scrutiny relating to Nike's use of child labour and general poor employment conditions, in order to promote the principles of human rights across businesses.[33] The military, security, and defence sectors appear to be omitted from categories of participating companies.[34]

The OECD's Guidelines for Multinational Enterprises are an instrument of Corporate Social Responsibility and consist of recommendations regarding social and environmental standards. The Guidelines are voluntary in nature and limited in scope.[35] The standards apply to multinational enterprises (MNEs) based in OECD states, which in turn agree to promote observance of the Guidelines among MNEs and 'good practice' in the spheres of human rights, labour standards, and the environment.[36]

A recent development by the Geneva Centre for the Democratic Control of Armed Forces (DCAF) and the International Committee of the Red Cross (ICRC) is the Toolkit for Addressing Security and Human Rights Challenges in Complex Environments.[37] The Toolkit is a guidance document which addresses real-life security and human rights challenges identified through engagement with many stakeholders. For each listed "Challenge", the Toolkit outlines good practice and recommendations, offering practical tools such as checklists, templates, and case studies.[38]

Most prominent and widely accepted amongst industry standards is the International Code of Conduct for Private Security Service Providers (ICoC). The ICoC is an international, industry-driven initiative that originated from a 2005 Swiss Federal Council report on private military and security companies that "recommended pursuing further dialogue and action in this area".[39] While based on the Montreux Process, its purpose and content are aimed at businesses, rather than states. It is also administered by the industry, making it a self-regulatory body. The objective of the ICoC is to set out a range of industry-developed principles and standards to guide PMCs on matters of international human rights and humanitarian law:

> Signatory Companies will exercise due diligence to ensure compliance with the law and with the principles contained in this Code, and will respect the human rights of persons they come into contact with, including, the rights to freedom of expression, association, and peaceful assembly and against arbitrary or unlawful interference with privacy or deprivation of property.[40]

Furthermore, the Code stipulates that signatory companies must comply with the outlined grievances procedures,[41] as well as ensure that they have "sufficient financial capacity in place at all times to meet reasonably anticipated commercial liabilities for damages to any person in respect of personal injury, death or damage to property".[42] The issue arising from this liability clause is the implication that human rights violations can be mitigated or punished through a financial settlement. In other words, if a company is found to have committed a human rights offence that under the ICoC is considered inadmissible, this company would have to undergo a self-imposed grievance procedure, and, as a result, establish the amount of a 'reasonable' financial damage, while not being legally bound to do so.

While the Code states that "the procedures must allow complaints to be brought by personnel or third parties",[43] the only practical repercussions against violations of the Code is aimed at PMC personnel and could result in dismissal.[44] The ICoC contains provisions concerning PMC respect for human rights and mandates that "Signatory Companies will adhere to the Code whether or not the Code is included in a contractual agreement with a Client".[45] However, another conflict of regulation arises. According to contract law, the contracting party is obliged to follow only those provisions that are explicitly listed in the contract. In other words, if the human rights provisions are not stated in the contract, the client cannot expect them to be adhered to.[46]

The concluding paragraph in the liability section reinforces this point, stating that the provisions listed in the Code cannot replace or override any contractual requirements or specific Company policies or procedures concerning wrongdoings.[47] This provision presents a moot point, as it highlights the obvious fact of a legally binding contract between a PMC and its client prevailing over a set of voluntary norms. Since the drafting of the ICoC, certain states[48] as well as the UN agencies[49] referenced the ICoC adherence as one of the obligatory provisions in contracts with PMSCs. However, if the voluntary Code is to be adhered to, the only binding way of ensuring its acceptance of the parties, is for it to be consistently incorporated into contracts.[50]

The language used in the ICoC is extremely important as it inflates the legal significance of the document. The ICoC creates a false sense of legitimacy by referencing IHL and including extracts from the Rome Statute on the definition of war crimes.[51] Despite its legitimising framework and in the absence of legally binding instruments to invoke corporate responsibility, the ICoC currently lists over 700 companies, including the above-mentioned DynCorp and Academi (former Blackwater).[52]

In the efforts to further and solidify a self-proclaimed status of initiator of a process towards better governance, compliance, and accountability of PSCs, the ICoC adopted Articles of Association[53] which led to creation of the International Code of Conduct Association (ICoCA).[54] A Swiss non-profit association, the ICoCA was established in September 2013. Intended to be representative of the private security industry,[55] the ICoCA currently lists ninety-two companies, thirty civil society organisations, and nine states[56] with all members publicly identified on the ICoC Association website.[57]

While the aim of this external governance and oversight mechanism was to improve accountability in the sector and provide a forum for third party complaints, currently the Association does not have the necessary resources to fulfil this opportunity.[58] It has, nevertheless been issuing certification to participating PMSCs, with companies such as Academi (former Blackwater), Triple Canopy (awarded contracts that were previously under Blackwater USA in Iraq,[59] currently under Academi consortium), and Olive Group (currently under Academi consortium[60]) receiving ICoCA's stamp of approval. In fact, the ICoCA certification is reinforced by the International Organization for Standardization (ISO) as it incorporates the existing ISO standards relating to private security. Both published in 2015, ISO 18788 Management System for Private Security Operations[61] and ISO 28007 Private Maritime Security Certification,[62] the guidelines provide PMCs and their clients with a business and risk management framework ensuring compliance with law, human rights, and relevant voluntary regulatory measures ISO is party to. ISO standards have earned a strong and healthy reputation across a number of industries, from finance to manufacturing.[63] Requiring PMCs to obtain ISO certification before they can contract out their services, could replace the vague vetting process of the UN Guiding Principles and help standardisation across the sector. Yet, although incorporating ISO standards into the ICoC governance could form a solid complementary foundation for measures of quality, the industry alone is not robust enough to regulate private military providers and invoke corporate responsibility.

In analysing the future of PMC impunity, scholars like Liu and White are concerned with the effectiveness of self-regulation, suggesting that the industry would create the appearance of regulation, and could even prevent other, more robust, enforcement mechanisms from emerging in the realm. While Liu acknowledges that self-regulation could lead to greater compliance to industry standards, he notes that its extralegal nature leaves the question of PMC accountability unresolved. Indeed, the significance of industry self-regulation, in particular, the ICoC and the Association should not be underestimated as it points to a number of pertinent conclusions. First, it has potential for streamlining regulatory standards and by incorporating ISO standards and providing certification on that basis. Furthermore, the challenges of respecting human rights and compensating victims could, to an extent, be addressed by including the ICoC in the service contracts, although the enforcement mechanism remains unclear. Second, industry self-regulation establishes itself as an internationally recognised regulatory body as national governments and international organisations reinforce its authority. This, in turn, contributes to a growing legitimacy of private security industry, by reinforcing a professional industry association, whereby the industry and PMC-welcoming states are operating a governance framework with a DCAF seal of approval and with no overarching oversight or any legally binding accountability mechanisms in place.

Corporation as a form of governance

This leads me to another important issue that the industry self-regulation raises in the context of a changing governance. Similar to the exercise of identifying different historic types of governance, the use of politically agnostic concepts of power and legitimacy[64] allows us to see beyond the traditional (Westphalian) association of governance with public governmental authorities. It furthermore enables us to recognise a contemporary form of governance, transpiring parallel to that of a neoliberal state; a type of 'governance without government'[65] whereby corporations command transnational relations, wielding power (political, economic, military) and making claims to legitimacy through self-regulation and the framework of CSR.

In 1522, Chief Justice Fineux referred to the Parliament of King, Lords, and Commons as a 'corporation by the common law'. For Fineux, the essence of corporateness was, thus, encapsulated in the establishment and permanent existence of an organised group, forming 'the body of members'.[66] Despite possessing legal personality, contemporary corporations are not recognised as actors under international law in the same way states or individuals are.

Nevertheless, since the 1980s states have been transferring functions and services to the private sector through privatisation and deregulation. The companies that have subsequently taken on the functions formerly owned by states have also inadvertently acquired a form of governance. As echoed in Cutler, Singer, and Avant, outsourcing creates such a form of governance (or sovereignty) whereby power is shared between the public and the private sphere and the exact balance of authority between the two is undefined or fluctuating.[67] In the case of PMCs, we can trace the shift in governance from the state to a corporation, whereby PMCs perform the bureaucratic functions of logistics, organising security operations, training and, ultimately, killing.

With the expansion of authority of private sectors and private institutions, grew the importance and prominence of private sources of law.[68] Along with the military power that these companies possess, PMCs are also making claims to a form of legitimacy by locating themselves within the corporate framework and associating with regulatory mechanisms of corporate social responsibility. As argued by Edwin Mujih[69] and Saleem Sheikh,[70] the lack of an authoritative definition of the concept of CSR poses a problem to understanding its legal application. CSR can broadly be understood as a corporation's responsibility to be socially aware, ensuring plausible working standards for its employees and their families,[71] ethical conduct towards society and the company's stakeholders[72] beyond the maximisation of profit, and basic regulatory standards with the purpose of making a positive contribution to the society.[73] What CSR implies in the context of my argument and beyond the mere need for punishing corporate misconduct is that companies have established such an extent of power and governing authority that, just like states and international actors, they ought to carry a responsibility equivalent to their status and the scope of their activity.[74]

The unhelpful effects of self-regulatory voluntary bodies become apparent as they create a false sense of legitimacy and regulation. By applying the concepts of power and legitimacy, industry self-regulation can be viewed not only as a step towards the commodification of security to fit the framework of the free market, but also as an attempt by PMCs to extend their authority without adequate oversight in place.

Conclusion

The non-binding 'responsibilisation' approach currently dominates the stage of PMC regulation while the development of a legally binding instrument has been protracted if not largely futile. Yet, the coexistence of these competing regulatory mechanisms is problematic as it puts policy choice at a crossroad. The issue may not be immediate, as each address a different audience, with the Draft Convention aimed at states, and the ICoC at the industry. However, in the long term the opposing approaches to PMC regulation are likely to create a divide and prevent the development of coherent norms and standards internationally. The polarisation of regulatory models is challenging and is unlikely to produce a coherent solution for PMC regulation. According to White, "states connected to the industry are more likely to stick with and entrench the Montreux Process, and those opposed to PMCs as a modern form of mercenarism are more likely to support the Draft Convention process".[75] Same applies to the companies themselves, so, unless a domestic legal system has reach over unlawful PMC activity, there is no legally binding way to invoke corporate liability. The corporate status of PMCs presents both constrains and opportunities for establishing criminal responsibility for PMCs. Albeit hamstrung by the transnational dimension of PMC activity and by the nonexistence of the norm for international criminal responsibility, PMC newly acquired legal personality offers a whole new body of law that can be explored to better understand existing and potential future mechanisms for PMC regulation.

Notes

1 See Chapter 2.
2 Accounts that consider the relationship between CSR and law: Segerlund (2010); Zerk (2006); McBarnet (2009); Olufemi (2011).
3 Guiding Principles, p. 1; A/HRC/17/31.
4 Ruggie (2011, p. 12).
5 Guiding Principles, p. 5.
6 Guiding Principles, pp. 8–9.
7 Guiding Principles, pp. 25–26.
8 Established at the 26th HRC session in June 2014, by adopting resolution 26/9, A/HRC/RES/26/9, p. 2.
9 A/HRC/32/39, p. 10.
10 A/HRC/31/50, p. 7.
11 A/HRC/31/50, p. 5, p. 12.
12 This concern was also raised during the session's panel on state obligations; Panel V. Obligations of States to guarantee the respect for human rights by transnational corporations and other business enterprises, including extraterritorial obligation, A/HRC/31/50, pp. 13–15.
13 A/HRC/31/50, p. 19b.

14 A/HRC/31/50, p. 11.
15 UN HRC
16 The Working Group on the use of mercenaries as a means of violating human rights and impeding the exercise of the right of peoples to self-determination.
17 Cutler and Law(2017, p. 259); White (2011, pp. 133–151).
18 Draft Convention, Article 20 (1) Liability of legal persons and entities.
19 Or a combination of all three.
20 Draft Convention, Article 20 (2).
21 Draft Convention, Article 20 (3).
22 Draft Convention, Article 20 (4).
23 White (2011, p. 29).
24 United Nations Convention against Transnational Organized Crime and the Protocols thereto, 2004
25 United Nations Convention against Transnational Organized Crime, Article 31 (2).
26 UN Convention against Transnational Organized Crime, Article 31 (2)(d)(i)–(iii).
27 A/HRC/30/47, Art. 39, p. 11.
28 Cutler (2017, p. 259).
29 A/HRC/32/39, p. 19.
30 Stewart (2014, pp. 66–67).
31 Pillay (2009, pp. 63–68).
32 White and MacLeod (2008, p. 978); see UN Global Compact and UN Economic and Social Council.
33 UN Global Compact.
34 White and MacLeod (2008, p. 980).
35 White and MacLeod (2008, p. 978).
36 OECD, *Guidelines for Multinational Enterprises*, Revision 2000, note 62, I(1) and II(1) and (2).
37 Addressing Security and Human Rights Challenges in Complex Environments Toolkit, Third Edition, DCAF and ICRC, June 2016.
38 See section 3 on "Working with Private Security Providers".
39 ICoC, p. 5.
40 ICoC, para. 21, pp. 25–26.
41 ICoC, 66–68, pp. 51–53.
42 ICoC, para. 69, p. 53.
43 ICoC, para. 66, p. 51.
44 ICoC, para. 67 (f), p. 52.
45 ICoC, para. 19.
46 Liu (2015, p. 199).
47 ICoC, para. 68, p. 53.
48 US State Department, 2013 "State Department to Incorporate International Code of Conduct into Worldwide Protective Services Contracts".
49 UN Department for Safety and Security 2012 Guidelines on the Use of Armed Security Services from Private Security Companies.
50 Cutler (2017, p. 267).
51 ICoC, pp. 27–31.
52 708 as of 1 October 2013, see: https://business-humanrights.org/en/conflict-peace/special-initiatives/initatives-on-private-military-security-companies/international-code-of-conduct-for-private-security-service-providers-icoc-a-process-aimed-at.
53 See www.icoca.ch/en/articles_of_association
54 See www.icoca.ch/en/history
55 Cutler (2017, p. 265).
56 These include Australia, Canada, Norway, Sweden, Switzerland, the UK, and the US.
57 See www.icoca.ch/en/membership
58 A/HRC/32/39, p. 11.

59 See www.mercenaryjobs.org/triple-canopy-security-jobs.html
60 See www.academi.com/pages/about-us
61 See www.iso.org/iso/home/store/catalogue_tc/catalogue_detail.htm?csnumber=63380
62 See www.iso.org/standard/63166.html
63 Bowen (2000, pp. 26–31).
64 A method developed throughout this monograph, see Chapters 2, 3 and 4.
65 See Rosenau and Czempiel (1992).
66 Maitland (1900, p. 8).
67 See Avant (2004; 2005); Singer (2004); Cutler (2017).
68 Cutler and Dietz (2017); Cutler (2003).
69 Mujih (2012, pp. 23–24).
70 Sheikh (1996, pp. 14–15).
71 Regelbrugge (1999, p. 32).
72 Watts and Holme (1999, p. 3).
73 Khan (1997, p. 628); Slaughter (1997, p. 321).
74 Drawing on the concepts of power and legitimacy as per the historical chapters of the thesis.
75 White (2011, p. 150).

References

A/HRC/30/47.

A/HRC/31/50.

A/HRC/32/39.

A/HRC/32/39.

A/HRC/32/39.

A/HRC/RES/26/9.

Addressing Security and Human Rights Challenges in Complex Environments Toolkit, Third Edition, DCAF and ICRC, June 2016, available at: www.securityhumanrightshub.org/content/toolkit.

Avant, D.: *The Market for Force: The Consequences of Privatising Security*, CUP, Cambridge, 2005

Avant, D.: "The Privatisation of Security and Change in the Control of Force", 2004, Vol. 5 (2), *International Studies Perspectives*, pp. 153–157.

Bowen, R. D.: "ISO 9000 is the New 'Gold Standard' for Banking" June, 2000, *ISO News*, pp. 26–31.

Business and Human Rights, available at: https://business-humanrights.org/en/conflict-peace/special-initiatives/initatives-on-private-military-security-companies/international-code-of-conduct-for-private-security-service-providers-icoc-a-process-aimed-at.

Cutler, A. C.: *Private Power and Global Authority: Transnational Merchant Law in the Global Political Economy*, CUP, Cambridge, 2003.

Cutler, A. C. and Dietz, T. (eds.): *The Politics of Private Transnational Governance by Contract*, Routlegde, London, 2017.

Cutler, A. C. and Law, S.: "Regulating Private Military Security Companies by Contract. Between Anarchy and Hierarchy?" in Cutler, A. C. and Dietz, T. (eds.) *The Politics of Private Transnational Governance by Contract*, Routledge, London, 2017.

Draft Convention, Article 20 (1) Liability of legal persons and entities.

Guiding Principles, *supra*, p. 1; A/HRC/17/31.

www.mercenaryjobs.org/triple-canopy-security-jobs.html.

www.academi.com/pages/about-us.

www.icoca.ch/en/articles_of_association.
www.icoca.ch/en/history.
www.icoca.ch/en/membership.
www.iso.org/standard/63166.html.

International Organisation for Standardisation, available at: www.iso.org/iso/home/store/catalogue_tc/catalogue_detail.htm?csnumber=63380.

Khan, F.: "Pandora's Box: Managerial Discretion and the Problem of Corporate Philanthropy", 1997, Vol. 44 (3), *UCLA Law Review*, pp. 579–676.

Liu, H.-Y.: *Law's Impunity: Responsibility and the Modern Private Military Company*, Hart Publishing, Oxford, 2015.

Maitland, F.: "The Corporation Sole", 1900, Vol. 16, *Law Quarterly Review*, pp. 335–354.

McBarnet, D., Voiculescu, A. and Campbell, T.: *The New Corporate Accountability: Corporate Social Responsibility and the Law*, CUP, Cambridge, 2009.

Mujih, E. C.: *Regulating Multinationals in Developing Countries: A Conceptual and Legal Framework for Corporate Social Responsibility*, Routledge, Abingdon, 2012.

OECD, *Guidelines for Multinational Enterprises*, Revision 2000, note 62, I(1) and II(1) and (2).

Olufemi, A. (ed.): *Corporate Social Responsibility, Human Rights and the Law*, Routledge, Abingdon, 2011.

Pillay, N.: "The Corporate Responsibility to Respect: a Human Rights Milestone", *International Labour and Social Policy Review*, Geneva, 2009.

Regelbrugge, L. (ed.): *Promoting Corporate Citizenship: Opportunities for Business and Civil Society Engagement*, Kumarian Press, Lynne Rienner Publishers, 2000.1999.

Rosenau, J. and Czempiel, E. O. (eds): *Governance without Government. Order and Change in World Politics*, CUP, Cambridge, 1992.

Ruggie, J.: Report of the Special Representative of the Secretary-General on the Issue of Human Rights and Transnational Corporations and Other Business Enterprises, Guiding Principles for the Implementation of the United Nations "Protect, Respect and Remedy" Framework, 2011.

Segerlund, L.: *Making Corporate Social Responsibility a Global Concern: Norm Construction in a Globalised World*, Ashgate, Surrey, 2010.

Sheikh, S.: *Corporate Social Responsibility Law and Practice*, Cavendish Publishing, London, 1996.

Singer, P. W.: *Corporate Warriors: The Rise of the Privatized Military Industry*, Cornell University Press, 2004.

Slaughter, C.: "Corporate Social Responsibility: A New Perspective", 1997, Vol. 18 (10), *The Company Lawyer*, pp. 313–329.

Stewart, J. G.: "The Turn to Corporate Criminal Liability for International Crimes: Transcending the Alien Tort Statute", 2014, Vol. 47 (1), *New York University Journal of International Law and Politics*, pp. 121–206.

The International Code of Conduct for Private Security Service Providers, Geneva Academy, August 2013, available at: www.geneva-academy.ch/docs/publications/briefing4_web_final.pdf.

United Nations Convention against Transnational Organized Crime and the Protocols thereto, 2004, available at: www.unodc.org/documents/middleeastandnorthafrica/organised-crime/UNITED_NATIONS_CONVENTION_AGAINST_TRANSNATIONAL_ORGANIZED_CRIME_AND_THE_PROTOCOLS_THERETO.pdf.

UN Department for Safety and Security 2012 Guidelines on the Use of Armed Security Services from Private Security Companies, available at: www.ohchr.org/Documents/Issues/Mercenaries/WG/StudyPMSC/GudielinesAnnexBModelContract.pdf.

UN Economic and Social Council: Norms on the Responsibilities of Transnational Corporations and Other Business Enterprises with Regard to Human Rights, UN Doc. E/CN.4/Sub.2/2003/12/Rev.2 of 26 Aug. 2003.

UN HRC, available at: www.ohchr.org/en/hrbodies/hrc/wgmilitary/pages/oeiwgmilitaryindex.aspx

United Nations Global Compact, available at: www.unglobalcompact.org/AboutTheGC/TheTenPrinciples/index.htmlwww.unglobalcompact.org/AboutTheGC/TheTenPrinciples/index.html.

US State Department: "State Department to Incorporate International Code of Conduct into Worldwide Protective Services Contracts", 2013, available at: https://2009-2017.state.gov/r/pa/prs/ps/2013/08/213212.htm

Watts, P. and Holme, L.: *Meeting Social Expectations: Corporate Social Responsibility*, World Business Council for Sustainable Development, Geneva, 1999.

White, N. and MacLeod, S.: "EU Operations and Private Military Contractors: Issues of Corporate and Institutional Responsibility", 2008, Vol. 19 (5), *European Journal of International Law*, pp. 965–988.

White, N. D.: "The Privatisation of Military and Security Functions and Human Rights: Comments on the UN Working Group's Draft Convention", 2011, Vol. 11 (1), *Human Rights Law Review*, pp. 133–151.

Zerk, J.: *Multinationals and Corporate Social Responsibility: Limitations and Opportunities in International Law*, CUP, Cambridge, 2006.

7 Limitations and opportunities arising from the corporate status of PMCs

Domestic and transnational procedure for invoking corporate responsibility

There are a number of regulatory bodies that make provisions for private military company (PMC) regulation; some are international, some domestic, some binding, and others self-regulating and voluntary. The outcome of such an active regulatory response concerning private military conduct is a complex network of binding and voluntary provisions that all claim to regulate the private military space. What complicates this picture further is the domestic jurisdiction enacted by the corporate status of PMCs, therefore introducing company law, contract law, and tort law into the mix.

There exist domestic and transnational avenues for invoking criminal and social corporate liability. However, each mechanism is not without doctrinal or territorial limitations, thus obstructing access to an effective corporate criminal procedure. These challenges are also epitomised through the disparity of PMC and mercenary-specific provisions in a number of domestic legal systems. Nevertheless, a selection of case studies where PMCs were sued as companies, rather than as individual contractors and an evolving precedent of CACI International can be found in tort law.

This chapter continues to examine the bodies of law that attempt to regulate PMCs as corporations, and the ways in which they invoke corporate responsibility through domestic and transnational legal procedure. The importance of this analysis lies in the problem posed by PMCs' corporate legal status, coupled with the voluntary nature of existing international regulation and the absence of strong international criminal accountability mechanisms applicable to legal persons. With state responsibility being a highly theoretical matter,[1] and individual criminal responsibility only able to address PMC contractors or directors, there appears to be a strong case to better understand how PMCs, as companies, can be liable for gross human rights violations or crimes of international significance. Furthermore, the newly acquired legal personality of PMCs should be scrutinised to identify opportunities for corporate accountability in the sources of law, formerly unavailable and inapplicable to private military actors.

Procedural obstacles

The corporate status of the company poses a number of issues to its recognition and treatment under criminal law. In countries like France and Germany, for example, the principle of *societas delinquere non potest* – "a legal entity cannot be blameworthy" – long prevented imposition of criminal liability at all.[2] In *Ferguson v. Wilson* (1886), Lord Cairns concluded that "a company cannot act in its own person for it has no person, it can only act through directors, who are the agents of the company".[3] Described by Viscount Haldane L. C. in the judgement of the civil case of *Lennard's Carrying Co. Ltd v. Asiatic Petroleum Co. Ltd*[4] as "an abstraction", a corporation could only bear liability through its agent, who carries out its acting and directing will.[5] If corporations are understood as inanimate tools run by individuals, the responsibility will be placed on natural rather than juridical persons.[6] Not only does such an approach pose doctrinal obstacles to holding companies criminally liable, but it also defeats the purpose of assigning corporations with a legal personality.[7] However, as early as 1522 Chief Justice Fineux argued that "a corporation is an aggregation of head and body: not a head by itself, nor a body by itself; and it must be consonant to reason, for otherwise it is worth nought".[8] Indeed, a legal positivist approach creates significant limitations to corporate criminal liability,[9] as, according to Kramer, "recognition of the corporation as a legal person has largely carried with it protections without the imposition of corresponding responsibilities and obligations".[10]

Individuals and corporations alike can bear vicarious liability, when liable for the acts of another, or personal, when liable for their own actions. Until 1944, all cases brought forward against corporations concerning criminal responsibility in England were based on vicarious liability.[11] In the context of PMCs, the application of vicarious liability transfers criminal responsibility from an individual employee to the corporation itself, while the agent or employee remains responsible for the crime committed.[12] However, three cases, *DPP v. Kent & Sussex Contractors Ltd*,[13] *R. v. ICR Haulage Co. Ltd*,[14] and *Moore v. Bresler Ltd*,[15] demonstrated that companies can have direct personal liability, as it was established that acts of certain employees can under certain circumstances be viewed as the acts of a company itself.[16] The doctrinal value of these cases lies in their introduction of the 'doctrine of identification' to criminal law in the cases of personal liability for corporations.[17] This meant that the courts recognised that the acts of a company's agents can be viewed as the acts of the company.[18]

Criminal liability for a corporation is made problematic by the 'black letter' reading of the law. For example, it is considered that a company cannot commit murder, because only an individual can bear the lawful sentence, life imprisonment, for such crime.[19] It is complicated further by the definition of homicide, whereby it is understood as "the killing of one human being by another human being".[20] The same logic applies to crimes such as bigamy, incest, rape, and conspiracy with a company's sole director. While most jurisdictions stipulate that a company cannot commit a murder per se, it can be found guilty as a secondary party.[21] Nourse L. J. in *Odyssey Re (London) Ltd & Another v. OIC Run Off Ltd*[22] established that "there would be an unacceptable shortcoming in company law if evidence given on behalf of a company was incapable of being treated as the evidence of the company". Moreover, legal persons cannot be compared to physical individuals like for like. So, why should jurists attempt to apply the same jurisdictional methods to these incomparable legal personalities? Indeed, part of the problem arises from attempting to apply the same legal framework to physical and legal persons. While the law recognises both individuals and companies, the legal treatment and approach to responsibility ought to be tailored to suit the social construction of both subjects.[23] Given that criminal law and its liability mechanisms are focused on the individual, its literal and unchanged application to a corporation could prove problematic and ineffective.

Furthermore, procedural complexities of corporate indictment were also linked to the need of a defendant being present in court. In the UK, procedural obstacles of criminal prosecution were addressed by the s. 33 (3) Criminal Justice Act 1925, which allowed a corporation to enter a plea through a representative.[24] On the practical side, limited budgets and the costs of litigation can be an obstacle that discourages public prosecutors from investigating and indicting what tend to be complex matters.[25] Drawing on the work of John Braithwaite and Brent Fisse,[26] a significant development has been introduced in Australian criminal law to that end. Criminal courts can convict companies of offences based on a body corporate's failure "to create and maintain a corporate culture that required compliance with the relevant provision".[27]

In 2007, the UK Corporate Manslaughter and Corporate Homicide Act was published to create a new offence in relation to corporate responsibility.[28] It shifted the focus of liability from individual guilt to identifying gross negligence in the way a corporation organises and conducts its activities. Under the Act, a company could be criminally liable if its conduct "causes a person's death, and amounts to a gross breach of a relevant duty of care owed by the organisation to the deceased".[29] As a corporation, a PMC would owe a relevant duty of care in regards to its contractors in the event of a corporate manslaughter offence. However, contract law would interject, establishing in most cases that only parties to a contract can invoke liability as a result of a breach. It is, therefore, debatable whether or not a PMC would owe a relevant duty of care to individuals outside of company employees. On the other hand, PMCs that are signatory parties to the International Code of Conduct (ICoC) commit to upholding human rights values. Perhaps it could be argued that this commitment to conduct their activities in adherence with human rights values could be sufficient to establish a relevant duty of care in regards to non-employees. However, in regards to private military activity a "relevant duty of care" is limited. An offence committed by private military contractors who are incorporated in state forces, or if the PMC is contracted by the Ministry of Defence, does not invoke a "relevant duty of care" and, therefore, would not be subject to this legislation.[30] This example demonstrates the complexity and the fundamental inefficacy of overlapping laws and regulations concerning PMC activity. As a result, the hard laws prevail, while the human rights norms and industry self-regulation create only a veneer of legality. Notwithstanding the ascribed legal personality that companies have acquired, the account of rationality and autonomy, explored by Wells, appears to exclude corporations from the legal realm based on the assumption that they are not persons in a metaphysical sense.[31]

This juxtaposition between the corporate immunity of *societas delinquere non potest* and deniability of corporate criminal responsibility is one of the origins of PMC (and other company) impunity with regard to criminal law. What a PMC status of a corporation could achieve, is the potential to attribute responsibility to a legal person. However, without a more granular definition, the attribution on its own fails to clarify and solidify the process of holding a corporation liable.[32] Peter French argues that "corporations are not just organised crowds of people [...] they have metaphysical-logical identity that does not reduce to a mere sum of human members".[33] When examining the nature of PMC activity and the failure to adequately punish significant wrongdoings, such as human rights violations or war crimes, this approach becomes extremely relevant. Take the infamous Blackwater case, for example. The company committed crimes that no one disputes, yet its founder and former CEO moved on to a new endeavour in the same sector, while the company itself has been renamed, sold, and then once again renamed. It continues to offer military and security services, and, ironically, is also a signatory company to the ICoC. The only outcome of the Nisour Square atrocities is a few contractors behind bars, while the company that facilitated the intelligence, the arms, and other means, continues to prosper, albeit under a different name.

Territorial limitations and examples of domestic jurisdiction on PMCs

Domestic criminal legal systems are often challenged by the extraterritorial nature of PMC activity. For example, the world's largest private security company, G4S, employs more than 623,000 people on six different continents, of whom more than three-fifths are in Asia, the Middle East, and Africa.[34] When the two components of criminal liability, *actus reus* (criminal act) and *mens rea* (criminal intent), are identified to be in the same place, the place of the crime and, therefore, acting jurisdiction, is straightforward.[35] However, when it comes to the corporate liability of PMCs, in most scenarios the criminal act would occur in a different country to that of the PMC headquarters or incorporation address.

In 1988, the Council of Europe urged its member states to support the practice of corporate criminal responsibility due to the limitations of individual criminal liability of corporate officers, which left a regulatory gap that corporate criminal responsibility could fill.[36] Although today a number of member states allow for extraterritorial legislation concerning human rights, most of the laws do not extend to companies.[37] To tackle this gap, the UK enacted the International Criminal Court Act of 2001. While not specific to PMCs, it can impose criminal liability on corporations acting both in and outside of British territory.[38] In addition, the UK Security Industry Authority was set up under the Private Security Industry Act 2001, which is "responsible for regulating the private security industry by, *inter alia*, operating a licensing regime for individual security operatives and a voluntary approvals scheme for security businesses".[39] In France, national legislation encompasses corporate criminal liability for businesses that operate abroad. The same legal framework exists in Canada, Norway, and the US.[40] In the US, "corporations – as entities – can be criminally tried and convicted for crimes committed by individual directors, managers, and even low-level employees".[41] While in the US companies are criminally liable and could face criminal prosecution, in reality the risk of an actual trial is very low. Edward Diskant explains this phenomenon through shifting liability from corporation to individuals. The companies forfeit any protections and avoid criminal liability in exchange for agreements to waive their privilege, to deny indemnification to employees, and to cease any support provided to those individuals under investigation.[42]

Since developing the Draft Convention in 2011, the Working Group (WG) on the use of mercenaries has been conducting a study across a number of states on domestic laws that are aimed specifically at regulating private military and security companies.[43] For the purposes of the review, the WG defined PMCs as "a corporate entity which provides on a compensatory basis military and/or security services by physical persons and/or legal entities".[44] To date, it has reviewed national legislation of twenty-one African states,[45] eight selected countries in Asia and the Middle East,[46] eight countries in Central America and the Caribbean,[47] eight countries in South America,[48] as well as the US and Switzerland,[49] and France, Hungary, and the UK.[50] The study found that, with the exception of South Africa, none of the African, Asian, or Central and South American countries reviewed had legislation that covered the export of military or security services.[51] Equally, French law does not contain relevant provisions on the direct participation of private military and security company personnel in hostilities.[52] In the meantime, the Belgian legislature revoked provisions for extraterritorial corporate liability in 2003,[53] as a result of the US threat to move the NATO headquarters out of Brussels.[54] A similar trend was noted in the Spanish legal system, as the Parliament "acted to limit the jurisdiction over human rights cases in 2009".[55]

Given its extensive history concerning mercenary and private military activity, South Africa provides an example of a national legislation that is actively seeking to regulate PMC activity. To address the growing numbers of South Africans with military skills and experience offering their services abroad in the post-apartheid era, South Africa passed the Regulation of Foreign Military Assistance Act No. 15 in 1998, which covers both mercenary activity and PMCs.[56] While the definition of a 'mercenary' in South African legislation differs from that in international or regional regulations, it specifically outlaws mercenary activities and "requires permission for the rendering of military or security services to a party to an armed conflict or to a designated country".[57] When it became known that a number of South African citizens participated in a coup attempt in Equatorial Guinea in 2004,[58] stronger legislation was adopted.[59] In 2007, the Prohibition of Mercenary Activities and Regulation of Certain Activities in the Country of Armed Conflict Act came into force. The extraterritorial jurisdiction of the Act applies to individuals as well as corporations, therefore criminalising both mercenaries or private military contractors as well as the companies they work for.[60]

Domestic criminal jurisdictions are often limited by the extraterritorial nature of PMC and mercenary activity.[61] Even those domestic legal systems that cater for extraterritoriality are frequently dependent on transnational cooperation. In the thirtieth session of the Human Rights Council (HRC) as part of the open-ended intergovernmental working group, the South African delegation expressed their disappointment at the lack of cooperation among countries where foreign military activities had taken place, which were often those countries involved in the Montreux Document and ICoC processes.[62] Non-cooperation renders the enforcement of the Regulation of Foreign Military Assistance Act No. 15 of 1998 impossible, and the Act itself ineffective. Nonetheless, South Africa has got one of the most (if not the most) elaborate and comprehensive domestic legal frameworks to regulate mercenaries and PMCs. The country is openly opposed to private security in a military context, and their stance was presented in the abovementioned HRC session. The South African delegation suggested that "norms should be elaborated in international law to (a) define private military and security companies; and (b) hold such companies accountable under international humanitarian and international human rights law".[63]

The Swiss draft law on the provision of private security services abroad is one of the most recent national efforts to address the issues of PMC regulation. The draft law prohibits selected activities, such as direct participation in hostilities in an armed conflict, and the hiring, training, and provision of security personnel for direct participation in hostilities. However, it does not ban PMCs per se.[64] In the US, besides the Military Extraterritorial Jurisdiction Act that invokes individual criminal responsibility, legislation covers "possible criminal charges under the False Claims Act for those private security companies which falsely stated that they were in compliance with the required standard".[65] None of the other states reviewed by the WG have appropriate laws or regulations to address military-like activities or Private Military and Security Companies (PMSCs), nor do they provide extraterritorial jurisdiction for companies.[66] The laws of the Russian Federation currently do not cater for extraterritorial PMC activities. In the HRC's thirtieth session, the Russian delegation argued that this is due to those functions being deemed inherently governmental and only being undertaken by state institutions.[67] There was no mention of the PMCs registered and domiciled on the territory of the Russian Federation, nor was this statement challenged at any point during the session.[68] The WG plans to continue its enquiry and analysis of domestic legislations with the purpose of highlighting the legislative gaps in national jurisdictions and establishing a legally binding international regulatory instrument as a way of ensuring consistent regulation.[69]

Civil procedure in establishing corporate accountability in tort law

The corporate identity of PMCs creates a legal gap for regulation. On the one hand, corporate law assigns juridical personhood to companies, legitimising their status to the extreme of *societas delinquere non potest*. On the other, IL does not characterise corporations as subjects with rights and respective responsibilities for their wrongful acts. This challenge is both evident and addressed within the jurisdiction of the Alien Tort Statute (ATS). The 1789 Alien Tort Statute, also known as the Alien Tort Claims Act (ATCA), is a legislation that enables US federal courts to assert jurisdiction over "any civil action by an alien for a tort only, committed in violation of the law of nations or a treaty of the United States".[70] The torts committed by a company, however substantial, are limited to being a civil wrong under the ATS.[71] Although the ATS does not ascribe criminal responsibility, it is an important mechanism that has been repeatedly deployed in the efforts of establishing corporate accountability, including for PMCs.

There are a number of cases that were brought specifically against PMCs under the ATS. DynCorp was contracted to combat production of illicit drugs in Colombia by aerially spraying cocaine and poppy plantations with the herbicide glyphosate. In September 2001, a group of bordering Ecuadorian farmers, who claimed to be affected by the spraying, filed a class action against the company, known as *Arias v. DynCorp*. The suit was filed under the ATS, the Torture Victim Protection Act, and state law claims in US federal court.[72] The court found that the claims raised by the plaintiffs were outside the scope of the Congressional authorisation of DynCorp's contract.[73] In addition, the plaintiffs raised an international legal question, by claiming that defendants were operating as a "wilful participant in joint activity with the State or its agents", were "controlled by an agency of the state", or were "entwined with governmental policies".[74] They claimed that the "Defendants' activity which allegedly caused plaintiffs' harm was cloaked in the authority of the U.S. State Department and the Colombian government".[75] In February 2013, the court ruled in favour of the PMC, and the District of Columbia judge dismissed all claims.[76] However, a parallel complaint (*Quinteros v. DynCorp*) was filed in 2006 by Ecuadorian citizens before the Inter-American Commission of Human Rights for the lack of enforcement of a ruling of the Constitutional Court, ordering all relevant ministries to adopt all necessary measures to remedy the damage suffered by communities on the northern border of Ecuador, as a consequence of the aerial herbicide sprayings on the Colombian side of the border, and to prevent further damage from being caused. However, a decision on the admissibility of the complaint is still pending.[77] *Aerial Herbicide Spraying (Ecuador v. Colombia)* was then brought before the International Court of Justice (ICJ) in March 2008. Ecuador subsequently moved to discontinue the case in September 2013, following an agreement between the parties "that fully and finally resolves all of Ecuador's claims against Colombia" in the case.[78]

One of the most infamous and media-covered PMC lawsuits was the Blackwater case of the 16 September 2007 Baghdad incident. During the proceedings of this case, individual, corporate, and state responsibility were examined. From the corporate liability perspective, however, a very limited result was achieved. The case was filed under the ATS in a US federal court against Blackwater, its parent company The Prince Group, and Blackwater founder and chairman Erik Prince. The company was charged with opening fire on unarmed civilians, which constituted extrajudicial killings and a war crime.[79] In December 2010, Blackwater argued that the US government, and not the company itself, should be held accountable for the shooting incident because it was providing security to State Department personnel. As demonstrated in the previous section, this argument did not stand due to technical grounds, and was thereafter dismissed by the court. Blackwater consequently settled the wrongful-death lawsuit out of court in 2012 for an undisclosed sum.[80]

Despite its capacity to try corporate cases, the extent and capacity of the ATS have been hamstrung over the years. First of all, in a 2004 case, *Sosa v. Alvarez-Machain*, the scope of the statute was narrowed to include only claims based on fundamental principles of customary IL on the basis that they could be incorporated into American federal common law.[81] In other words, a claimant must bring forward a "cause of action in international law sufficiently fundamental to have developed into a customary norm".[82] Second, historically, there has not been a coherent view on the applicability of the ATS to legal persons, and after *Kiobel v. Royal Dutch Petroleum Co. PLC* it has reduced significantly. According to the claim, Nigerian military and police forces attacked Ogoni villages, committing atrocities and looting the property of the residents. Meanwhile the respondents, the Royal Dutch Petroleum Company and Shell Transport and Trading Company, aided and abetted these offenses by "providing the Nigerian forces with food, transportation, and compensation, as well as by allowing the Nigerian military to use respondents' property as a staging ground for attacks".[83]

In 2002 Royal Dutch/Shell was sued in a US Federal court for illegal detention, torture, extrajudicial killing, and other violations pursuant to the ATS. The court dismissed the motion in 2010 on the basis that a direct business relationship between the US and its Nigerian subsidiary (the Petroleum Development Company of Nigeria) had not been established in order for ATS to apply.[84] After numerous appeals, the Second Circuit dismissed the entire complaint in 2013, reasoning that the law of nations does not recognise corporate liability.[85] Judge Cabranes's statement in *Kiobel v. Royal Dutch Petroleum Co. PLC* provides a strong normative insight regarding the readiness of US courts to arbitrate corporate responsibility. He concluded that "modern international tribunals make it abundantly clear that, since Nuremberg, the concept of corporate liability for violations of customary international law has not even begun to 'ripen' into a universally accepted norm of international law".[86]

In principle, corporate liability under ATS is permissible, but the statute cannot be breached by private action alone without the 'colour of law'.[87] There has been requirement for a related state action to be established in order to punish a corporate entity under the ATS. This provision immunises corporations that directly violate human rights, reducing PMC responsibility to the mode of complicity and liability as an accessory. Furthermore, the liability of a state actor is undercut by sovereign immunity that the state could choose to extend to the PMC in question.[88] Arguably, the ATS is not fit to address human rights violations by PMCs. The structure of its jurisdiction only allows for social/civil liability, which in effect reduces gross criminal violations to mere civil wrongs that can be financially reimbursed. To paraphrase James Stewart, if former military and political leaders indicted at the International Criminal Court (ICC) for war crimes deserve criminal punishment, how can a company, that participated in the same crimes, circumvent criminal charges simply by paying a fine?[89]

However, despite the procedural trajectory of ATS cases brought against corporations and adjudicated in their favour, recently there has been an important development for ATS resulting from Abu Ghraib lawsuits against CACI and Titan.[90] On 28 June 2017, a US court ruled[91] that claims for torture; cruel, inhuman, and degrading treatment; and war crimes can be brought under Alien Tort Statute against private actors.[92] Following a motion to dismiss the case, on 22 September 2017, a district court judge denied the defendants' request and ruled that the case could proceed. Nearly fifteen years after the abuses at the Abu Ghraib "hard site" prison in Iraq came to light, a Virginia federal judge ruled that the mistreatment of three Iraqi plaintiffs who were detained there constitutes torture, war crimes, and cruel, inhuman, and degrading treatment. A district judge later ruled that CACI could not be held directly liable for torture at Abu Ghraib prison due to an insufficient connection between the plaintiffs and the company.[93] However, the ruling held that the PMC can be held liable for its employees conspiring to commit and aiding and abetting these crimes, rejecting the company's decade-long claim it should be shielded from liability. Building a precedent, this ruling importantly concludes that a company can be held liable for the crimes committed internationally.[94]

Considering that historically the court judgements swayed in favour of the corporations sued under the ATS, the outcome of this case could determine the pathways for establishing international criminal responsibility for corporations, and PMCs in particular. Additionally, academic and legal coverage of these cases helps to create a new historical narrative which is an important first step towards formulating corporate responsibility and addressing impunity.[95] PMCs may not have declared wars and initiated hostilities but, due to the nature of their business, they have and are capable of perpetrating serious human rights abuses. This, in turn, signals a need for criminal corporate responsibility which can be invoked domestically, but also transnationally. Drawing on the discussions from previous chapter, it becomes increasingly more important to recognise the power and legitimacy that corporations wield and to recognise corporations' legal status as transnational actors, claiming a certain degree of governance. Corporate accountability is also pertinent because states would not be responsible for every offence committed by PMCs they hire, and individual responsibility does not prevent the company from continuing to conduct their business, and potentially committing future crimes.

(Establishing) Corporate responsibility for international crimes

International crimes have a particular meaning within the framework of International Criminal Law (ICL). Under the Rome Statute of the ICC, international crimes comprise exclusively of genocide, crimes against humanity, crime of aggression, and war crimes.[96] Another nuance is in the application of the ICC mandate, extending to natural persons only, and not states or corporations. While domestic legal systems are inconsistent and patchy when it comes to corporate responsibility and specific PMC provisions, the absence of a strong norm of international criminal liability for corporations creates another major regulatory gap. In reality, the realms of international and domestic bodies of law are not strictly separated. As discussed throughout, the transnational nature of PMCs, and corporations more generally, enacts a myriad of overlapping regulations to accommodate both the actor (domestic, transnational, or international; parent company or subsidiary; incorporated into armed forced or governed by a contract) and the act (tort, human rights violation, manslaughter, international crime, participation in hostilities in IAC/NIAC). Besides adding to the complexity of effectively regulating private military actors, sometimes these different bodies of law give rise to valuable lessons, interdependencies, and lineages for evolving precedents. Importantly, the *Tadic case* contributed to the construction of an essential element in the criminal liability for corporations, namely joint criminal enterprise.[97] The principle of this collective liability depends on lowering the culpability threshold as one individual may be deemed liable for another's actions when operating in a group. It also changed the perception of war crimes dating back to Nuremberg, to an idea that crimes against humanity can also occur outside of international conflict.[98]

To take this argument further, not only could international crimes occur outside of an international conflict, but they could also be perpetrated by entities other than individuals and states. A joint project of the International Peace Academy and the Norwegian think tank Fafo on Assessing the Liability of Business Entities for Grave Violations of International Law (Fafo report) identified the premise for criminal liability for corporations in many jurisdictions.[99] The report lists recent cases brought against corporations that were believed to have committed war crimes. Amongst them are cases of *Presbyterian Church of Sudan v. Talisman Energy*[100] and *Sarei v. Rio*,[101] whereby the defendant corporations are charged with aiding and abetting certain war crimes including military bombings and assaults on civilian targets, torture, rape, and genocide.[102] Additionally, the cases of *Doe v. Unocal*, *Wiwa v. Royal Dutch Petroleum Co.* (*Wiwa*), *Bowoto v. Chevron* (*Bowoto*), *John Does v. Exxon Mobil Corp* (*Exxon Mobil*), and *Rio Tinto*, and *Beanal v. Freeport-McMoran Inc.*[103] were brought forward on the bases of crimes against humanity.[104] Also, in Argentina there are currently a number of criminal proceedings pending against large Argentine as well as EU and US companies concerned with corporate complicity in dictatorship crimes.[105] The added value of identifying precedent of corporations charged on the basis of complicity in international crimes is that it builds a strong scholarly and case-based demand for corporate liability that could help shape legal debate and policy decisions with regard to corporate accountability.

Pertinent to the limitations of territoriality, corporate law produces another source of impunity that is highly relevant in the realm of PMCs, namely the company law doctrine of "separate corporate personality" that most jurisdictions recognise. According to this doctrine, a parent company and its subsidiaries are considered to be separate legal entities. Such a construct of legal separation and limited liability allows for impunity, commonly referred to as the 'corporate veil', whereby a parent company will not be held liable for acts or offenses committed by its subsidiary merely on the basis of shareholding.[106] The HRC recognises the discrepancies across national jurisdictions of parent companies' legal responsibilities to identify, prevent, and mitigate human rights abuses, and acknowledges the associated barriers to remedying them, through added legal costs and delays.[107] While this liability gap is recognised by Human Rights Law, it is in the early stages of development and is currently unable to address the challenges of the corporate veil.[108]

However, in June 2018, French cement giant LafargeHolcim, also one of France's biggest companies, was placed under formal investigation on the charges of terrorist financing and aiding and abetting crimes against humanity as the company continued their operations in the midst of Syrian civil war.[109] The case was co-filed in 2016 by a Paris-based human rights group Sherpa and the European Centre for Constitutional and Human Rights, marking a pivotal step towards establishing corporate accountability for companies operating in conflict zones. Furthermore, this indictment is the first time a parent company has been charged with complicity in crimes against humanity, based on the actions carried out by its subsidiary in Syria.[110] In practical terms, a French court will have to determine if the company had violated international sanctions and, most importantly, whether it was complicit in committing crimes against humanity by financing terrorism and enabling IS. In order to prove complicity of parent company, the link to the principal perpetrators' ideology is not required.[111] Instead, it is sufficient to demonstrate the knowledge of the crimes being carried out and that one's conduct would contribute to these crimes being committed.[112] If found guilty, the sentence would constitute a fine only for the company, while the individuals may serve a prison sentence for up to ten years.

Conclusion

Evidently, criminal responsibility may be as relevant to other businesses as much as it is to PMCs, whose activities and employees have a close connection with hostilities and the use of lethal force. While there is a need to ensure parity of legal obligation for corporations, currently prospective international codification of corporate criminal liability is made problematic by the inconsistencies across national legislation. Nonetheless, there is a strong scholarly and case-based demand for corporate liability that cannot and will not be left unnoticed. As Andrew Clapham argues,

> as long as we admit that individuals have rights and duties under customary international human rights law and international humanitarian law, we have to admit that legal persons also have the necessary international legal personality to enjoy some of these rights and conversely be prosecuted or held accountable for violations of their international duties.[113]

Therefore, any corporation, including PMCs, should be accountable for any breaches of IL, in particular war crimes and violations of human rights.[114] The existing legally binding mechanisms, such as domestic criminal jurisdictions and the Alien Tort Statute, are insufficiently effective in their current form to address the international extent of corporate criminal liability. However, given the emerging precedent of corporate complicity in international crimes and the attempt to ascribe responsibility on that basis, the intersection with international criminal law (ICL) is important and noteworthy to explore.

Notes

1 Simpson (2002, p. 56).
2 Diskant (2008, p. 129).
3 *Ferguson v. Wilson*, 1866, Chamber of Appeals 77, p. 89.
4 1915, A. C., 705.
5 1915, A. C., 713.
6 Moore (2010, pp. 246–247, 623).
7 Liu (2015, p. 248).
8 Maitland (1900, p. 8).
9 See Cutler (2002).
10 Kramer (1989, p. 157).
11 Pinto and Evans (2008, p. 39).
12 A/HRC/32/39, p. 19.
13 1944, 1 K. B. 146.
14 1944, K. B. 551.
15 1944, 2 K. B. 515.
16 Pinto and Evans (2008, pp. 39–42).
17 Pinto and Evans (2008, p. 44).
18 Pinto and Evans (2008, p. 39).
19 Pinto and Evans (2008, p. 5).
20 *R. v. P&O European Ferries (Dover) Ltd*, 1991, 93 Criminal Appeal Reports, p. 72.
21 Pinto and Evans (2008, p. 90).
22 Formerly Sphere Drake Insurance Plc and Orion Insurance Co. Plc, respectively.
23 Wells (2001, p. 74).
24 Pinto and Evans (2008, p. 19).
25 Chatham House (2015, p. 5).
26 Fisse and Braithwaite (1993).
27 Section 12.3(2)(d) Commonwealth Criminal Code Act of 1995, Australia.
28 In 2015 New sentencing guidelines for corporate manslaughter were introduced.

29 Corporate Manslaughter and Corporate Homicide Act 2007, Chapter 19, Art. 1 (1) (a), (b), p. 1.
30 Corporate Manslaughter and Corporate Homicide Act 2007, p. 5.
31 Wells (2001, p. 65).
32 Wells (2001).
33 French (1984, p. 32).
34 See: G4S Company Website.
35 Pinto and Evans (2008, p. 91).
36 Council of Europe, Recommendation no. R (88) 18 of the Committee of Ministers to Member States Concerning Liability of Enterprises Having Legal Personality for Offences Committed in the Exercise of Their Activities.
37 Kirshner (2015, p. 19).
38 International Criminal Court Act, 2001, c. 17, § 4 (UK).
39 A/HRC/30/47, Art. 23, p. 7.
40 Fafo Report (2005, p. 12).
41 Diskant (2008, p. 128).
42 Diskant (2008, pp. 133–134).
43 See: A/HRC/24/45, A/HRC/27/50, and A/HRC/30/34.
44 A/HRC/27/50, p. 4.
45 Results on Botswana, Ghana, the Gambia, Kenya, Lesotho, Mauritius, Namibia, Nigeria, Sierra Leone, South Africa, Swaziland, Uganda, Zimbabwe presented in A/HRC/24/25; results on Burkina Faso, Cameroon, Côte d'Ivoire, the Democratic Republic of Congo, Mali, Morocco, Senegal, Tunisia presented in A/HRC/27/50.
46 China, India, Malaysia, Pakistan, the Philippines, Singapore, Sri Lanka, and the United Arab Emirates covered in A/HRC/27/50.
47 Costa Rica, Cuba, El Salvador, Guatemala, Honduras, Mexico, Nicaragua, and Panama covered in A/HRC/30/34.
48 Argentina, Bolivia, Brazil, Chile, Colombia, Ecuador, Peru, and Uruguay covered in A/HRC/30/34.
49 Presented in A/HRC/21/43.
50 Presented in A/HRC/30/34.
51 A/HRC/24/25, p. 6.
52 A/HRC/30/34, Art. 28, p. 7.
53 Ratner (2003, pp. 888, 889); Murphy (2003, pp. 984, 986–987).
54 Black and MacAskill (2003); Wastell (2003).
55 Kirshner (2015, p. 16).
56 A/HRC/21/43, p. 8.
57 A/HRC/24/25, p. 7.
58 See Roberts (2006); see also A/HRC/18/32/Add.2.
59 A/HRC/21/43, p. 8.
60 Prohibition of Mercenary Activities and Regulation of Certain Activities in the Country of Armed Conflict Act, Art. 11, p. 10.
61 Kirshner (2015, p. 12).
62 A/HRC/30/47, Art. 19, p. 7.
63 A/HRC/30/47, Art. 13, p. 5.
64 Smith (2013).
65 A/HRC/30/47, Art. 18, p. 6.
66 A/HRC/27/50, Art. 16, p. 7.
67 A/HRC/30/47, Art. 25, p. 8.
68 Russian PMCs include: Center-Alfa, Moran Security Group, Viking, RSB Group.
69 A/HRC/30/47, Art. 131, p. 23.
70 See Global Policy.
71 Liu (2015, p. 266).

72 *Arias v. DynCorp*, 517 F.Supp.2d 221 (2007), United States District Court, District of Columbia.
73 Business and Human Rights Resource Centre (c).
74 Arias v. DynCorp, 517.
75 Arias v. DynCorp, 517.
76 *Arias v. DynCorp*, 752 F.3d 1011 (2014), United States Court of Appeals, District of Columbia Circuit.
77 The DynCorp Case in Colombia, Environmental Justice Organisations, Liabilities and Trade (EJOLT), August 2015, p. 2, n. 5.
78 *Aerial Herbicide Spraying (Ecuador v. Colombia)*, International Court of Justice, No. 2013/20, 2013.
79 See Business and Human Rights Resource Centre (a).
80 Apuzzo (2014).
81 542 U.S. 692, 732 (2004).
82 Kirshner (2015, p. 9).
83 *Kiobel v. Royal Dutch Petroleum*, 569 U.S. 2013, p. 2.
84 See Business and Human Rights Resource Centre (b).
85 569 U.S. (2013, p. 3).
86 *Kiobel v. Royal Dutch Petroleum Co. PLC*, 2010, United States Court of Appeals for the Second Circuit, p. 137.
87 Liu (2015, p. 280).
88 Liu (2015, p. 281).
89 Stewart (2014, p. 55).
90 Abu Graib lawsuits against CACI, Titan (now L-3).
91 US District Court for the Eastern District of Virginia, Alexandria Division: Suhail Najim Abdullah Al Shimari, et al., v. CACI Premier Tech, Inc., 28 Jun 2017.
92 Centre for Constitutional Rights 2018.
93 US District Court for the Eastern District of Virginia, Alexandria Division: Suhail Najim Abdullah Al Shimari, et al., v. CACI Premier Tech, Inc., [opinion on lack of subject matter jurisdiction on conspiracy claims] 25 June 2018.
94 Next court hearing is scheduled to start on 23 April 2019.
95 Kaleck and Saage-Maasz (2015).
96 Art. 25 Statute of the International Criminal Court UN Doc./A.CONF.183.9*, 2187 UNTS 1998, p. 90.
97 Simpson (2002, p. 120).
98 Schabas (2001, p. 12); *Tadic*, Decision on the Defence Motion for Interlocutory Appeal on Jurisdiction, 2 October 1995.
99 Business and international crimes 2005.
100 US Court of Appeals for the Second Circuit, United States.
101 US Court of Appeals for The Ninth Circuit, United States.
102 Fafo Report (2005, p. 17).
103 All the above-mentioned cases were heard in the US courts.
104 Fafo Report (2005, p. 17).
105 Kaleck and Saage-Maasz (2015).
106 A/HRC/32/19, Art. 22, p. 9; Schutter (2006, p. 36).
107 A/HRC/32/19, Art. 23, p. 10.
108 A/HRC/32/19, Art. 22, p. 9.
109 *Daily Nation* (2018).
110 Waldie (2018).
111 In the Nazi collaborator "Papon" case of 1997, the French Supreme Court's judgment established that complicity in crimes against humanity does not require supporting the ideology of the principal perpetrators, nor is it necessary for the accomplice to know the specific crime was being planned and actually perpetrated; See Cour de Cassation, Chambre criminelle, 23 January 1997, 96–84.822.

112 Tixeire (2018).
113 Clapham (2000, pp. 139, 190).
114 Stewart (2014, pp. 1–78); see also Stewart's work on corporate accountability and criminal justice at: http://jamesgstewart.com/category/blog/corporate-accountability/; White and MacLeod (2008, p. 967).

References

1915, A. C., 705.

1915, A. C., 713.

1944, 1 K. B. 146.

1944, 2 K. B. 515.

1944, K. B. 551.

542 U.S. 692, 732 (2004).

569 U.S. (2013).

A/HRC/18/32/Add.2.

A/HRC/21/43.

A/HRC/24/45.

A/HRC/27/50.

A/HRC/27/50.

A/HRC/30/34.

A/HRC/30/47.

A/HRC/30/47.

A/HRC/32/19.

A/HRC/32/39.

Abu Graib Lawsuits against CACI, Titan (now L-3), available at: www.business-humanrights.org/en/abu-ghraib-lawsuits-against-caci-titan-now-l-3-0.

Aerial Herbicide Spraying (Ecuador v. Colombia), International Court of Justice, No. 2013/20, 17 September 2013 at: www.icj-cij.org/docket/files/138/17526.pdf.

Apuzzo, M.: "Blackwater Guards Found Guilty in 2007 Iraq Killings", 22 October 2014, *The New York Times*, available at: www.nytimes.com/2014/10/23/us/blackwater-verdict.html?_r=0.

Arias v. DynCorp, 517 F.Supp.2d 221 (2007), United States District Court, District of Columbia.

Arias v. DynCorp, 752 F.3d 1011 (2014), United States Court of Appeals, District of Columbia Circuit.

Black, I. and MacAskill, E.: "US Threatens NATO Boycott over Belgian War Crimes Law", 13 June 2003, *The Guardian*, available at: www.theguardian.com/world/2003/jun/13/nato.warcrimes.

Business and Human Rights Resource Centre (a), available at: https://business-humanrights.org/en/blackwater-usa-lawsuit-re-16-sep-2007-baghdad-incident-1.

Business and Human Rights Resource Centre (b), available at: https://business-humanrights.org/en/shell-lawsuit-re-nigeria-kiobel-wiwa#c9306.

Business and Human Rights Resource Centre (c), available at: http://business-humanrights.org/en/dyncorp-lawsuit-re-colombia-ecuador-0.

Centre for Constitutional Rights: "Private Corporation May be Sued for Role in Abu Ghraib Torture, Judge Rule, Judge Rules", 21 Feb 2018, available at: https://ccrjustice.org/home/press-center/press-releases/private-corporation-may-be-sued-role-abu-ghraib-torture-judge-rules.

Chatham House: "Corporate Responsibility for International Crimes", Chatham House International Law Programme, Meeting Summary, 19 May 2015, London.

Clapham, A. "The Questions of Jurisdiction under International Criminal Law over Legal Persons: Lessons from the Rome Conference on an International Criminal Court" in Kamminga, M. T. and Zia-Zarifi, S. (eds): *Liability of Multinational Corporations under International Law*, The Hague, Kluwer, 2000.

Commonwealth Criminal Code Act of 1995, Australia.

Corporate Manslaughter and Corporate Homicide Act 2007.

Council of Europe, Recommendation no. R (88) 18 of the Committee of Ministers to Member States Concerning Liability of Enterprises Having Legal Personality for Offences Committed in the Exercise of their Activities.

Cour de Cassation, Chambre criminelle, 23 January 1997.

Cutler, A. C.: "Critical Historical Materialism and International Law: Imagining International Law as Praxis" in Hobden, S. and Hobson J. M. (eds.): *Historical Sociology of International Relations*, CUP, Cambridge, 2002.

Daily Nation: "French Cement giant Lafarge Indicted on Terror Financing in Syria", 29 June 2018, available at: www.nation.co.ke/business/Cement-giant-Lafarge-indicted-on-terror-financing-Syria/996-4637936-yj5svfz/index.html.

Diskant, E. B.: "Comparative Corporate Criminal Liability: Exploring the Uniquely American Doctrine through Comparative Criminal Procedure", 2008, Vol. 118, *The Yale Law Journal*, p. 128.

Environmental Justice Organisations, Liabilities and Trade (EJOLT): The DynCorp Case in Colombia, August 2015, available at: www.ejolt.org/wordpress/wp-content/uploads/2015/08/FS-47.pdf.

Fafo Report, Business and International Crimes: Assessing the Liability of Business Entities for Grave Violations of International Law (2005), available at: www.fafo.no/index.php?option=com_zoo&task=item&item_id=3742&Itemid=927&lang=en.

Ferguson v. Wilson, 1866, Chamber of Appeals 77.

Fisse, B. and Braithwaite, J.: *Corporations, Crime and Accountability*, CUP, Cambridge, 1993.

French, P.: *Collective and Corporate Responsibility*, Columbia University Press, New York, 1984.

G4S company website, available at: www.g4s.com/en/Who%20we%20are/Our%20people/Our%20employees/.

Global Policy, available at: www.globalpolicy.org/international-justice/alien-tort-claims-act-6-30.html.

International Criminal Court Act, 2001, c. 17, § 4 (UK), available at: www.legislation.gov.uk/ukpga/2001/17/2005-06-07.

Kaleck and Saage-Maasz: "The Expressive Value of Corporate Prosecutions", 30 April 2015, available at: http://jamesgstewart.com/author/wolfgang-kaleck/.

Kiobel v. Royal Dutch Petroleum Co. PLC, 2010, United States Court of Appeals for the Second Circuit.

Kiobel v. Royal Dutch Petroleum, 569 U.S. (2013), p. 2, available at: www.supremecourt.gov/opinions/12pdf/10-1491_l6gn.pdf.

Kirshner, J. A.: "A Call for the EU to Assume Jurisdiction over Extraterritorial Corporate Human Rights Abuses", 2015, Vol. 13, (1), *Northwestern Journal of International Human Rights*, pp. 1–26.

Kramer, R.: "Criminologists and the Social Movement against Corporate Crime", 1989, Vol. 16 (2), *Social Justice*, pp. 146–164.

Liu, H.-Y.: *Law's Impunity: Responsibility and the Modern Private Military Company*, Hart Publishing, Oxford, 2015.

Maitland, F.: "The Corporation Sole", 1900, Vol. 16, *Law Quarterly Review*, pp. 335–354.

Moore, M.: *Causation and Responsibility: An Essay in Law, Morals, and Metaphysics*, OUP, Oxford, 2010.

Murphy, S. D. (ed.): "Contemporary Practice of the United States Relating to International Law", 2003, Vol. 97 (4), *American Journal of International Law*, pp. 962–991.

Pinto, A. and Evans, M.: *Corporate Criminal Liability*, 2nd edition, Thompson, Sweet & Maxwell, London, 2008.

Prohibition of Mercenary Activities and Regulation of Certain Activities in the Country of Armed Conflict Act, Art. 11, available at: www.gov.za/sites/www.gov.za/files/a27-06.pdf.

R. v. P&O European Ferries (Dover) Ltd, 1991, 93 Criminal Appeal Reports.

Ratner, S. R.: "Belgium's War Crimes Statute: A Postmortem", 2003, Vol. 97 (4), *American Journal of International Law*, pp. 888–897.

Roberts, A.: *The Wonga Coup*, Profile Books, London, 2006.

Schabas, W. A.: *An Introduction to the International Criminal Court*, CUP, Cambridge, 2001.

Schutter, O. D.: "Extraterritorial Jurisdiction as a Tool for Improving the Human Rights Accountability of Transnational Corporations", December 2006, p. 36, available at: http://198.170.85.29/Olivier-de-Schutter-report-for-SRSG-re-extraterritorial-jurisdiction-Dec-2006.pdf.

Sentencing Guidelines for Corporate Manslaughter 2015, available at: www.sentencingcouncil.org.uk/news/item/new-sentencing-guidelines-introduced-for-corporate-manslaughter-health-and-safety-and-food-safety/.

Simpson, S.: *Corporate Crime, Law, and Social Control*, CUP, Cambridge, 2002.

Smith, R.: "Switzerland Checks Mercenaries, Partially", 18 February 2013, *Inter Press Services*, available at: www.ipsnews.net/2013/02/switzerland-checks-mercenaries-partially/.

Statute of the International Criminal Court UN Doc./A.CONF.183.9*, 2187 UNTS 1998.

Stewart, J. Blog on Corporate Accountability and Criminal Justice at: http://jamesg-stewart.com/category/blog/corporate-accountability/.

Stewart, J. G.: "The Turn to Corporate Criminal Liability for International Crimes: Transcending the Alien Tort Statute", 2014, Vol. 47 (1), *New York University Journal of International Law and Politics*, pp. 121–206.

Tadic, Decision on the Defence Motion for Interlocutory Appeal on Jurisdiction, IT-94-1-ES, 2 October 1995.

Tixeire, C.: "Can the Lafarge Case be a Game Changer? French Multinational Company Indicted for International Crimes in Syria", 2018, *Business and Human Rights Resource Centre*, available at: www.business-humanrights.org/en/can-the-lafarge-case-be-a-game-changer-french-multinational-company-indicted-for-international-crimes-in-syria.

US Court of Appeals for The Ninth Circuit, United States.

US Court of Appeals for the Second Circuit, United States.

US District Court for the Eastern District of Virginia, Alexandria Division: Suhail Najim Abdullah Al Shimari, et al., v. CACI Premier Tech, Inc., 28 June 2017.

US District Court for the Eastern District of Virginia, Alexandria Division: Suhail Najim Abdullah Al Shimari, et al., v. CACI Premier Tech, Inc., [opinion on lack of subject matter jurisdiction on conspiracy claims] 25 June 2018.

Waldie, P.: "Lafarge under Formal Investigation in France over Allegations of Terrorist Financing", 28 June 2018, *The Globe and Mail*, available at: www.theglobeandmail.com/business/international-business/european-business/article-lafarge-under-formal-investigation-in-france-over-allegations-of/.
Wastell, D.: "America Threatens to Move NATO after Franks Is Charged", 18 May 2003, *Sunday Telegraph*, available at: www.telegraph.co.uk/news/worldnews/europe/belgium/1430468/America-threatens-to-move-Nato- after-Franks-is-charged.html.
Wells, C.: *Corporations and Criminal Responsibility*, OUP, Oxford, 2001.
White, N. and MacLeod, S.: "EU Operations and Private Military Contractors: Issues of Corporate and Institutional Responsibility", 2008, Vol. 19 (5), *European Journal of International Law*, pp. 965–988.

8 Exploring the mechanisms of international criminal law to develop corporate accountability for PMCs

Although corporations do not currently possess an international legal personality, insofar as they are not considered to be actors under international law (IL), private military company (PMC) activity extends internationally. Therefore, PMC regulation has to be considered an international issue where the military and civilian realms meet and overlap. Having considered existing international regulatory bodies and legal frameworks that are tasked with PMC regulation, it transpires that none of them take into consideration the mode of shared governance that private military actors operate in. More answerable regulation and a legally binding mechanism to invoke corporate responsibility for international crimes and serious human rights violations for companies, and PMCs in particular, is thus required for a number of reasons.

Social liability is not sufficient to address gross human rights violations, war crimes, or crimes against humanity. While there are self-regulatory industry bodies that take concrete steps towards raising the standards of PMC services and spread human rights awareness, they cannot tackle serious violations adequately or bring justice to victims. And although cases of corporate complicity in international crimes were found in some of the other sectors, due to the military nature of their activity and an inherent proximity to conflict, PMCs ought to be treated with greater scrutiny. Finally, the formulation of international criminal liability for corporations would reinforce state responsibility and drive down impunity for PMCs. This, in turn, will ensure a more efficient and controlled use of private military resources by states and international organisations.

Though disparate and territorially restricted, the field of domestic criminal corporate responsibility is rapidly developing with valuable precedents emerging in the area of corporations indicted for international crimes. The corporate status of PMCs and their transnational activity provides an ingress into exploring accountability mechanisms available within international criminal law. The potential opportunity here is twofold: first, understanding and evaluating the potential trend of international corporate criminal responsibility into the future, and second, exploring possible and more suitable ways of establishing corporate accountability for PMCs.

International criminal law and possible lineages of corporate responsibility

One of the practical advantages of using international criminal law (ICL) and universal jurisdiction (UJ) as criminalisation tools is that these avenues allow for the trial of international crimes potentially committed by PMCs, such as war crimes[1] and crimes against humanity. However, neither the International Law Commission nor the International Criminal Court (ICC) is competent for the international criminal regulation of companies. This is mainly due to the fact that historically, the main purpose of IL was to regulate relations between states. As principal actors, states were sanctioned in the event of violation of norms or treaties through political, economic, or territorial measures.[2] This was the case until the end of the Second World War, when the idea of international criminal responsibility for individuals materialised through the establishment of the Nuremberg and Tokyo military tribunals.[3] Unlike individuals and states, who can be tried at the ICC (and the ad hoc Tribunals) and the International Court of Justice respectively, corporations cannot be held criminally liable on an international level. Equally, the UJ doctrine has only ever been applied to natural rather than legal persons.

The international personality of companies (in the context of governance and transnational mode of operation, rather than in a strict international law sense) has developed over a lengthy period of time. As found in the examples of the British and Dutch East India Companies, these companies operated as sovereign entities managing their respective empires abroad as early as the seventeenth century.[4] On the basis of Royal Charters these companies exercised governance and governmental functions including local administration, tax collection, and the control of armed forces. The British East India Company had "the right to have its contracts treated as international treaties and the right to make war".[5] As a result, the international corporate personality of the East India Companies can be evoked as a valid precedent to formulate the establishment of international corporate criminal responsibility.[6] Cameron and Chetail believe that the Nuremberg Trials provide grounds for a theory of corporate criminal liability on an international level.[7] According to the Charter of the International Military Tribunal, in cases where a group or organization is declared criminal by the Tribunal, the competent national authority of any Signatory shall have the right to bring individuals to trial for membership therein before national, military or occupation courts.[8]

The criminality of corporations was, therefore, used in order to establish individual criminal responsibility.[9] Contrary to Cameron and Chetail, Liu references the Nuremberg Trials as he traces the normative roots of corporate impunity. He argues that by criminalising civilian industry leaders of German arms production rather than the corporations that facilitated the war crimes, the Nuremberg international legal proceedings set the precedent in favour of individual criminal responsibility over the corporate one.[10] According to Bush, corporate criminal liability was explored in depth at Nuremberg, and was never rejected as legally unsound.[11] However, he disagrees with those who claim that Nuremberg signalled a normative move towards the establishment of corporate criminal liability.[12] Bush argues that the reasons for not criminalising German armaments companies were economic rather than legal. US prosecutors did not want to hamper the reconstruction of the German economy.[13]

In addition, Cameron and Chetail have identified the preparatory works of the Rome Statute as the foundation of international corporate criminal liability. It is important to note that to this day the ICC has no jurisdiction over corporate entities, nor was the act of mercenarism codified as an international crime under the Rome Statute, therefore leaving the ICC toothless in exercising any jurisdiction over PMCs. Notwithstanding this, the question of corporate criminal responsibility was raised in the early International Law Commission (ILC) discussions on the creation of an international criminal legislative body.[14] However, the notion faced significant criticism and was rejected due to its novel and controversial nature.[15] Ironically, while private armies dominated the security landscape at many periods throughout history, PMCs are often considered a novelty under the different bodies of IL.[16] The first preliminary statute of the ICC (1998) contained provisions for criminal corporate responsibility. However, consensus could not be reached, mainly for technical reasons.[17] In 2000, a reference to the liability of legal persons was made in Article 10 of the UN Convention against Transnational Organised Crime,[18] although it was removed in later revisions.

There have been some instances of institutional practice within the international criminal law of recognising criminal corporate responsibility. There are emerging exceptions that support international criminal liability for corporations. One example is the Special Tribunal for Lebanon (STL), which charged and prosecuting two media corporations for contempt of court.[19] The Defence challenged the Tribunal's jurisdiction and the Contempt Judge found that the Tribunal lacked jurisdiction over legal persons (i.e., the corporate media entity Akhbar Beirut). However, this decision was subsequently overturned by an Appeals Panel, finding that the case could proceed against Akhbar Beirut. The accused was found guilty of the sole count in the order in lieu of an indictment and sentenced to a fine.[20] However, as this does not amount to a core crime under the STL's statute, it is arguable that the precedent for international corporate liability in this case is weak.[21]

A more prominent regional example that could amount to a strong precedent in IL is found in the African Court of Justice and Human Rights. Following the struggles of national liberation from the 1960s onwards, the Court has emerged as the driving force behind the establishment of international and regional anti-mercenary norms. It is therefore not surprising that it became the first international court to recognise and criminalise corporate liability for international crimes.[22] In June 2014, members of the African Union (AU) approved a protocol that extended the Court's jurisdiction "over legal persons, with the exception of States". While the Court's legislation does not contain any clauses specific to PMCs, its international criminal jurisdiction does recognise the crime of mercenarism.[23] Sadly, as noted above, there is a significant disconnect, whereby the Statute defines only a mercenary, and not mercenarism as an activity. In addition, the Statute's definition of a mercenary derives from the International Convention against the Recruitment, Use, Financing and Training of Mercenaries of 4 December 1989, which is narrow and contextual.[24]

Arguably, until the act of mercenarism is defined, it cannot be used to criminalise private military companies for the crime of mercenarism under the jurisdiction of the Statute. In its current form, it can only be applied to individuals and does not prevent a company from incorporation with the purpose of delivering private military services. Nonetheless, the list of other crimes under the Court's jurisdiction includes crimes against humanity, war crimes, corruption, and trafficking in persons, drugs, and hazardous wastes, all the serious violations which can potentially be committed by PMCs and can now be tried for as corporations. This regional precedent is highly promising as it can be replicated in order to contribute to the establishment of international legal personality for corporations in domestic and international legal systems.

Limitations of international criminal legal procedure

In the light of growing PMC activity and extensions of their power and legitimacy, there is a need for establishing accountability mechanisms that would enable the prosecution of international crimes committed by corporations. But to what extent can it be done in the absence of international legal personality for companies and an internationally recognised crime of mercenarism, not to mention the existing deficiencies of international regulation for PMCs and given the jurisdictional limits of international tribunals?[25] Contemporary international criminal law is normally associated with individual responsibility and is often envisaged through the ICC and the ad hoc Tribunals where this law is exercised.[26] While considering the limitations associated with the application of ICL through the ICC, it could be valuable to decouple the two and envisage ICL as the appropriate body of law that can address international crimes committed by corporations.[27] Just like the IMT at Nuremberg and the International Criminal Tribunal for the Former Yugoslavia (ICTY) in the case of *Tadic* asserted jurisdiction over individuals on the basis of commission of international crimes,[28] the international element is integral to PMC conduct and the subsequent offences that may occur.

According to Article 1 of the Rome Statute, the ICC is complementary to national jurisdictions, which is different from the primary relationship of the ICTY and ICTR tribunals.[29] It obliges domestic legal systems to prosecute international crimes, and steps in if national courts are unwilling or unable to do so. Although it puts more pressure on national systems to develop an international criminal legal procedure, it also allows for some flexibility in classifying the crimes, which are narrowly defined at the ICC level. It also decouples ICL from the context of international courts and tribunals, allowing it to shift between the domestic and international domains.[30] While the ICC is a forum for the prosecution of the most serious crimes,[31] it was not set up to adjudicate isolated cases. So, it is important to establish whether the offences committed by PMCs could fit within the current categorisation of the Rome Statute. Crimes under the jurisdiction of the Court include genocide, aggression, war crimes, and crimes against humanity.[32] The crime of aggression,[33] defined at the Kampala Conference in 2010, is directly linked to state armed forces, and are therefore unlikely to be applied to PMCs who are always contracted to deliver services on behalf of a client. The crime of aggression could only be extended to PMCs if they were formally incorporated into state national forces, or if their conduct could otherwise be attributed to the acts of the state (in which case, at least theoretically, state responsibility would be enacted).[34]

Arguably, it is also less possible that genocide could be perpetrated by a PMC and its employees, as it requires "intent to destroy, in whole or in part, a national, ethnical, racial or religious group",[35] which is unlikely to occur, especially systematically, under the contracted services of the company. Individual acts associated with war crimes and crimes against humanity, such as murder, hostage-taking, rape, or torture, are more likely to occur and do not necessitate the special intent (intent to destroy) of the international crime of genocide.[36] However, the definition by the Rome Statute of crimes against humanity imposes a limitation by considering these acts "as part of a widespread and systematic attack directed against any civilian population".[37] Article 8 further stipulates that in order for the ICC to exercise its jurisdiction over war crimes, these ought to be part of a broader "plan or policy", or identified as "part of a large-scale commission of such crimes".[38] This would potentially require amendments in order to apply more broadly to individual incidents carried out by corporations such as PMCs.

Furthermore, trying corporations would also make criminal court processes longer and more expensive.[39] Critics of international criminal law have questioned the autonomy and impartiality of international courts and prosecutors, the respect for the accused's rights of pretrial release, and the quality of the punishment.[40] Amongst the main critiques of international criminal justice is also the selectivity of crimes that reach the tribunals.[41] The lack of justice following the Hiroshima and Nagasaki atomic bombings in 1945, NATO's bombing raids on Serbia, Vojvodina, and Kosovo in 1999, are only a few examples that characterise the bias of so-called victors' justice.[42] Gerry Simpson disagrees with the victors' justice frame and considers war crimes trials to be political, as he claims the concept of what is political is at play all the time. Compromising between idealism and realism, war crimes trials set out to carry out prosecutions in the political realm while also guaranteeing immunity to the hegemons.[43] To an extent, victors' justice and increased politicisation are present across all aspects of IL.[44] Although limiting the 'universality' of ICL and UJ, these concerns should not prevent the development of the international criminal justice system. Daniele Archibugi sees all existing bodies of ICL as "the embryos of more robust ones that will be needed to guarantee global legality", and argues that "a fully fledged international criminal court needs to be set up".[45] Furthermore, companies operate on a different plane to individuals and so ICL could tackle the corporate veneer that is currently producing corporate impunity in the absence of criminal responsibility norms for corporations. For the same reasons, the implementation of the principles of UJ may clash with political interests and diplomacy, and this could hinder its development.[46]

Lessons from addressing international crimes through ICL and possible lineages of international criminal responsibility

The question remains as to how could international criminal law be deployed in order to invoke corporate criminal responsibility? ICL is based on the principle that certain human rights are so widely acknowledged in IL that abuses should be punished regardless of the location of the offence.[47] In other words, the prosecution of serious international crimes naturally enjoys extraterritorial application. Another part of the attraction of ICL is that it largely circumvents customary IL and common law.[48] Lessons found in historical examples of exercising universal jurisdiction could be applicable to contemporary corporations in the way that international crimes are prosecuted. Given the absence of a relevant international legislation with regard to corporate entities, these examples could provide possible lineages and future opportunities for building a more robust case for corporate accountability for PMCs.

Universal jurisdiction and piracy

Another method adopted by ICL to address the problem of international crimes is through the application of universal jurisdiction (UJ). Stephen Macedo describes UJ as "part of a wider set of political and legal movements to expand legal accountability and the global rule of law, and thereby to end impunity for serious crimes under international law".[49] The purpose of UJ is its ability to invoke criminal responsibility "in respect of certain crimes irrespective of the location of the crime and the nationality of the perpetrator or the victim".[50] Approximately 150 of the 197 UN member states provide for UJ for at least one of the four recognised international crimes.[51] Also, cases such as *Demanjuk*[52] in 1985, *Pinochet*[53] in 1999, *Butare Four*[54] in 2001, *Pascal Simbikangwa*[55] in 2014, and most recently the *Hissène Habré* trial by the Extraordinary African Chambers in 2015,[56] validate the practical applicability of UJ as a method of trying international crimes.[57] However, there is an ongoing debate amongst states as to its sources, scope, and application. In the sixty-fourth UN General Assembly (GA) session in 2009,[58] the delegations disagreed on whether the principle had become part of customary IL, or if the crimes covered under the principle of UJ belong to treaty law.[59] Some delegations raised concerns about an expansion of the crimes covered under UJ and suggested that it should only be used as a last resort, while disagreeing on the scope of crimes under the jurisdiction.[60]

For centuries, the doctrine of UJ was applied only to the prosecution and punishment of the crime of piracy, whereby any nation could capture and try pirates it found on the high seas.[61] The pirate was regarded as *hostis humani generis* or *hostis omnium*, an "enemy of all mankind".[62] This lay the foundation for the principle that piracy should be considered a paradigmatic crime for which IL authorises and even requires universal enforcement and punishment.[63] What makes the crime of piracy a universal one is the indiscriminate harm that pirates cause to their victims and trade regardless of political views, geographies, or nationality. This means that piracy affects all states without discrimination, except for those states who used pirates as a policy vehicle, providing state harbour and creating the category of privateers. According to Kontorovich and Art, piracy concerns even the countries not directly involved in shipping, as pirate attacks raise the prices of commodities.[64] In this respect, piracy is rather different to mercenarism, as there is always a state (or non-state) party that deliberately wishes to hire a private military force to further its own political conduct. Even though, as with mercenaries and private military contractors, pirates fall in the grey zone between military combatants and civilians,[65] the political drive behind the private security demand could be a serious obstacle to the criminalisation of mercenary activity.

There is also a second pillar that supports the universality of the crime of piracy. According to Christopher Staker the purpose of UJ is to deliver justice against crimes that would otherwise go unpunished.[66] The issue of corporate impunity persists in cases of private military activity, and it has several roots. The problem is not only the lack of a universal definition of a mercenary, but also the situational and political context of existing definitions. In addition, while the AP I outlined a number of narrow scenarios that criminalises mercenaries, the act of mercenarism had not been criminalised. On that premise, PMCs were able to be incorporated as companies, and continue to operate under the legitimising shield of their legal personality. If mercenarism as an activity was criminalised, this could have two possible benefits. First, civilian participation in hostilities on behalf of a private company without a proper incorporation into a state's army would be forbidden, which, as demonstrated throughout the monograph, has never been achieved through hard law, even if the general normative sentiment of the twentieth century claimed otherwise. Second, PMCs will no longer be able to form corporations that provide military services, as civilian participation in hostilities will be illegal. The criminalisation of mercenarism would not come without its challenges, which are discussed in more detail in the final section below on considerations and opportunities for future regulation.

War crimes and crimes against humanity

According to David Hirsh, the notion of crimes against humanity marks a "recognition that there is no sovereign right to commit such crimes and that the claim made by cosmopolitan law, that it has jurisdiction within all sovereign states in relation to such crimes is legitimate".[67] Falling under the UJ, these international crimes could potentially be extended to PMC misconduct. In May 1960 Mossad, the Israeli intelligence service, captured Adolf Eichmann from his hiding place in Argentina and transported him to Jerusalem to be tried in an Israeli court.[68] By May 1960, the statute of limitation meant that only first degree murder could be prosecuted with other offences reduced to twenty years of imprisonment.[69] Ironically described by Gerry Simpson as "a latter-day pirate" with his crimes "against all states",[70] Eichmann was charged with crimes against the Jewish people, crimes against humanity, and war crimes committed under the Nazi regime during the Second World War.[71] The jurisdiction to try the accused in Eichmann's case was the Nazis and Nazi Collaborators (Punishment) Law 5710-1950,[72] which is equivalent to the "enforcement through universal jurisdiction of prohibitions under the rules of war against the commission of crimes against humanity".[73] What undermines the universality of this case is the focus on the Jewish people, rendering it an experience of "particular groups at the hands of other groups" instead of a "universal experience subject to universal laws".[74] While Eichmann had insisted that he was only "aiding and abetting" in the commission of the abovementioned crimes, the District Court of Jerusalem reached a decision that could set precedent to address the limitation currently posed by complicity in IL. The Court concluded that

> in such an enormous and complicated crime as the one we are now considering, wherein many people participated at various levels and in various modes of activity – the planners, the organizers and those executing the acts, according to their various ranks – there is not much point in using the ordinary concepts of counselling and soliciting to commit a crime. [...] On the contrary, in general, the degree of responsibility increases as we draw further away from the man who uses the fatal instrument with his own hands.[75]

This judgement set a precedent for the comprehensiveness of war crimes and crimes against humanity or, more generally, international crimes. Therefore, it allows ICL to address the entire 'supply chain' of crimes. Currently the parent company is protected by corporate law from any responsibility over the indiscretions of its subsidiaries. Building a tangential link to PMC accountability, if extended to corporations, ICL could address the challenges posed by the corporate veil and ensure the parent company's liability is also invoked.

Eichmann was a bureaucrat who, prior to his position as head of the Centre for Emigration of Austrian Jews in 1938, had had a rather insignificant career as a travelling sales person. A déclassé son of a solid middle-class family,[76] he was never truly interested in the Nazi ideology, nor had he read Hitler's *Mein Kampf*.[77] The 'banality of evil', according to Hannah Arendt, lies in the way Eichmann's lack of professional fulfilment and his natural talent for organisation and negotiation led him to setting in motion "forced emigration" and all subsequent stages of the Nazi Solution to the Jewish Question.[78] The bureaucratic background to a series of war crimes can be comparable with the banality of a company operating in politically sensitive and high risk regions.[79] To quote

Diane Amann, "corporations are being used as instrumentalities for great and unimaginable suffering".[80] The corporate structure removes the element of aggression, intervention, and civilian participation in hostilities. It also obscures all those rules and norms that international humanitarian lawyers have worked so methodically to establish. Beyond the principle of the nature of crime[81] that characterised the UJ of the "Eichmann model", the case also demonstrated a form of bureaucratic power on the part of an individual who worked for the government and executed the state's policy through his role as a functionary. In the case of PMCs, we can trace the shift in governance from state to corporation, whereby PMCs in particular perform the bureaucratic functions of logistics, organising security operations, training, and, ultimately, killing.

By drawing on the historical typology of forms of governance, we observe a transformation in the extent of states power, whereby their functions have been limited or modified through privatisation and outsourcing to the private sector. The companies which have subsequently taken on the functions formerly owned by states have also inadvertently acquired a form of governance, making claims to legitimacy through self-regulation. This newly acquired governance on the part of PMCs could be viewed as building a rationale against an overarching criminal responsibility for corporations. In other words, companies make sovereignty claims by establishing international regulatory frameworks within the industry that promote human rights values on the one hand, and do not have to answer to any judicial or state authority, on the other. It could be argued, in a similar vein, that the 'responsibilisation' approach of voluntary norms and industry standards falls in line with the neoliberal framework of the free market.

However, to follow my claim for normative regulation, PMCs alongside any other corporations preforming inherently governmental functions and operating in zones of conflict or political tension, ought to answer to an independent overarching authority, accepting criminal responsibility for the acts committed by the legal entity. In other words, the 'business of killing' should not be self-regulated; instead PMCs' increasing claims to sovereignty signal the need for criminal responsibility that ought to recognise corporations as independent actors, and tackle their misconduct directly.

Considerations and opportunities for future regulation

Having reviewed the existing regulatory landscape for corporations, and PMCs as a specific category, I conclude that there is a strong need to establish a mechanism to invoke criminal responsibility for PMCs for crimes and human rights violations committed transnationally. The need for corporate criminal responsibility does not negate the value brought by the standard-setting regulatory mechanisms, such as ISO and the ICoC. On the contrary, this would enable a more effective functioning of existing industry self-regulation, complementing industry standards with an enforcement mechanism that would also have a deterrent effect and a clear binding monitoring and accountability framework. However, if to remain unbinding and entirely voluntary, industry-led self-regulatory processes, such as the ICoC and the Montreux Process, will continue to act as a distraction from the legal vacuum of the PMC space. Ultimately, voluntary regulation can only be meaningful and beneficial in controlling private force if there is an enforcement and accountability mechanism that could step in, should the soft law fail to govern.

In addition to tackling corporate impunity, the ability to invoke corporate criminal responsibility internationally would help ensure a more effective and responsible use of private security resources. In order to tackle the challenge of prosecuting international crimes committed by corporations, I consider opportunities within international criminal law. One of the many practical advantages of this is that ICL and UJ allow for the trial of international crimes.[82] ICL could offer a way of constructing a criminal corporate responsibility that is appropriate for the contemporary security landscape and which would be capable of adapting to changing governance structures. International crimes in ICL can address the entire 'supply chain' of crimes, thereby tackling the challenges posed by the corporate veil. As ruled in *Eichmann*, war crimes and crimes against humanity are comprehensive enough to extend responsibility beyond the individual firing the gun.[83] If transferred to corporations, this could ensure the parent company is also held responsible. An important precedent to follow will be the *Lafarge case* as it proceeds with an indictment of a French parent company for the acts of terrorist financing and complicity in crimes against humanity of its Syrian subsidiary abroad.

Yet, there several procedural considerations of establishing such a mechanism, as it could be achieved through different avenues. With that in mind, I consider four possible criminalisation options that explore different methods of employing ICL and exercising it in different fora, domestic, international, and transnational. Each method considers the advantages and possible challenges that may arise, mindful of the current 'shared' form of governance, the critique of the international justice system, the existing deficiencies of PMC regulation, and associated state practice.

The first option considers the feasibility and advantage of criminalising the act of mercenarism through universal jurisdiction. The following three options partially circumvent the need for state buy-in on criminalising mercenarism, adopting the framework of ICL to prosecute companies for already codified criminal acts under UJ and the Rome Statute. These recommendations should be treated as proposals that, while they could address the key loophole of the corporate impunity of PMCs, each require a deeper analysis to enable implementation.

Criminalising mercenarism

Many have connected the rise of PMCs at the turn of twenty-first century to the failure to criminalise the act of mercenarism through Geneva Conventions and other regional international legal fora.[84] Private military and security actors are recruited and deployed by a contracting party, meaning they need financing and direction in order to perform their function. This, in turn, would imply that a mercenary or a private military company are simply a tool in the arsenal of a contracting party. In order to establish responsibility under IL, it would therefore necessitate not only to criminalise a mercenary, but also to codify the act of mercenarism as a crime, as originally attempted by the OAU Convention and now codified under the jurisdiction of the African Court of Justice and Human Rights. The importance of codification lies in the blurred lines between mercenaries, PSCs, and PMCs. In order for this avenue to be implementable, it will be crucial to define the intended activity and not just the actor when approaching the question of regulation.

Although unlikely to be adopted due to an increasing privatisation trend, criminalisation of the act of mercenarism could nonetheless be considered a 'shortcut' mechanism. The criminalisation of mercenarism could not only prevent civilians from direct participation in hostilities, but could also limit the scope of activity for companies themselves. According to the provisions of corporate and contract law, companies cannot be formed with a purpose of engaging in illegal activities. If mercenarism, or the provision of private armed forces for combat purposes, is deemed criminal, then private military companies will not be incorporated to pursue belligerent goals. Of course, companies could fail to declare the provision of military services as part of their functions yet continue to supply these services covertly. And although such misconduct would give rise to liability, criminalisation of the act of mercenarism would not tackle the issue of corporate criminal responsibility, ignoring the shared governance trend and leaving a wide gap in PMC regulation from the corporate perspective.

Nevertheless, the universal jurisdiction could be used a vehicle for criminalising the act of mercenarism, by adding it to the list of grave crimes under the auspices of the UJ. This could be achieved by adopting the approach to UJ that justifies the principle based on the nature of crimes, allowing states to apply UJ jurisdiction if the act is a crime under IL. This option could materialise either through customary IL, or via a treaty process such as the Geneva Conventions.[85] The limitations of treaty-based regulation have been discussed at length in previous chapters, and the impotence of the UN Mercenary Convention is an indication as to how future efforts to criminalise mercenarism through treaty law will pan out. After the *Arrest Warrant Case* in 2000,[86] there has been a shift away from the "Eichmann model" which focuses on the nature of offence towards state behaviour, requiring a strong precedent to justify application of UJ.[87] Unlike the Princeton definition that solely emphasises the "nature of the crime, without regard to where the crime was committed",[88] more recent attempts to define UJ outline three state-focused conditions, in which at least one should apply to meet the legal principle. The infraction must either be committed in the territory of the state, or by a national of the state, or the victim must be a citizen of the state in question.[89] Possible challenges that would arise from this shift are related to the state-centric model of UJ, which, as discussed in *Chapter 6*, is unlikely to succeed under the current mode of shared governance.

Although both avenues are likely to face considerable challenges to state acceptance and implementation, UJ could be applicable to mercenary activity, given it is aimed at delivering justice in respect of crimes that would otherwise go unpunished. One of the possible outcomes could, therefore, entail a restricted civilian, or more accurately non-combatant, participation in hostilities. This would prompt states to incorporate private military contractors into national armed forces, thus enacting command and control responsibility and enabling the jurisdiction of the ILC Articles. In this way, criminalising mercenarism could also potentially increase state responsibility under IL with regard to private actors.

Another advantage of criminalising mercenarism through UJ is the strength of national commitment to the international community, as a state would have to take necessary measures to ensure the UJ can be exercised in national courts.[90] At the same time, this could also pose a serious challenge. There are other doctrinal limitations to this solution. Currently there is no legally neutral, universal definition of the act of mercenarism, while the existing definitions can be conflicting and restricted by political context. The same is seen in the failure to codify terrorism as an international crime. Due to the lack of consensus on the definition of terrorism amongst states, customary IL does not currently provide for the prosecution of 'terrorist' acts under the universality principle.[91]

As to state exercised precedent, reported numbers of cases brought under UJ illustrate momentum with 58 cases delivering accountability in 2017 through specialised international crimes units set up in a number of states.[92] To compare, in 2015 the principle of UJ was applied to forty cases, with arrests, indictments, or convictions achieved in twenty-seven cases, significantly exceeding the 2014 results.[93] Moreover, as part of the UN GA's seventy-first session on the scope and application of the principle of UJ,[94] Georgia advised that participation of mercenaries in armed conflicts or military actions is codified in Article 410 of chapter XLVII of the Criminal Code as part of specific legislation relating to UJ.[95] However, other recent examples of the exercise of UJ in Spain and Belgium have demonstrated the prevalence of sovereign interests over international justice.[96] In 2003, as a result of the US threat to move the NATO headquarters out of Brussels,[97] the Belgian legislature revoked provisions of its extraterritorial 1993 UJ law.[98] Meanwhile, the Spanish Parliament "acted to limit the jurisdiction over human rights cases in 2009".[99] The amendment stipulated that, in order for UJ to apply, the victims must be of Spanish nationality, the alleged perpetrators must be in Spain, or there should be an important connecting link with Spain, and that another jurisdiction or an international criminal court should not have initiated investigation and prosecution of those offences.[100] More recently, in 2014, a new amendment was issued, limiting the jurisdiction to cases initiated by public prosecutors and victims.[101]

Most importantly, the implementation of this option would be subject to the prevailing relationship between states and private military actors. The clear privatisation trend, coupled with the practice of 'small' government, signals the desire of states to use PMCs and incorporate private security into government policy. The limitation of governmental functions results in the outsourcing of various tasks to private companies, including security. In other words, states are unlikely to accept mercenarism as an international crime under UJ because they are leading PMC clients and willingly use private military resources.

Include corporations (or at least PMCs) in the jurisdiction of the Rome Statute

Another option for establishing criminal corporate responsibility for international crimes could be achieved through the international forum of the ICC. This could be achieved by recognising corporations as actors under international law, and therefore extending criminal liability to companies alongside individuals for crimes within the jurisdiction of the Rome Statute. Arguably, PMCs require a greater level of scrutiny due to the military nature of their business and the fact that their services are mostly delivered outside of their home state, so the international element is inevitable. By assigning corporations with an international legal personality, PMCs can then be held liable for war crimes committed in an international conflict, rather than only non-international; currently PMCs are treated as a civilian component of an operation, not military. This change in PMC status would expand the scope of potential violations and curtail corporate impunity.

The first underlying principle of the Rome Statute, the principle of complementarity, stipulates that the ICC may exercise jurisdiction only when national legal systems are unable or unwilling to do so.[102] This means that domestic courts prevail in cases of simultaneous jurisdiction. "The court is not intended to replace national courts, but operates only when they do not".[103] While it assumes that both domestic and international criminal justice systems ought to function in a subsidiary manner,[104] if this mechanism is to be implemented, it would not negate the need for recognition of international criminal responsibility for corporations, for two reasons. First, currently, corporate criminal liability is not consistently codified across all domestic legal systems, meaning that the ICC could be the sole avenue for such jurisdiction.[105] This, in turn, would render the system too lengthy, costly and, ultimately, inefficient in prosecuting legal entities for international crimes. Second, the principle of complementarity does not apply uniformly across all international courts. The ICTY and the ICTR ad hoc Tribunals both prevail over national courts in cases of concurrent jurisdiction.[106]

Alongside all the above-mentioned advantages of ICL application, the use of an international forum has the advantage of extraterritoriality. While the ICC is only applicable to state parties, the nationals of non-parties who committed a crime within the ICC's jurisdiction can be subjected to it.[107] The UN Security Council can also refer a case to the ICC involving non-party nationals, or the ICC can have jurisdiction if an act was committed on the territory of a state party by a non-party national.[108]

So, if the ICC's jurisdiction extended to corporations, or even PMCs specifically, this could overcome the territorial barrier of national jurisdiction. Unfortunately, this extraterritoriality is highly conditional. Although the ICC has jurisdiction over crimes against humanity, it does not exercise UJ as it was specifically rejected in the proceedings of the Rome Statute,[109] significantly limiting its extraterritorial reach. This means that the biggest PMC providers and clients, namely the US, China, and Russia, would not be subject to the ICC's jurisdiction, having not ratified the Rome Statute.[110] Furthermore, different immunity mechanisms shield UK and the US military personnel from ICC investigations.[111] What complicates matters further is that the ICC was not set up to deal with isolated cases of international crimes; instead it is perceived as a forum where only the most heinous and systematic crimes ought to be tried, such as genocide, crimes of aggression, war crimes, and crimes against humanity.[112] The need to prove that the offences were systematic could potentially obstruct the prosecution of one-off cases and continue to foster PMC impunity. Lacking the general requirement of being "widespread and systematic", the case of Baha Mousa,[113] an Iraqi civilian who was beaten to death while detained by British army soldiers in 2003, never made it to the ICC. The systematic element could pose an issue for PMC regulation, as single violations that do not form part of a large-scale action will not qualify as crimes against humanity and, therefore, will not be accepted by the Court. Equally, other serious crimes, such as human rights abuses, gross negligence, are currently not covered by the Statute, signalling the potential need for a new category, to ensure relevance and effectiveness of this criminalisation mechanism. Until codified by the international military tribunals at the end of the Second World War, the types of crimes committed by the Nazis, such as crimes against humanity and crimes of aggression, did not exist under IL.[114] Perhaps if corporations are recognised as actors under IL by the Rome Statute, a new type of crime, a corporate international crime, could henceforth be codified in order to reflect the gross misconduct of PMCs in military support operations abroad and human rights abuses perpetrated by all types of corporations.

Another hurdle that IL would have to overcome is the narrow responsibility of complicity for corporations,[115] as well as the narrow catalogue of crimes currently tried before the ICC. It is not sufficient for only the most important crimes to be tried before the ICC,[116] as it would leave less grave PMC misconduct unpunished. Without a doubt, not all PMC violations will require a criminal justice response, so there is still room for domestic criminal procedure and social corporate responsibility to regulate less serious violations. Whether this should be done on the domestic level, or brought to the international forum, is a question of implementation and subject to further research, as the challenge remains pertaining to PMC international reach and their uniqueness in comparison to other corporations based on the nature of their business.

Another limitation of IL as a forum for international criminal responsibility for corporations is the lack of widely recognised international criminal responsibility for corporations, outside of the African Court of Justice and Human Rights, and the very narrow precedent set by the Special Tribunal for Lebanon. Even if the jurisdiction of the international courts is extended to legal persons, the ICC and the Tribunals would have to develop or adopt legal procedures for the criminal trial of a corporation rather than a natural person. Here I refer to the existing procedural difficulties associated with corporations, addressed in detail in *Chapter 7.* Moreover, international legal space remains highly politicised as the ICTY and ICTR have limited jurisdictional reach, while the principle of the complementarity of the ICC tasks domestic courts with prosecuting international crimes.[117] So before corporations can be tried at the international courts, first, it appears, the international criminal procedure would need to be significantly amended.

'Pairing' ICL to domestic legal systems

A criminalisation mechanism could nevertheless be implemented through domestic legal systems.[118] If undertaken across a considerable number of states, this approach could arguably be more effective in terms of enforcement than that of the international courts, due to their tendency to take on only the most serious crimes. As demonstrated in *Chapter 7*, corporate criminal liability for international crimes is already available in many European jurisdictions and in the African Court of Justice and Human Rights without resort to customary IL. The legislative mandate for corporate criminal liability for international crimes is enabled through domestic legal systems by incorporating the language of ICL. Between 2004 and 2005, Fafo conducted a study of sixteen national jurisdictions across a variety of legal systems and traditions to identify the practice of corporate criminal liability. The results of the survey showed that eleven out of sixteen countries, namely Australia, Belgium, Canada, France, India, Japan, the Netherlands, Norway, South Africa, the United Kingdom, and the United States, have developed provisions for the criminal liability for corporations, while Argentina, Germany, Indonesia, Spain, and Ukraine currently do not recognise such liability.[119] These findings provide an indication of the growing inclusion of corporate persons into national criminal practice. At the same time, there has been an increasing trend of national courts extending their reach to international crimes.[120]

The method of applying ICL in a domestic legal forum could also leverage existing voluntary norms relating to PMC conduct and regulation. For example, as demonstrated in earlier chapters, by the means of the Montreux Process, seventeen states (including the US, the UK, China, and South Africa) officially agreed that the idea of superior responsibility, grounded in ICL, has a potential role in assigning responsibility for international crimes to PMC directors and their clients.[121] While lacking legal enforcement, the Montreux Process creates a clear norm concerning corporate responsibility, that can be leveraged through ICL.

By adopting ICL language in domestic legal systems, corporate responsibility could bypass the limitation of complicity posed by corporate criminal procedure, and potentially expose corporations to a greater level of criminal responsibility in the event of misconduct. Furthermore, a 'domestic' solution could overcome the resistance of international law practitioners to the recognition of corporate legal personality without compromising the ability to cover the transnational realm of PMC operation. Given the international nature of PMC activity, domestic case law could then provide grounds for developing customary international law. In addition, choosing a national legal system as the criminal liability forum for corporate bodies gives domestic courts a relative freedom of interpretation, which would not be the case on the international level, where consensus would have to be reached on a number of provisions, including definitions and enforcement. According to Stewart, if international crimes are defined by IL and incorporated into domestic legal systems, then more varied standards of blame attribution could be applied to these "international-crimes-made-national".[122] Aiding and abetting, or complicity, was the most prominent method of attributing responsibility to corporations both in domestic legal systems and through the ATS.[123] ICL, on the contrary, offers a much wider selection of "modes of liability", including superior responsibility, joint criminal enterprise, and more.[124]

Importantly, the availability of a domestic accountability mechanism for PMC corporate conduct would strengthen the validity of voluntary industry regulation, providing the enforcement mechanism to the existing standard-setting and monitoring structures. Finally, this issue of extraterritoriality could be resolved under UJ for the most serious international crimes, as opposed to the first option which suggests codifying the crime of mercenarism as a new offence under UJ.[125] By applying UJ to PMCs as corporations who are found to have committed grave international crimes, such as war crimes, crimes against humanity, etc., companies could be tried at any national court without having to rely on the geographical coverage of domestic legal systems. On the other hand, it could mean continued disparity in the treatment of PMC violations and a lack of coherent regulation standards for corporate crimes. Divergence amongst states as to how they define the crime and what jurisdiction they assert over it could, in fact, pose difficulties for the emergence of a customary international law rule. The territorial limitation would leave room for impunity, as not all states would be willing to embrace international criminal responsibility for corporations. This could also exacerbate corporate impunity should PMCs shift their business to the states where corporate criminal liability is not recognised.

Employing transnational law to construct corporate criminal responsibility

Similar to the previous option of tacking international crimes for corporations in a domestic forum, transnational criminal law suggests "the indirect suppression by international law through domestic penal law of criminal activities that have actual or potential trans-boundary effects".[126] Forming part of ICL, transnational criminal law (TCL) still benefits from the international dimension in which the crimes are committed, but is not limited to the core international crimes[127] and reliance on customary international law.[128] Due to PMCs operating mostly in post-war environments, it may be problematic to argue for serious systematic crimes in many cases of PMC offences. As part of a broader misconduct, acts of murder, torture, rape, and so on, all constitute a crime against humanity[129] and are on the ICC Rome Statute list of international crimes. TCL could, however, overcome this limitation as the catalogue of transnational crimes[130] covers of a wide variety of offences, including organised, white-collar and political crime.[131]

By employing transnational law, this solution could be seen as loosely replicating the principle of Alien Tort Statute (ATS), only through criminal, not purely social corporate responsibility. In its current form, transnational criminal law is arguably more suitable to corporations than international law as it does not require the same extent of adjustments or recognition of international legal personality. According to Bassiouni, transnational crimes are those committed by private or non-state actors.[132] Such classification is more tailored to PMC conduct as it removes the necessity of establishing the link to state bodies in order for PMC crimes to be recognised as international or as part of state conduct in a different state.

However, a great extent of scholarly and practical development is necessary to realise this recommendation as private military activity does not fall organically within the realm of transnational criminal law. TCL predominantly targets the criminal market,[133] while the PMC activity is a priori legitimate and only becomes an unregulated issue when human rights abuses and other serious offences occur. TCL is limited to offences covered by a suppression convention,[134] so state buy-in is still necessary to willingly suppress a particular form of conduct. For PMC regulation it could either mean following the existing framework of transnational crimes,[135] or designing a new category of human rights violation by PMCs transnationally. While such convention requires governmental consent, it does not prevent the use of PMCs or demand the criminalisation of PMC activity as such. Instead, it would specifically target gross misconduct and offences that would call for criminal liability on the domestic level, or if committed by an individual. Therefore, criminalisation of serious PMC offences through transnational criminal law could offer the most tailored approach to regulation in the context of shared governance.[136] Similarly to the previously discussed option of a domestic forum, this approach would act in synergy with emerging industry regulation, and would help build corporate accountability beyond national borders.

While the disparity in prosecuting legal persons exists on the national level and should, without a doubt, be recognised as a limitation, the private nature of transnational crimes makes the inclusion of corporate liability in the suppression conventions more feasible. For instance, the United Nations Convention against Corruption (UNCAC) and the United Nations Convention against Transnational Organized Crime (UNTOC) both oblige state parties "consistent with its legal principles, to establish the liability of legal persons".[137]

This mechanism would naturally be enforced through a domestic forum. Alternatively, the precedent of the Extraordinary African Chambers[138] allows for the ad hoc establishment of a new special tribunal while national courts streamline the corporate prosecution procedures. This solution, coupled with the 'domestic' option described above, would produce comprehensive coverage while overcoming doctrinal difficulties and taking into consideration the governance trends.

Notes

1 Due to PMC's civilian status, it is unlikely that their conduct can be considered as part of an international conflict. Article 3 in each of the 1949 Conventions provides a description of war crimes that are applicable to non-international conflicts.

2 Zolo (2009, p. ix); also: Germany following the Treaty of Versailles; a more recent example is the US in the *Nicaragua case*.
3 Nuremberg Prosecutor Jackson claimed there was precedent for the idea of individual criminal responsibility under customary IL in cases of piracy, see: Lauterpacht (1944, pp. 61, 64); Heller-Roazen (2009).
4 See Chapter 2.
5 Garrett (2008, p. 133).
6 White and MacLeod (2008, p. 969); see also: Robins (2006); Stone (1975, p. 15).
7 Cameron and Chetail (2013, p. 584).
8 Agreement for the Prosecution and Punishment of the Major War Criminals of the European Axis, and Charter of the International Military Tribunal, London, 8 August 1945, Article 10.
9 Cameron and Chetail (2013, p. 585).
10 Liu (2015, pp. 252–254).
11 Bush (2009, p. 1239).
12 Bush (2009, p. 1237).
13 Bush (2009, p. 1240).
14 1951/53 Reports of the Committee on International Criminal Jurisdiction of the ILC.
15 Clapham (2000, pp. 171–172).
16 Liu (2015, p. 289).
17 Clapham (2000, p. 191); Schabas (2011, p. 81).
18 225 United Nations Convention against Transnational Organized Crime 275.
19 Prosecutor v. Mohamed et al., STL-14-05 (2014); Prosecutor v. Al Amin et al., STL-14-06 (2014).
20 Akhbar Beirut S.A.L. & Mr Al Amin (STL-14-06).
21 Chatham House (2015, p. 6).
22 Draft Protocol on Amendments to the Protocol on the Statute of the African Court of Justice and Human Rights, May 15, 2014, STC/Legal/Min/7(I) Rev. 1, Art. 46C; see also the Decision on the Draft Legal Instruments, Doc. Assembly/AU/8(XXIII), at 1 in African Union, Decisions, Declarations And Resolution, Assembly/AU/Dec.517-545(XXIII).
23 STC/Legal/Min/7(I) Rev. 1, Article 28A, International Criminal Jurisdiction of the Court, p. 15.
24 See Chapter 3.
25 For example, the ICC's limit to territory of state parties and nationals of state parties.
26 On the ICL procedure and the ICC see: Schabas (2011); Cryer, et al. (2014); Schwobel (2014).
27 Echoed in Schwarzenberger (1950, pp. 263–296).
28 Simpson (2007, pp. 44–45).
29 Rome Statute, Art. 1.
30 Simpson (2007, p. 53).
31 Bassiouni (2001, p. 82); Cryer (2014, p. 754).
32 Rome Statute, Art. 5 (1).
33 Rome Statute, Art. 8 *bis*, inserted by resolution RC/Res.6 of 11 June 2010.
34 See ILC Articles on attribution of conduct.
35 Rome Statute, Art. 6.
36 Simpson (2007, pp. 68–69).
37 Rome Statute, Art. 7 (1).
38 Rome Statute, Art. 8 (1).
39 Amann (2000, p. 334).
40 Zolo (2009, p. 140).
41 Cryer (2005); McCormack and Simpson (1997); Bull (1977); Kelsen (1947, pp. 153–171); Kelsen (1944); Roling (1973).

42 Zolo (2009, p. xi).
43 Simpson (2007, pp. 18–19).
44 Greene (1957); Koskenniemi (2002, pp. 1–35).
45 Archibugi (2002, p. 36).
46 Philippe (2006, p. 376); Langer (2011, pp. 1–49).
47 Thompson, Ramasastry, and Taylor (2009, pp. 845–846).
48 Stewart (2014, p. 40).
49 Macedo (2004, p. 5).
50 International Law Association Committee on International Human Rights Law and Practice (2000, p. 2).
51 Universal Jurisdiction Annual Review 2016, p. 4; note that, e.g., Reydams is critical of NGO data collection; see: Reydams (2004).
52 *Demanjuk v. Petrovsky*, US Court of Appeal, 6th Cir., 31.10.1985, ILR 79, 546.
53 House of Lords, 24 March 1999, 2 WLR 827.
54 Cour d'Assises de Bruxelles, 8 June 2001.
55 See: Trial International.
56 See: "The Trial of Hissène Habré", *Human Rights Watch*.
57 Langer (2015, pp. 245–256).
58 See: United Nations General Assembly, 64th session, 15 September 2009.
59 Following *Pinochet*, a debate arose over whether the authority to prosecute the crime of torture derived from universal jurisdiction, or if it was the principle of customary international law (*aut dedere aut judicare*).
60 UN GA 64th Session, 2009; UN GA 67th Session, 2012.
61 United Nations Convention on the Law of the Sea Arts 3, 56(1), Dec. 10, 1982, 1833 U.N.T.S. 397, 400, 418; Legal Framework for the Repression of Piracy Under UNCLOS, updated 9 September 2010.
62 Neocleous (2015, p. 29); an alternative view, argued in the Harvard Research Draft Convention on Piracy, considers piracy a municipal offence that gave rise to an exception to exclusivity of territorial jurisdiction; see: Bingham (1932, p. 757).
63 Kontorovich and Art (2010, p. 246).
64 Kontorovich and Art (2010, p. 252).
65 Kontorovich and Art (2010, p. 245); pirates who were hired by states were not considered criminals, instead state practice legitimised privateering and distinguished it from piracy.
66 Staker (2014, p. 322).
67 Hirsh (2003, p. 152).
68 *Attorney General v. Adolf Eichmann*.
69 Arendt (1994, p. 14).
70 Simpson (2007, p. 41).
71 *Attorney General v. Adolf Eichmann*, Criminal Case No. 40/61, District Court of Jerusalem, Judgement
72 Israel Ministry of Foreign Affairs.
73 International Committee of the Red Cross, Customary IHL, Practice Relating to Rule 157: Jurisdiction over War Crimes, available at: https://ihl-databases.icrc.org/customary-ihl/eng/docs/v2_cou_il_rule157; the Israeli courts also cited passive personality jurisdiction and protective jurisdiction; see: Lasok (1962, p. 368).
74 Simpson (2007, p. 51).
75 Attorney General v. Adolf Eichmann, para. 197.
76 Arendt (1994, p. 31).
77 Arendt (1994, p. 33).
78 Arendt (1994, see in particular chapters 2 and 3, pp. 21–55).
79 Such as Lafarge example illustrated in previous chapter, whereby the company was charged with complicity in crimes against humanity and terrorist financing.
80 Amann (2000, p. 336).

81 Princeton University (2001, p. 28).
82 Philippe (2006, p. 377).
83 On different forms of criminal liability see chapter 15 "General Principles of Liability" in Cryer, et al. (2014, pp. 353–397).
84 See Chapters 3 and 4.
85 There is a debate in legal academic literature over whether treaty-based UJ is a separate principle of *aut dedere aut judicare*; see: Da Rocha Ferreira (2013, pp. 204–205).
86 Democratic Republic of the Congo v. Belgium.
87 Reydams (2004); Reydams (2011, pp. 337–354).
88 Princeton University (2001, p. 28).
89 Universal Jurisdiction Annual Review 2016, Make Way for Justice 2, p. 3.
90 Philippe (2006, p. 387).
91 See: *United States v. Yousef*, 327 F.3d 56, 97 (2nd Circuit, 2003); in the Spanish UJ case of Pinochet, one of the crimes he was charged with was terrorism, as defined in Spanish law; see: Wilson, R. J.: "Prosecuting Pinochet in Spain", available at: www.wcl.american.edu/hrbrief/v6i3/pinochet.htm.
92 Redress (2018).
93 Universal Jurisdiction Annual Review (2016, p. 7).
94 A/71/111, Item 85 of the preliminary list, 28 June 2016.
95 A/71/111, Table 2.
96 Simpson (2007, p. 42).
97 Ratner (2003, pp. 890–891).
98 Human Rights Watch (2003); Reydams (2003, pp. 679–689).
99 Kirshner (2015, p. 16).
100 See: *Boletín Oficial Del Estado* (2009); Kern (2014).
101 Article 23 (4) of the 1985 Organic Law of the Judicial Power; Molto (2015, pp. 1121–1144).
102 Rome Statute, Article 17(2).
103 Arsanjani (1999, pp. 24–25).
104 Philippe (2006, p. 380).
105 However, the key rationale behind Art. 17 on complementarity is to urge states into getting their domestic legal order into shape.
106 Article 9 of the ICTY Statute: International Tribunal for the Prosecution of Persons Responsible for Serious Violations of International Humanitarian Law Committed in the Territory of the Former Yugoslavia since 1991, p. 7; Article 8 of the ICTR Statute: Statute of the International Criminal Tribunal for the Prosecution of Persons Responsible for Genocide and Other Serious Violations of International Humanitarian Law Committed in the Territory of Rwanda and Rwandan Citizens Responsible for Genocide and Other such Violations Committed in the Territory of Neighbouring States, between January 1, 1994 and December 31, 1994.
107 See Bassiouni (2001, p. 92): "in the territory of a state party or against citizens of a state party, and are found in the territory of a state party or in the territory of a non-party willing to cede jurisdiction to the ICC."
108 Rome Statute, Article 13.
109 Simpson (2007, p. 47).
110 In October 2016 Burundi, South Africa, and Gambia withdrew from the ICC. Experts believe that Kenya, Namibia, and Uganda could be among the next countries to leave the Court. Sieff (2016).
111 Simpson (2007, p. 17).
112 Rome Statute, Art. 5, also reflected in the IMT Charter at Nuremberg.
113 Williams (2013).

114 Schabas (2011, p. 6); Simpson (2007, p. 40).
115 See: Clapham and Jerbi (2000–2001, pp. 339–349); Clapham (2008, pp. 899–926).
116 Philippe (2006, p. 384).
117 Simpson (2007, p. 50).
118 An example of a purely domestic proposal is to replicate US Foreign Corrupt Practices Act in Ganesan 2015.
119 Ramasastry and Thompson (2006, p. 13).
120 Simpson (2007, p. 134).
121 The Montreux Document (2008).
122 Standards of attribution would depend on and vary by domestic legal system; Stewart (2014, p. 40).
123 See: Talisman, Khulumani, etc.
124 See: Sepinwall (2008, pp. 251–304); Damaska (2001, pp. 455–496); Van Sliedregt (2012); Jain (2014); Ohlin (2007, pp. 69–90).
125 I use the interpretation that reads UJ as 'any state' can prosecute, as per the *Eichmann case*, practices in Belgium, Randall (1988, pp. 785–841).
126 Boister (2003, p. 955).
127 Articles 5–8 of the Rome Statute.
128 Boister (2012, p. 18).
129 Rome Statute, Art. 7; in *Tadic*, amongst other charges, the Appeals Chamber found Dusko Tadic guilty of one count of murder as a crime against humanity and one count of murder as a violation of the laws of war; IT-94-1-ES, Decision of the President, para. 7.
130 The term was first used at the Fifth UN Congress on Crime Prevention and the Treatment of Offenders in 1975; see: Williams and Vlassis (2001).
131 Boister (2012, p. 4).
132 Bassiouni (1974, p. 421).
133 Such as drug and human trafficking, cross border contraband, money laundering etc., see Boister (2012, p. 15).
134 See Boister (2002, pp. 199–227).
135 E.g.: The International Convention for the Suppression of Counterfeiting of Currency, 20 April 1929; UN Convention against Illicit Traffic in Narcotic Drugs and Psychotropic Substances, 20 December 1988, the 1950 European Convention for the Protection of Human Rights and Freedoms, etc.
136 Drawing upon the relationship between the form of governance and the type of power, analysed in Chapters 2, 3, and 4.
137 Article 26 of UNCAC and Article 10 of UNTOC.
138 See: Chambres Africaines Extraordinaires.

References

1945 Charter of International Military Tribunal, Nuremberg, available at: www.un.org/en/genocideprevention/documents/atrocity-crimes/Doc.2_Charter%20of%20IMT%201945.pdf.

1951/53 Reports of the Committee on International Criminal Jurisdiction of the ILC, available at: http://legal.un.org/diplomaticconferences/1998_icc/.

Agreement for the Prosecution and Punishment of the Major War Criminals of the European Axis, and Charter of the International Military Tribunal, London, 8 August 1945.

Akhbar Beirut S. A. L. & Mr Al Amin (STL-14–06), available at: www.stl-tsl.org/en/the-cases/contempt-cases/stl-14-06.

Amann, D. M.: "Capital Punishment: Corporate Criminal Liability for Gross Violations of Human Rights", 2000, Vol. 24, *Hastings International and Comparative Law Review*, pp. 327–337.

Archibugi, D.: "Demos and Cosmopolis", 2002, Vol. 13, *New Left Review*, pp. 24–38.

Arendt, H.: *Eichmann in Jerusalem: A Report on the Banality of Evil*, revised and enlarged edition, Penguin Books, Harmondsworth, 1994.

Arsanjani, M. H.: "The Rome Statute of the International Criminal Court", 1999, Vol. 93 (1), *The American Journal of International Law*, pp. 22–43.

Attorney General v. Adolf Eichmann, Criminal Case No. 40/61, District Court of Jerusalem, Judgement.

Bassiouni, C. M.: "An Appraisal of the Growth and Developing Trends of International Criminal Law", 1974, Vol. 45, *Revue Internationale de Droit Penal*, pp. 405–433.

Bassiouni, C. M.: "Universal Jurisdiction for International Crimes: Historical Perspectives and Contemporary Practice", 2001, Vol. 42 (1), *Virginia Journal of International Law*, pp. 81–157.

Bingham, J. W.: "Part-IV Piracy", 1932, Vol. 26 (1, Supplement: Research in International Law), *The American Journal of International Law*, pp. 739–885.

Boister, N.: *An Introduction to Transnational Criminal Law*, OUP, Oxford, 2012.

Boister, N.: "Human Rights Protections in the Suppression Conventions", 2002, Vol. 2 (2), *Human Rights Law Review*, pp. 199–227.

Boister, N.: "'Transnational Criminal Law'?", 2003, Vol. 14 (5), *European Journal of International Law*, pp. 953–976.

Boletín Oficial Del Estado, No. 266, 4 November 2009.

Bull, H.: *The Anarchical Society*, Macmillan, London, 1977.

Bush, J.: "The Prehistory of Corporations and Conspiracy in International Criminal Law: What Nuremberg Really Said", 2009, Vol. 109, *Columbia Law Review*, pp. 1094–1242.

Cameron, L. and Chetail, V.: *Privatizing War: Private Military and Security Companies under Public International Law*, CUP, Cambridge, 2013.

Chambres africaines extraoridnaires, available at: www.chambresafricaines.org.

Chatham House: "Corporate Responsibility for International Crimes", Chatham House International Law Programme, Meeting Summary, 19 May 2015, London.

Clapham, A.: "Extending International Criminal Law beyond the Individual to Corporations and Armed Opposition Groups", 2008, Vol. 6 (5), *Journal of International Criminal Justice*, pp. 899–926.

Clapham, A.: "The Questions of Jurisdiction under International Criminal Law over Legal Persons: Lessons from the Rome Conference on an International Criminal Court" in Kamminga, M. T. and Zia-Zarifi, S. (eds): *Liability of Multinational Corporations under International Law*, The Hague, Kluwer, 2000.

Clapham, A. and Jerbi, S.: "Categories of Corporate Complicity in Human Rights", 2000–2001, Vol. 24, *Hastings International & Comparative Law Review*, pp. 339–349. Consejo General del Poder Judicial: Organic Law of the Judicial Power, 1985.

Cour d'Assises de Bruxelles, 8 June 2001, available at: www.legal-tools.org/en/browse/record/a70d94/.

Cryer, R.: "International Criminal Law" in Evans, M. D. (ed.): *International Law*, 4th edition, OUP, Oxford, 2014.

Cryer, R.: *Prosecuting International Crimes: Selectivity and the International Criminal Law Regime*, CUP, Cambridge, 2005.

Cryer, R., et al.: *An Introduction to International Criminal Law and Procedure*, 3rd edition, CUP, Cambridge, 2014.Da Rocha Ferreira, A. et al.: "The Obligation to Extradite or Prosecute (*aut dedere aut judicare*)", 2013, Vol. 1, International Law Commission, *UFRGS Model United Nations Journal*, pp. 202–221.

Damaska, M. R.: "The Shadow Side of Command Responsibility", 2001, Vol. 49 (3), *American Journal of Comparative Law*, pp. 455–496.

Decision on the Draft Legal Instruments, Doc. Assembly/AU/8(XXIII), at 1 in African Union, Decisions, Declarations And Resolution, Assembly/AU/Dec.517–545(XXIII), available at: www.au.int/en/sites/default/files/decisions/9661-assembly_au_dec_517_-_545_xxiii_e.pdf.

Demanjuk v. Petrovsky, US Court of Appeal, 6th Cir., 31.10.1985, ILR 79, 546.

Democratic Republic of the Congo v. Belgium.

Draft Protocol on Amendments to the Protocol on the Statute of the African Court of Justice and Human Rights, May 15, 2014, STC/Legal/Min/7(I) Rev. 1, Art. 46C, available at: www.iccnow.org/documents/African_Court_Protocol_-_July_2014.pdf.

Ganesan, A.: "One of the Missing Pieces in the Accountability Puzzle", 11 April 2015, *Human Rights Watch*, available at: http://jamesgstewart.com/one-of-the-missing-pieces-in-the-accountability-puzzle/.

Garrett, A.: "The Corporation as Sovereign", 2008, Vol. 60 (1), *Maine Law Review*, p. 130–164.

Greene, T. P.: *Wilson at Versailles: Problems in American Civilization*, D.C. Heath and Company, Lexington, 1957.

Heller-Roazen, D.: *The Enemy of All: Piracy and the Law of Nations*, Zone Books, New York, 2009.

Hirsh, D.: *Law Against Genocide: Cosmopolitan Trials*, Glasshouse Press, London, 2003.

House of Lords, 24 March 1999, 2 WLR 827.

Human Rights Watch: "The Trial of Hissène Habré", available at: www.hrw.org/tag/hissene-habre.

Human Rights Watch: Belgium: *Universal Jurisdiction Law Repealed*, 1 August, 2003, available at: www.hrw.org/news/2003/08/01/belgium-universal-jurisdiction-law-repealed.

ICTR Statute: Statute of the International Criminal Tribunal for the Prosecution of Persons Responsible for Genocide and Other Serious Violations of International Humanitarian Law Committed in the Territory of Rwanda and Rwandan Citizens Responsible for Genocide and Other such Violations Committed in the Territory of Neighbouring States, between January 1, 1994 and December 31, 1994.

ICTY Statute: International Tribunal for the Prosecution of Persons Responsible for Serious Violations of International Humanitarian Law Committed in the Territory of the Former Yugoslavia since 1991

International Committee of the Red Cross, Jurisdiction over War Crimes, available at: https://ihl-databases.icrc.org/customary-ihl/eng/docs/v2_cou_il_rule157.

International Law Association Committee on International Human Rights Law and Practice: "Final Report on the Exercise of universal jurisdiction in respect of gross human rights offences", 2000.

International Law Commission, 2001 Article 8, available at: http://legal.un.org/ilc/texts/instruments/english/commentaries/9_6_2001.pdf.

International Tribunal for the Prosecution of Persons Responsible for Serious Violations of International Humanitarian Law Committed in the Territory of The Former Yugoslavia since 1991, Decision of the President, available at: www.legal-tools.org/doc/01079f/pdf/.

Israel Ministry of Foreign Affairs, available at: www.mfa.gov.il/mfa/mfa-archive/1950-1959/pages/nazis%20and%20nazi%20collaborators%20-punishment-%20law-%20571.aspx.

Jain, N.: *Perpetrators and Accessories in International Criminal Law: Individual Modes of Responsibility for Collective Crimes*, Hart, Oxford, 2014.

Kelsen, H.: *Peace through Law*, The University of North Carolina Press, Chapel Hill, 1944.

Kelsen, H.: "Will the Judgement at Nuremberg Constitute a Precedent in International Law?", 1947, Vol. 1 (2), *International Law Quarterly*, pp. 153–171.

Kern, S.: "Spain Rethinks Universal Jurisdiction", 31 January 2014, *Gatestone Institute International Policy Council*, available at: www.gatestoneinstitute.org/4149/spain-universal-jurisdiction.

Kontorovich, E. and Art, S.: "An Empirical Examination of Universal Jurisdiction for Piracy", 2010, Faculty Working Papers, Paper 38, Vol. 98 (1), *California Law Review*, pp. 243–276.

Koskenniemi, M.: "Between Impunity and Show Trials", 2002, Vol. 6, *Max Planck Yearbook of United Nations Law*, pp. 1–35.

Langer, M.: "The Diplomacy of Universal Jurisdiction: The Political Branches and the Transnational Prosecution of International Crimes", 2011, Vol. 105 (1), *American Journal of International Law*, pp. 1–49.

Langer, M.: "Universal Jurisdiction is Not Disappearing. The Shift from 'Global Enforcer' to 'No Safe Haven' Universal Jurisdiction", 2015, Vol. 13 (2), *Journal of International Criminal Justice*, pp. 245–256.

Lasok, D.: "Eichmann Trial", 1962, Vol. 11 (2), *International and Comparative Law Quarterly*, pp. 355–374.

Lauterpacht, H.: "The Law of Nations and Punishment of War Crimes", 1944, Vol. 21, *British Yearbook of International Law*.

Legal Framework for the Repression of Piracy Under UNCLOS, updated 9 September 2010, available at: www.un.org/depts/los/piracy/piracy_legal_framework.htm.

Liu, H.-Y.: *Law's Impunity: Responsibility and the Modern Private Military Company*, Hart Publishing, Oxford, 2015.

Macedo, S. (ed.): *Universal Jurisdiction: National Courts and the Prosecution of Serious Crimes Under International Law*, University of Pennsylvania Press, Philadelphia, 2004.

McCormack, T. and Simpson, G. (eds): *The Law of War Crimes: National and International Approaches*, Kluwer Law International, The Hague, 1997.

Molto, J. E. E.: "The 'Great Leap Forward' to Impunity. Burying Universal Jurisdiction in Spain and Returning to the Paradigm of Human Rights as '*domaine reserve*' of States", 2015, Vol. 13 (5), *Journal of International Criminal Justice*, pp. 1121–1144.

Neocleous, M.: "The Universal Adversary /ll Attack: Pigs, Pirates, Zombies, Satan and the Class War", 2015, Vol. 8 (1), *Critical Studies on Terrorism*, pp. 15–31.

Ohlin, J. D.: "Three Conceptual Problems with the Doctrine of Joint Criminal Enterprise", 2007, Vol. 5 (1), *Journal of International Criminal Justice*, pp. 69–90.

Philippe, X.: "The Principles of Universal Jurisdiction and Complementarity: How Do the Two Principles Intermesh?", 2006, Vol. 88 (862), *International Review of the Red Cross*, pp. 375–398.

Princeton Principles on Universal Jurisdiction, Princeton University, New Jersey, 2001.

Prosecutor v. Mohamed et al., STL-14–05 (2014); Prosecutor v. Al Amin et al., STL-14–06 (2014).

Ramasastry, A. and Thompson, R. C.: "Commerce, Crime and Conflict. Legal Remedies for Private Sector Liability for Grave Breaches of International Law. A Survey of Sixteen Countries", Fafo report 536, 2006, p. 13, available at: http://biicl.org/files/4364_536.pdf.

Randall, K. C.: "Universal Jurisdiction under International Law", 1988, Vol. 66 (4), *Texas Law Review*, pp. 785–841.

Redress: "Make Way for Justice", 12 March 2018, available at: https://redress.org/news/report-make-way-for-justice-4-signals-momentum-towards-accountability/.

Reydams, L.: "Belgium Reneges on Universality: The 5 August 2003 Act on Grave Breaches of International Humanitarian Law", 2003, Vol. 1 (3), *Journal of International Criminal Justice*, pp. 679–689.

Reydams, L.: "The rise and fall of universal jurisdiction" in Schabas, W. and Bernaz, N. (eds): *Routledge Handbook of International Criminal Law*, Routledge, Abingdon, 2011.

Reydams, L.: *Universal Jurisdiction: International and Municipal Legal Perspectives*, OUP, Oxford, 2004.

Robins, N.: *The Corporation that Changed the World: How the East India Company Shaped the Modern Multinational*, Pluto Press, London, 2006.

Roling, B. V. A.: "The Nuremberg and Tokyo Trials in Retrospect" in Bassiouni, C. and Nanda, U. P. (eds): *A Treatise on International Criminal Law*, Charles C. Thomas, Springfield, 1973.

Rome Statute of the International Criminal Court, available at: http://legal.un.org/icc/statute/99_corr/cstatute.htm.

Schabas, W.: *Introduction to the International Criminal Court*, 4th edition, CUP, Cambridge, 2011.

Schwarzenberger, G.: "The Problem of an International Criminal Law", 1950, Vol. 3 (1), *Current Legal Problems*, pp. 263–296.

Schwobel, C. (ed.): *Critical Approaches to International Criminal Law: An Introduction*, Routledge, Abingdon, 2014.

Sepinwall, A. J.: "Failures to Punish: Command Responsibility in Domestic and International Law", 2008, Vol. 30 (2), *Michigan Journal of International Law*, pp. 251–304.

Sieff, K.: "Gambia Is the Latest African Country Deciding to Pull Out of International Criminal Court", 26 October 2016, *The Washington Post*, available at: www.washingtonpost.com/world/gambia-latest-african-country-deciding-to-pull-out-of-international-criminal-court/2016/10/26/7f54d068-c4ca-440f-848f-e211ba29dc34_story.html?utm_term=.d33089cea7d2.

Simpson, G.: *Law, War and Crime: War Crimes Trials and the Reinvention of International Law*, Polity Press, Cambridge, 2007.

Staker, C.: "Jurisdiction" in Evans, M. D. (ed.): *International Law*, 4th edition, OUP, Oxford, 2014.

STC/Legal/Min/7(I) Rev. 1, Article 28A, International Criminal Jurisdiction of the Court.

Stewart, J. G.: "The Turn to Corporate Criminal Liability for International Crimes: Transcending the Alien Tort Statute", 2014, Vol. 47 (1), *New York University Journal of International Law and Politics*, pp. 121–206.

Stone, C.: *Where the Law Ends: The Social Control of Corporate Behaviour*, Harper and Row, New York, 1975.

The 1950 European Convention for the Protection of Human Rights and Freedoms, available at: www.echr.coe.int/Documents/Convention_ENG.pdf.

The International Convention for the Suppression of Counterfeiting of Currency, 20 April 1929, available at: https://treaties.un.org/PAGES/LONViewDetails.aspx?src=LON&id=556&chapter=30&clang=_en.

The Montreux Document on Private Military and Security Companies, 17 September 2008, available at www.eda.admin.ch/eda/en/home/topics/intla/humlaw/pse/psechi.html.

The United Nations Convention against Corruption, available at: www.unodc.org/documents/brussels/UN_Convention_Against_Corruption.pdf.

Thompson, R. C., Ramasastry, A. and Taylor, M. B.: "Translating UNOCAL: The Expanding Web of Liability for Business Entities Implicated in International Crimes", 2009, Vol. 40 (4), *George Washington International Law Review*, pp. 845–846.

Trial International, available at: https://trialinternational.org/latest-post/pascal-simbikangwa/#section-2.

UN Convention against Illicit Traffic in Narcotic Drugs and Psychotropic Substances, 20 December 1988, available at: www.unodc.org/unodc/en/treaties/illicit-trafficking.html.

UN GA 64th Session, 2009, available at::://www.un.org/en/ga/sixth/64/UnivJur.shtml.

UN GA 67th Session, 2012, available at: www.un.org/press/en/2012/gal3442.doc.htm.

UN GA 71st Session, 2016, available at: www.un.org/press/en/2016/gal3525.doc.htm.

United Nations Convention against Transnational Organized Crime and the Protocols Thereto, available at: www.unodc.org/unodc/en/organized-crime/intro/UNTOC.html.

United Nations Convention on the Law of the Sea, 10 December 1982, available at: www.un.org/depts/los/convention_agreements/convention_overview_convention.htm.

United Nations General Assembly A/71/111, available at: https://undocs.org/A/71/111.

United Nations General Assembly, 64th session, 15 September 2009.

United States v. Yousef, 327 F.3d 56, 97 (2nd Circuit, 2003).

Universal Jurisdiction Annual Review 2016, Make Way for Justice 2.

Van Sliedregt, E.: *Individual Criminal Responsibility in International Law*, OUP, Oxford, 2012.

White, N. and MacLeod, S.: "EU Operations and Private Military Contractors: Issues of Corporate and Institutional Responsibility", 2008, Vol. 19 (5), *European Journal of International Law*, pp. 965–988.

Williams, A.: "Baha Mousa will never get justice while the army investigates itself", 12 September 2013, *The Guardian*, available at: www.theguardian.com/commentisfree/2013/sep/12/baha-mousa-justice-army-lawrence.

Williams, P. and Vlassis, D. (eds.): *Combatting Transnational Crime: Concept, Activities, Responses*, Frank Class, London, 2001.

Wilson, R. J.: "Prosecuting Pinochet in Spain", available at: www.wcl.american.edu/hrbrief/v6i3/pinochet.htm.

Zolo, D.: *Victors' Justice: From Nuremberg to Baghdad*, Verso, London, 2009.

Conclusion

Thinking critically about historical forms of governance and militaries allows us to identify regulation in previously unsuspected places, "history may appear arbitrary, but its dynamics are dominated by laws".[1] Given the scarcity of historically informed literature in international law on PMCs, most approaches treat this subject as an entirely new area of study. Furthermore, existing approaches produce temporary or incomplete regulatory frameworks as they fail to take into consideration the question of constantly changing governance structures.

This monograph has surveyed an extensive terrain, identifying various forms of private power from the feudal lords and fifteenth-century Italian *condottieri* who contracted their own troops in local wars, to the professional mercenary soldiers of the absolute monarchies of continental Europe, to the outsourced governance of the East India Company, to the modern-day PMC contractors working for legitimate private corporations. The manifestations of private violence in different governance models and the corresponding responses to this private force were identified and analysed in order to demonstrate a range of different normative standpoints concerning mercenaries, private armies, and PMCs.

The historical analysis enabled a critical reading of international law, demonstrating the use of private military forces by different types of governance both in the past and today. It afforded me the broader benefit of understanding the suitability and efficacy of existing and future regulatory mechanisms that administer this relationship between the state and military force. It also revealed that the policy of the use and regulation of violence is not legally neutral; instead it is shaped by the various expressions of power and is articulated through the language of legitimacy. In the context of this research, legitimacy is best envisaged in terms of acceptance and validation of authority, while power is understood as the military force that prevails in any given form of governance.

The contemporary relationship between power and legitimacy also revealed a number of conflicts between legitimate systems. As private military companies are growing in authority and sharing power with states, they are also making claims to legitimacy. Companies attain their legitimacy from different sources of law, such as international self-regulation and industry standards, but also from the corporate status of PMCs as companies. Indeed, private force has always found room to exist within different forms of governance; only now the shift from mercenaries to properly incorporated companies marked the shift of private security into a realm administered by national jurisdictions. Furthermore, the coexistence of domestic, international and industry-level regulatory systems is not complementary. Instead, these conflicting legitimising systems claim authority over the private sources of power without a true effective and coherent enforcement. Deconstructing the overlapping regulations in the realm of private security, reveals the legal gap that arises from the lack of a strong norm of corporate responsibility. PMC impunity is fortified through the absence of a norm recognising international legal personality for corporations, while simultaneously creating a veneer of legitimacy of being a properly incorporated company.

In order for regulation to fulfil its purpose and establish accountability, it needs to be applied to the entire supply chain of private security, and implemented at a level that is less likely to generate impunity. An effective regulation of private military actors also needs to take account of the historical context. By assessing the prevailing form of governance and the role that private security plays in state policy, it becomes clear that states are the main PMC clients and they rely on companies for the provision of security services. Subsequently, due to their bias and reliance on private security providers, states are arguably not the best placed actors to carry out the regulation of PMCs. Neither is the industry, as it tends to treat military activity just like any other commodity that can be self-regulated by the free market. In order to close the gap of PMC impunity, an international legal response is required that has the capacity to act beyond the state and invoke criminal corporate responsibility.

Current regulation of private military space highlights the fact that power is out of synchronisation with the demands of legitimacy and cannot be adequately managed. There is, therefore, a need for legitimacy that responds to new and changing forms of power in the context of state-military relations. The regulation of killing and human rights violations needs to be taken seriously, whether these are committed by individuals, a state, or a corporation. Social corporate responsibility is insufficiently strong to single-handedly fulfil the function of creating responsibility. It lacks legally binding instruments to criminalise wrongful behaviour. Nor are the control mechanisms of state responsibility always reliable, due to the biased relationship and frequent reliance of states on PMCs. Referring to the historical analysis, it is unlikely that this reliance, at least for the biggest PMC client states, will diminish in the next few decades. In order to overcome the problem of corporate immunity, an international criminal response ought to be freed from the state responsibility limitation.

The legal analysis identified the gap between existing regulation and justice, while the historical patterns of relationships between states and military force provided insight into the effectiveness of existing and future regulatory responses. PMC regulation, current and developing, can be broadly divided into the 'responsibilisation' and criminalisation approaches. Although the soft norms of 'responsibilisation' are aimed at raising standards and PMC respect for human rights, they run a risk of creating a veneer of false legitimacy while lacking legal enforcement and any tangible mechanisms of delivering justice. The proposed criminalisation efforts, on the other hand, are state-centric and are likely to create a divergence between the states in the two opposing regulatory camps.

By examining the questions of the use and regulation of PMCs, this monograph also highlighted the main source of impunity, namely the lack of a strong norm of corporate responsibility and, particularly, international criminal liability for corporations. The proposal to deploy international criminal law as an appropriate PMC criminalisation mechanism is based on a number of principles. International criminal responsibility for corporations shifts the focus from states to PMCs as companies. By taking on functions that are considered to be inherently governmental, PMCs have acquired a new, more significant role in their relationship with states, a role that needs to be appropriately governed. State reliance on outsourced, privatised security is unlikely to diminish in the foreseeable future, while the model of small, relatively decentralised government prevails.

Furthermore, PMC activity is international, making PMC regulation an international issue of a merged military-civilian realm. Due to the military nature of their activity, international criminal responsibility for PMCs is relevant in order to address human rights violations, war crimes and crimes against humanity, and other international crimes. Finally, the formulation of international criminal liability for corporations would reinforce state responsibility and, coupled with selected industry standards, could bridge the legal gaps created by problems with contract law and the legal personality of PMCs.

While the above considerations could address key gaps in PMC regulation and improve accountability mechanisms, it is important to remember that the current form of governance poses an inherent limitation on the notion of the state monopoly of force. The rise of competing actors in international relations, as well as the conscious changes in government policy to limit the role of the state and outsource some of its functions, inevitably creates space for private military actors to exist. International law will struggle to fully criminalise and eliminate the risk of the unethical use of private force. However, by identifying the key sources of impunity across the supply chain of private military power, we can target the issues of corporate responsibility of PMCs. International criminal law offers a number of possible complementary avenues to implement a more robust mechanism to try and punish companies that to date have escaped liability for gross offences and violations by virtue of their corporate legal personhood.

Although the implementation of the abovementioned mechanisms requires further scrutiny, the criminalisation of gross corporate misconduct could ensure a more efficient and controlled use of private military resources by states and international organisations, making PMCs a welcome, rather than a feared, addition to the security landscape.

Note

1 Tar (1997).

Reference

Tar, Z.: *The Frankfurt School: The Critical Theories of Max Horkheimer and Theodor Adorno*, Wiley Press, New York, 1977, p. 27.

Index